THE
FRESHWATER
FIVE

THE FRESHWATER FIVE

5 MEN, 104 YEARS IN PRISON, AND THE QUEST FOR JUSTICE

AS TOLD TO MIKE DUNN AND NICKY GREEN

Front cover: the *Galwad-Y-Mor* (©Nicky Green)

First published 2021

The History Press
97 St George's Place, Cheltenham,
Gloucestershire, GL50 3QB
www.thehistorypress.co.uk

British Library Cataloguing in Publication Data.
A catalogue record for this book is available from the British Library.

ISBN 978 0 7509 9247 3

Typesetting and origination by The History Press
Printed and bound in Great Britain by TJ Books Limited.

MIX
Paper from
responsible sources
FSC® C013056

CONTENTS

1	The Arrest	7
2	Hooked	12
3	'Mor' the Merrier	18
4	Russian Roulette	26
5	Nikki's Sentence	31
6	Held at Gunpoint	39
7	'You're up to Running Drugs'	45
8	Hard Labour	54
9	Vic	59
10	Ships in the Night	66
11	Black Objects	81
12	Prison	92
13	Torn Apart	100
14	Did You Do it?	104
15	Ghost Plane	116
16	Don't Upset the Police	121
17	Altered Statements	129
18	Coopering	137
19	They'd Never Lie	150
20	Mr Anything-is-Possible	160
21	Tied up in Knots	169

22	It's Impossible	180
23	Spoilt	185
24	Who's that Man?	196
25	The Verdict	205
26	5 Men, 104 Years	212
27	Rigged	220
28	Terrorists	222
29	Innocent from Every Angle	234
30	The Missing Log	241
31	Fighting Back	248
32	Named and Shamed	256
33	Handcuffed in the Pulpit	261
34	Victims	274
35	Proving Our Innocence	280
36	Failures	288
37	The White Ember	292
38	Non-Disclosure	298
39	The Promise	309

| Support the Fight for Justice | 317 |
| About the Author | 319 |

Chapter 1

THE ARREST

I never saw the violence coming; I never saw the first arm lash out. I just felt a numb pain shivering through my body as the blow connected across my exposed throat and neck.

I never anticipated the rugby tackle, either, the one that must have sent me crashing to the floor. I was hauled down in seconds, everything suddenly upended, nothing making sense. *What the fuck?*

I heard angry, menacing voices barbed with threats. Someone barked: 'You ... don't move.' I tried to tilt my face upwards but an oversized palm instantly pressed heavily into my right cheek, grinding down, bone against bone, until the left side of my face felt like it was being forcibly squashed into the wooden decking below. That hurt.

My heart started pounding so ferociously it felt ready to explode at any moment; I gasped frantically for air but my rapid, panic-fuelled gulps weren't enough to calm me down.

'What the hell?' I yelled. 'What's all this?'

I could sense tightening grips around my ankles and arms and I could feel a crushing weight in the small of my back, like three or four sumo wrestlers had decided to pin me down. Their combined weight made movement impossible. I tried desperately to wriggle clear but the more I squirmed, the heavier the pressure on my back and the tighter the grips on my immobile limbs. *Shit, these guys mean business.*

There must have been around twelve of them. Moments earlier, I'd watched them approaching, blokes dressed casually in jeans with designer shirts hanging over their arses, and I thought to myself *'bloody yachties, why do they always come down the wrong pontoon?'* I even shouted over: 'You can't come down here, this is private.'

Dan and I had finished off at the *Galwad* and were just messing around, having a giggle. Vic was around somewhere although I didn't care where. I'd had enough of him. Scott had already headed off to the restaurant with a basket of lobsters. I'd told him to pick out the best because Maisy had booked a table. Her boyfriend's parents were over and she wanted to impress them. Dan had just kicked the fish pen back into the water and we were heading back to the quay as the blokes walked towards us.

I remember turning to Dan, just behind me, and muttering: 'Just look at these tossers.' I even gave them another warning: 'Hoy, you can't come down here, this is for the fishing crews only.' But they kept on walking – and that's when the arms suddenly lashed out and, within the blink of an eye, I was poleaxed on the pontoon floor.

'Fuck off,' I yelled. 'Who the hell are you lot?'

One of them – the one still pressing his hand down into my cheek – lowered his head closer. I could feel his stale breath pouring over my face and into my nostrils as he spat: 'Police … you're under arrest.' As he said that, I watched legs and boots running past me. They were going for Dan, too.

Next, I felt my arms being bent back and cold steel pressing against my wrists. I was being cuffed. There was nothing I could do, I was practically paralysed and totally at their mercy. So I carried on cursing and swearing because it was the only resistance I had left. 'What the fuckin' hell is this shit all about?'

Once they were happy I couldn't take a swipe at them, I was dragged back up to my feet. Two of them were now gripping the back of my arms, real tight, until it felt like their hands would leave permanent indentations in my skin. 'You'll find out soon enough,' someone said, as I was half dragged along the pontoon towards the main quay area, just in front of where the Wightlink ferry to Lymington gets moored. For a fleeting second, I got a clear glimpse of his face and thought: '*I know you, don't I?*' But I couldn't think why, or where from.

Once we reached the quay area, I was hauled over to a bench, close to the toilet block – where the old, grey waste-oil tank used to stand, close to the Wheatsheaf pub. I got the impression the police wanted me out of sight; it was a Bank Holiday weekend, around 9 p.m. on Sunday night, and there were plenty of pissed-up holidaymakers and day trippers milling around, some of them with pints in their hands, others holding kids or queuing in cars for the next ferry back to the mainland.

Another copper came over – it was a warm evening by now and he was wearing dark shorts. His legs looked pasty white and ludicrous. It just added to my suspicion that the whole thing was a joke.

'Mr Green?' he asked, although it was pretty obvious he knew damn well who I was.

'Yeah?'

'You're under arrest for importing class-A drugs.'

That really ignited the touch paper. 'You having a laugh or something?' I replied. 'You wankers are pissing in the wind. What the fuck's your game then?'

I carried on swearing and cursing and shaking my head from side to side, wriggling manically, desperately hoping – I guess – that my cuffs would miraculously spring apart.

'We're SOCA – the serious crime agency,' he replied. He was stood, towering above me, yet even then I still looked up to his eyes just in case there was a hint of mischief in there somewhere. 'Do me a fuckin' favour,' I replied. 'Tell me straight, is this is a bloody joke?'

'No,' he replied. 'Importation of drugs – cocaine.'

'What?' I yelled. It suddenly dawned on me there was absolutely no sign of Dan – or Vic for that matter – and, as I looked over towards the quay, I could see the *Galwad* was now ablaze with lights. The blokes who had upended me on the pontoon were crawling all over the deck. 'What are those dozy twats doing on my boat?' I screamed. Deep down, a part of me wanted an audience; I was hoping the holidaymakers would hear my cries and come over to see what all the fuss was about.

The copper clearly sensed I was playing up. Within seconds, a couple of his colleagues turned up and I was frogmarched into a nearby car and shovelled on to the back seat. The doors were clicked shut; one of them sat next to me, the other in the front.

We sat there for at least a couple of hours. Eventually I packed in swearing and cursing and trying to cause a commotion and instead fell quiet. Why did they suspect me of this? Was it because I'd been out on the *Galwad?* There'd been a plane – *I'd seen a plane* – first through the gaps in the Needles, then – again – as we came back into the Solent. Was that something to do with it? And there'd been boats, out on the horizon. *What were they doing there?* I needed to relive the last thirty hours in my mind. What had happened, what on earth had I done, to suddenly be in this mess?

Immediately my mind focussed on Vic, or rather the two strangers he'd turned up with. *I hadn't been expecting them.* I couldn't even remember their names – one was called Dexsa, or something stupid like that. *Were they somehow involved in this? If so, why? And how?* It was impossible to make any sense of it, especially as Vic had done nothing but puke up the entire time.

OK, he was clearly no fisherman. But he'd been with me throughout and vomited to the point of begging me to make calls in the hope he could somehow get off the boat. The more I dwelt on that, the more convinced I was that he'd been simply trying to get work here illegally. *What's that got to do with cocaine?*

Just as all this was whirling around in my mind, a penny suddenly dropped. I realised who the bloke on the pontoon was when they all jumped me. I knew I'd seen him before and now I realised where.

He was one of the armed police officers who'd held me and Nikki up at Lymington. I can still see his fuckin' revolver poking out of the holster hanging lopsided against his hip.

Now, it was beginning to make sense. My name was on their system and someone had it in for me.

Chapter 2

HOOKED

I was hooked from the age of 8. Even when I was an angry, rebellious teenager who just wanted to get pissed and have a punch-up, fishing reeled me back in, time and again. Hell, I even studied it at college where, for once in my life, I actually shone academically. I was good at something.

Grandad Cyril introduced me to fishing when I was still at primary school. We'd go sit on Ryde pier, rod and line fishing for hours on end. He wasn't a fisherman by trade – he was a signwriter on the trains – but angling was his hobby and he taught me all the basics: how to set up a rod, what worms to use and all the different types of bait, and where we could land a bit of mackerel. He taught me about patience and he taught me how to be skilled. Sometimes I'd be transfixed by the speed of his hands, all gnarled and lined with age and yet incredibly quick and deft as he changed bait or reeled in a catch.

Sometimes we'd get a few pollock off the pier but the real fuck-me moment would be if one of us caught a seabass. I can still hear us whooping and cheering when that happened.

I can still see his toothless, cheesy grin. The thrill never left him despite his age. I was a teenager when he passed away and that's when I inherited most of his gear. By then, a few of my mates had also picked up fishing and we'd go down the beach in the evenings and spend all night with the old tilly lights casting their yellowy glow over the water. Happy days.

I'd always been outdoorsy right from childhood. School wasn't for me – I preferred to go rabbiting and ferreting. Sometimes I'd skip lessons altogether and go fishing with a family friend, Charlie Bishop, who used to do a bit of small boat fishing with nets. My old man, who was a builder but also loved fishing, would occasionally join us, too.

I'd be about 15 years old by then. Another of my dad's pals, Jeff Williams, had a slightly bigger boat – a 27-footer that could handle rougher weather – and I'd go out with him in the winter months. It was Charlie, though, who persuaded us to get our own boat. He could see how captivated I was and one day, after we'd all been out, he turned to dad and I and said: 'Look, I've still got an old boat I ain't using over the other side of the island. Why don't you paint it? I'll give you some nets, and you can go dabble with it during the summer.'

It was only a 16-footer and although it looked a bit ship-wrecked and abandoned under the cliffs, we pulled it out and gave it a nice shiny coat of blue paint. Then we'd drag it over the beach and get it out on to the water. Next, we made up some pots from old scrap reinforcing bars off dad's building sites. We'd cut them up, weld them back together to make a D-shaped pot, which we'd wrap in netting. Then we'd create an entrance so the lobsters could climb in to get to the bait, and add some concrete at the bottom to weigh it down.

I guess I was learning the basics and something new nearly every day but I'd no idea where it was all leading until a careers' advisor came to our school. I was in my last year and we all had to see him one by one. 'So, Jamie, what do you want to do when you leave?' he asked.

I was going through a cocky know-it-all stage at the time and was convinced career advisors could do sod all for me. 'I want to be a fisherman,' I replied, half smirking and thinking: *What you going to do about that, then?*

'Ah, right' he replied, and scribbled down some notes. *Tosser.* I thought no more about it, then, to my astonishment he returned about two weeks later and collared me outside our classroom. 'Jamie. Jamie Green. I've got a college course for you.'

'You what?!' He explained there was a specialist YTS fishing course in Falmouth I could join. 'It lasts four months, you'll get £25 a week, and you'll get digs arranged and paid for.' Bloody hell.

I'll never forget the look on my parents' faces when I went home and announced: 'I'm going to college!'

'Get out of here, Jamie! You having a laugh with us? What college, where? Is this for real?'

'Down in Falmouth. They're even going to pay me!'

My parents were thrilled and I absolutely loved it. For the first time in my life, I was thriving in a classroom. I learned about boats, how to build them and how to strip out an engine, rebuild it and then keep it running. I'd always liked meddling around with old cars so the mechanical side of the course came easy. I learned about radio communications, areas to fish and what sort of fish you'd find and where. They told us how to make pots and nets and showed us proper knots and splicing for rope, as well as wire. Then we learnt about radars and mapping and handling weather and survival – even basics about business management. I gave it my all and ended up with a City and Guilds Distinction and some of the highest marks in college. It had never been like that for me at school.

I came back fired up and determined to build my own boat. My dad was up for it; we had pals who were building small fibreglass boats so we'd go along and watch how they did it. Our first proper boat was the *Lizzy-Jo*. We bought the shell, got it on a private slipway that we hired, then my old man employed a boat builder to customise it. I'd give him a hand and although I was only his gofer and labourer, I watched closely what he was doing.

I quickly understood the concept of fibreglassing, how to glass in the bulkheads and how to balance the right mix of resins, hardener and catalyst. Get that wrong and it'll go off real quick. We needed a boat with a stable platform to stack pots and a winch to haul them in; a boat that could get us out 6 to 7 miles quickly and handle rough weather.

I already knew, though, there were better areas to fish beyond that. Areas where we could land the really big stuff. We'd often get visiting Channel Islands boats stopping off overnight on the island. Their crews would come in for a beer and I'd quiz them about where they fished and the areas they liked. What they said stuck in my mind – there was a whole world to exploit further out there.

I also realised there was good money to be made from building boats, registering them and selling them on at a profit. It was becoming increasingly hard to get fishing licences and we were able to sell *Lizzy-Jo* to a bloke who simply wanted the licence for a trawler he owned. We very quickly started building *Lizzy-Jo 2* and by the time we'd sold that, we had enough money to build a catamaran – and get out beyond 6 miles.

I built the *John Edward* from fibreglass in 1996 and, compared to both *Lizzy-Jos*, it was the dog's bollocks. Naturally, I stretched the rules. I couldn't help myself. I wanted the catamaran to be bigger than was permitted. To get its licence, it had to measure 40ft, but I wanted longer. So I built long, pointed nose cones at the ends that could be hinged or bolted on – and detached when it came to physically measuring the length of the boat. I double-checked the rules, which clearly stated if attachments were detachable, they wouldn't be included in the structural measurement.

It was measured and passed, and that seriously pissed off my rivals, who kicked up a right fuss. Sure enough, the authorities came back, saying: 'We need to measure your boat again.'

'What do you mean? You've measured it once, what you need to measure it again for?'

'We need to double-check the length of it.'

I wasn't having that but the silly bastards turned up in Yarmouth and actually tried to seize the boat off me. I had a massive row with some pen-pusher down on the quay; in fact, I got so angry I almost threw him into the water. The next I knew I was being served with a whole load of notices: I couldn't go fishing, I couldn't go out, I couldn't use the boat, I couldn't do this, I couldn't do that.

That was a red rag. 'Right,' I bellowed. 'I'm taking the bow sections off completely, then you can't stop me.'

So that's what I did. The boat looked ridiculous but it measured 40ft and was therefore legal. We'd go off into a head sea and the water would come crashing over the front, straight at us. But I carried on and everyone got the right hump about it. They couldn't deny the *John Edward* was built to the maximum size permissible for its licence and, even with no nose cones, it remained quick and stable. It could handle loads of weather and it could carry loads of pots. Best of all, nobody else had anything like it.

The *John Edward* wasn't perfect but it was a giant step forward. It had no facilities for overnighting, although some-times we'd rough it and kip on two benches, down below at the back. It was always too damp and noisy down there to get any proper sleep, though.

I was in my own little bubble, earning a living, we had good times and we had some shit ones. Fishing goes in cycles like that. It was the mid-1990s, I was in my mid-20s and I had absolutely no inkling for anything else. I knew there were bigger and better areas to fish out there – but I hadn't worked out how to reach them.

I hadn't yet clapped my eyes on the *Galwad*.

Chapter 3

'MOR' THE MERRIER

The *Galwad Y Mor* was the world to me. I loved the fact its name was Welsh for *The Call of the Sea*. That sounded right. This wasn't just a boat, this was my life – the tangible proof that my business was doing OK, that my family had food on the table, that we could pay our bills and afford wages for a crew. I'd even taken out a £100,000 mortgage to buy it. That's how much it meant to me. I had a business plan and the *Galwad* was the embodiment of it, the heart and soul of everything I was and wanted to be.

I'll never forget the first time I clapped my eyes on the *Galwad*. I didn't own it then but I instinctively knew this was a boat I was destined to have. It was distinctive, with broad, horizontal stripes all the way round – dark Oxford blue immediately below the hand rails, then a vivid sky blue down to the water line. The top railings and wheelhouse were brilliant white and at the back, above its registration number, SU116, proudly stood the name *Galwad Y Mor*, printed in a posh, old-fashioned bright-red typeface.

I watched it sliding along the Solent and kept on watching it until it was no more than a distant dot on the horizon. That boat had everything I needed to expand my business – to take us into waters we couldn't reach – areas beyond the shipping lanes and closer to France where nobody else from the island went and where we could land bigger and more profitable catches.

Better than that, though. I knew something more: the *Galwad* was a boat that was just like me. It broke all the rules. It stuck two fingers up to authority. I loved it even more because of that.

I'd watched it being built by a family on the mainland in Lymington and I knew it was bigger than the 12m it was actually licensed for. In the old days, boats used to be officially measured from the pin on the rudder (its rudder stock) to the bow. Builders literally stretched the rules by extending the length of their boats some 4ft beyond the rudder stuck so the bodywork stuck out at the back.

The *Galwad* was built around 1988 and when measured she reached a mighty 44ft. It was a monster! The rules were eventually changed so licences would only be issued to boats that measured 12m overall – but those already on the register had the right to remain.

To my knowledge there were only three boats left in the United Kingdom that could cheat the system like this – and the *Galwad* was one of them. In the business it's known as Grandad's Rights. Once a boat is over 12m, the rules state it can only fish outside 6 miles from the island. The *Galwad* was considerably longer – yet nobody could stop it fishing right up to the beach, or absolutely anywhere else it wanted!

That boat was everything I stood for: a great, big, floating 'fuck off' to the rules. That's why I went after it. That's why I begged the bank to give me the £100,000 mortgage. I mean, banks on the Isle of Wight aren't exactly falling over themselves to lend you money to build a bloody boat. It's not like going to Newlyn or Grimsby where fishing is the bedrock of the entire community. The Isle of Wight is more about tourism and yachties than sweaty fishermen like me.

There aren't many of us left on the island fishing for a living. Go into a bank and say 'I want to build a boat' and their first reaction is to look at you like you're ravin' mad or something. But I showed them my turnover figures, my profits and costs, I talked to them about my business and how a new boat could help us expand big time. It wasn't easy for them – but they got it. They could see where I was taking my business and they knew I'd be out until Christ knows what time, seven days a week, to make it happen.

I also knew it would seriously piss off all my rival fishermen on the island. Even when I was arrested the local boats went straight to the fisheries office in Poole and tried to get the *Galwad* kicked out to 6 miles.

'It's too bloody big that boat, get it out,' they bleated. But the fisheries officer was stumped. All he could say was: 'Sorry, there's nothing we can do about it, it's under 12 metres from when it was built.'

Yes. That's why I bought the *Galwad*. It empowered me.

I'd just got into fishing as a livelihood when the *Galwad* was being built. But I was always at the mercy of the weather and how far out I could safely go. Winter would be too rough, which meant we'd be grounded and couldn't earn. My boat then – which I built – had no accommodation and no real cooking facilities. It had deck tanks to store product but they could only hold a ton and a quarter. Then I'd be full and we'd have to head back.

The *Galwad*, however, held 7 tons. It even had a vivier tank that pumped sea water through constantly, keeping the crab and lobsters alive and fresh – allowing me to stay out for as long as I wanted. It also had accommodation for five, a little shower and a proper galley. There was no toilet but that was a minor detail for us. We were used to either pissing over the side or crapping in a black plastic bucket.

Strange to think this detail would actually be debated in court years later as the police tried to shit all over us.

The *Galwad* went on sale in 2008 but I couldn't raise the money quickly enough and lost out to a fisherman up in the Shetlands. I knew the new owner's name, though. I got his number and rang him every couple of months or so, saying: 'If you ever want to sell, give me a call.'

Finally, in November the following year, he said, 'yes', so I headed up to Scotland, putting my own boat on the market in the hope I'd get a swift sale and have the cash to help pay for the *Galwad*. We haggled, the boat had deteriorated and needed work, but we finally agreed on £120,000. I thought that was fair-ish – he'd wanted 130 grand to start. Plus, a high side had been added that would protect us against crashing waves and help us work out on deck in bad weather.

I managed to sell my boat in time but I still needed the £100,000 mortgage to make up the difference. It didn't frighten me, though, because I knew it was my future. This was everything I wanted: if we put in the graft, we'd earn the money. I knew we'd be all right. I had the confidence.

I'm sure every skipper – when they've changed boats for something bigger and better – has that moment when he thinks 'I've made it.' That's what I was thinking as we headed back to the island in the *Galwad* for the first time. 'I've had to duck and dive but I've got here. I've taken on finance, I've put my neck on the line but I'm out here. I've done it, I'm up and running. This is going to be our year and we're going to earn a bit of serious money.' That's what I was thinking.

Usually, you're apprehensive steering a new boat for the first time. You have to get a feel for it, develop confidence and understand how it's going to handle, especially in weather. You have to get to know one another.

I instinctively knew the *Galwad*. We were connected already. It even had its own satellite phone – clapped out but even so, a step up from what I was used to.

I'd still got some money left over so I installed an Olex unit almost straight away. This was relatively new technology at the time but I knew, if I could master it, it would not only track my course, it would enable me to see 3D images of the seabed. This was massively important for me and cut to the core of everything I was aspiring towards.

On my other boats, I'd made do with an entirely inadequate echo sounder. Whenever we went to fresh grounds, we were practically fishing in the dark with no accurate picture of what was beneath us.

The Olex could change all that. Its monitor would let me build an image of the seabed below so I could see all the lumps and bumps. It enabled me to find hotspots other fishermen wouldn't know about, to open up grounds that would be good to fish. The craggier the seabed, the better. The unit had a basic, default template of what it assumed the seabed would look like. By repeatedly steaming up and down and over and over the same area, the Olex kept updating what it saw below, adding the new information to the template. The more I kept going over a piece of ground, the more accurate the picture on the monitor became until it looked entirely different from what it had started with.

The combination of this new-fangled device and the *Galwad* really was my dream ticket. The *Galwad* enabled us to have longer trips; the Olex empowered me to chart the seabed so I could physically see for myself the areas to go for. It was everything I wanted but it was also a lot to learn.

I didn't know anyone with an Olex so I had to teach myself how to use it.

I desperately wanted to master everything it could do. The more I could understand it, the more information it could give me – and that could be invaluable. I knew it could transform my business so, when we were out at sea, I'd spend as much time as possible in the *Galwad*'s wheelhouse playing with the Olex – while my crew were doing all the manual work on deck.

Looking for new ground was an all-consuming obsession, even before the *Galwad*. Fishermen always have to be on the move. You can't stay in the same places because once you've taken the cream off a new area, you're then fishing down and you don't get a good enough return. You always want fresh ground, then – after roughly two weeks there – you move on. The question was always the same: 'where next?'

The Olex would help me answer that by giving me a fuller insight into the ground and, because the *Galwad* enabled us to stay out longer, it gave me more time to map out an area while the lads got on with hauling in pots and shooting new lines.

The Olex I bought back then in 2009 was a bit like mobile phones were in their infancy – cumbersome and not very user-friendly. Today, they're streamlined, even more hi-tech and there isn't a credible boat on the water that doesn't have one.

My previous boat – the one I'd sold to help pay for the *Galwad* – was a catamaran and had no such electronic luxuries. It was more like a raft, banging up and down on top of the water. In weather, it'd literally shake your fillings out. If we hit a 40ft block of water, it'd be like driving into a brick wall. I've had lads out there petrified the boat would fall apart.

The *Galwad* was a completely different animal. It would roll, but its movements were a lot more conventional. It could handle steering straight into the waves without frightening my crew to death. It was steady rather than fast and could cruise comfortably between 5 and 8 knots.

It was still early days in a new boat, though, and we didn't always win. Winter 2009 was closing in and sometimes we'd come back almost empty handed. They'd be the worst days because the crew would still want paying and the restaurant would want its lobsters. Then there was the time when we had to call out the lifeboat.

We'd gone out to recover some pots. The weather was atrocious; when we eventually reached them, the back line, as we call it, had wrapped up on the seabed. The only option was to break the rope but when we did, it immediately shot straight back up and wound itself into the *Galwad*'s propeller.

We were basically screwed. There was nothing we could do to untangle it; the *Galwad* was rolling around uncontrollably and the lifeboat was our only option. It was late at night, hell, it's still embarrassing to even think about it; fishermen aren't supposed to call for help.

We were 30 miles out, the weather was really shitty, so I phoned the coastguard. What a humiliating conversation that was. They had to scramble a crew and there'd be no glory in it for them. Just a wretched all-nighter. It took them about an hour and a half to reach us, and then six hours to tow us back. By the time they rounded the Needles all of them, bar two, were spewing their heads off.

There were many other times, though, when the weather was blowing its arse out but instead of turning round – as we'd done before – the *Galwad* enabled us to carry on. We'd come home round the Needles with a really good catch on board – maybe 2 tons of crabs and some decent lobsters – and

I'd feel my chest pushing out and a little grin spreading across my face as Yarmouth came into view. I'd be proud of the crew and proud of what my family had achieved. There really was no finer feeling than that. That's what it was all about.

Chapter 4

RUSSIAN ROULETTE

I know what it's like to be hit by a cargo ship. I've never been so terrified in my life.

It still gives me shivers to think about it. A lad and I were out on the catamaran, fishing a lump of ground north of Cherbourg, close to the Westbound shipping lane. I was knackered and said, 'Take the wheel for a few minutes will you, while I get some kip.' I was so tired I didn't clock that he was barely awake himself.

I got down to my bunk and was slowly dozing off when suddenly I heard a high-pitched screech – so loud I can still hear it to this day. Everything plunged into darkness, the engine pitch switched from its familiar, contented hum to a piercing whine and I could sense the boat was no longer moving in the direction it was supposed to.

The screeching got worse and worse until the catamaran's skin was reverberating with the sickening sound of metal rubbing angrily against metal. It was like being stuck in a horror movie: I felt as though I was inside a waste-collection lorry that was about to clamp its enormous metal jaws shut at any moment and crush everything inside into a tiny ball of mangled fibreglass and metal.

I leapt off my bunk and clambered straight out the back door on to the deck at the rear of the boat, ready to take my chances and leap straight out into the Channel's freezing, black water. Something was seriously wrong, I'd never experienced or heard anything like it before but, as I hoisted myself on to the deck, I instinctively looked up.

It was like the world had been blanked out: all I could see was the arse end of a huge cargo ship, utterly obliterating the horizon as it towered over us, leaving behind a huge churning mass of boiling water that was tossing us around like we were a leaf in a hurricane.

I looked to the front of our boat: its crumpled nose told me instantly what had happened. The cargo ship had clearly pinched the front of the catamaran, pulled us around 90 degrees and then slammed us back into its rear end as it ploughed on. We were lucky, though. This particular ship had rounded cheeks at the back, so when we collided, the impact was slightly cushioned. If we'd hit it in the middle, we'd have sunk – probably without trace. Although the cargo ship pushed us down in the water as it carried on past us, it also let us go, dragging us further around in the process.

I found my mate, who was stood in a daze, barely moving, his jaw God knows how many fathoms below the water. Even in the dark, I could see his skin looked as white as a sheet. 'How the fuck did that happen?' I yelled, but he was too shell-shocked to speak.

Then I scrambled around lifting hatches to make sure we weren't sinking. Chunks had been ripped off the front but – as I desperately tried to push them back into jagged holes and gaps – I realised there was no sign that we were going under. The relief in that moment was overwhelming. It felt like we'd miraculously survived a bomb blast – and, as my senses clicked back into place and the adrenalin started to surge through my veins, I noticed the cargo ship slowly disappearing from sight and yelled: 'You didn't get us, you bastard!'

Deep down, I knew it hadn't got the faintest clue we were even there. That was the scariest bit.

It didn't half teach me a lesson. I was irresistibly drawn to the Channel's shipping lanes. There are two of them – Westbound and Eastbound. In many ways, they're a bit like a giant M25 of the seas, an endless procession of huge, hulking ships – like great, big, articulated lorries – ploughing up and down, weaving in and out, slaloming with each other and pushing their heaving engines ferociously as they carry colossal crates and cargo, usually between mainland Europe and the entire American continent.

Between the two lanes is a 5-mile stretch of sea, a bit like the central reservation on a motorway I suppose. I call it the separation zone and it's somewhere very few fishermen are prepared to enter, mainly because their boats aren't big enough to reach that far – and they don't want to run the risk of smashing into a passing container ship like we had.

The alarm bells always rang in my head whenever I saw one of these big beasts in the area. I'd see them approaching as we'd be heading north to south, pulling pots, and I'd watch them closely, thinking, *They'll see us in a moment, they'll have someone on watch, they can't miss us, surely?*

It was a bit like a game of cat and mouse but the rule of the sea is simple and universal: they have to give way to fishing boats. So long as they see us, that is.

Sometimes my nerve would crack and I'd get on to Channel 16 – a communication frequency every boat tunes in to – and, even though I wouldn't know the cargo ship's name, I'd say something like, 'This is fishing vessel *Galwad Y*

Mor, this is my position (my latitude and longitude) – you are to my starboard side, 1.5 miles off, travelling at a speed of 15 knots. Please give way, we are a fishing vessel in the process of retrieving crab pots. Please respond on Channel 16.'

They have to give way to us. It's the law. Sometimes they come back straight away, saying: 'Hi mate, yeah we see you, you're fine, we'll come across your bow.' When they make that contact, you know it's all OK and you can breathe freely again. But sometimes they don't come back to you at all and you're thinking, *Has this fucker seen me?*

Then you have a right dilemma. You still carry on hauling the pots because that's the business and there's money at stake, but you definitely slow down a bit and get back on the radio. If that fails, you finally call the Solent coastguard. 'Fishing vessel *Galwad Y Mor* here, I'm in position such and such, I've got a vessel 1.2 miles away from me, travelling this course, can you please try to raise him.'

Usually, when you call the coastguard like that on Channel 16, the cargo ship hears the call and suddenly bursts into life, mid-conversation. They'll come in over the top of the coastguard, insisting: 'Oh, fishing vessel *Galwad Y Mor*, yeah, we've seen you, there's no problem.'

The last thing they want is the coastguard on their backs because they can get done for it. But even then, there are no guarantees.

Sometimes you get no response at all, even after you've alerted the coastguard. There have been times when I've stopped trawling, and I'm about to order Scott to cut the string of pots because we need to get out of the way quickly or else we'd be done for.

Cutting the rope is the last thing I want to do because that's going to cost us time – and me money – to get it back later. It's better, though, than seeing your buoys getting severed off their lines and watching months, if not years, of hard graft sink irretrievably.

It's my call and sometimes we've been so close, the nippers have been on deck hooting and hollering at the cargo ship, even picking up crabs and hurling them in a bid to get noticed. Sometimes we've looked up to actually see the container crew waving back at us, smiling and laughing without a care in the world!

Christ, your old heart is racing and going ten to the dozen, and you're cursing when that happens. It's even worse in the middle of the night, or in a storm, or when there's a dense fog out there and you can't even see the end of your own boat. When it's like that, I'm on the radio all the time, calling the coastguard and leaving absolutely nothing to chance.

Once you've actually experienced being hit by one of these bastards, you swear you'll never let it happen again. In fact, I made damned sure it never did, especially once I'd got the *Galwad*.

After all, why would I take such an insane gamble with a boat I'd waited a lifetime to buy?

No, I'd *never* play Russian roulette with the *Galwad* just when it was about to turn my life around. I'd *never* take it out in a fierce storm and steer it perilously close to 66,500 tonnes of heaving steel ploughing past me at 20 knots.

Never.

Chapter 5

NIKKI'S SENTENCE

Sometimes I close my eyes and try to recall the good stuff: the laughs and the happiness and the love but it always ends the same way. A dark shadow creeps in and spreads and spreads until all that's left – in cruel, vivid detail – is the moment my wife was told, 'You have six months left to live.'

You what?

We were sat in a little office inside the island's main hospital at Newport. Nikki's oncologist was stood behind a desk stacked high with grey wire-mesh files stashed with piles of paper. It dawned on me that each piece of paper was a declaration of who got to live and who got to die.

The oncologist looked weary and uncomfortable and I wondered why she didn't sit down like us. In front of her was an open report and she kept running a pen down the pages, pausing at certain points as if she were digesting some important information. Her face rarely looked up.

'If we do nothing, you've got six months.'

She sounded calm, like it was a matter-of-fact sentence devoid of emotion. Silence filled the room; I turned to Nikki

– her cheeks, usually bright and rosy, had instantly turned sickly white, her face frozen as the devastation sank in. Before we could react and protest and say *surely there's been a mistake*, the oncologist continued.

'However, if we get you straight on to chemotherapy then you might survive another year beyond that.'

You what?

It was January 2010. Four months later I was arrested. Back then, though, it was Nikki getting sentenced.

We walked out in a daze, holding hands ferociously, like we were desperately clinging on to the rest of our lives. In fact, I turned to Nikki and said: 'Sorry luv, but I need to go back and hear that again.'

I found the specialist standing in one of those bleak-yet-functional hospital corridors, extra wide so trollies carrying bodies to operations and wards could be pushed down them. She was leaning against a grubby whitewashed wall, pock-marked with black smears where the trollies had no doubt scraped against them. She looked exhausted. Maybe telling us had knocked the stuffing out of her as well. I wasn't in the mood for pleasantries, though.

'What's going on?' I asked. 'Are you telling me my wife has terminal cancer and the good side might be eighteen months if she takes the treatment, and the bad side is six months if she doesn't?'

'Yes, that's correct.'

How could it be? My Nikki was indestructible. She had more balls than me. In fact, I called her 'Stormin' Norman' because nothing – absolutely nothing – got in her way.

I first spotted Nikki when she was working in the Mary Rose pub in Ryde High Street. I was about 19 and a pisshead. I'd gone in with some mates, saw her behind the bar, and said to one of them: 'Who's that then, she's a bit of all right, ain't she.'

'That's my cousin. She's called Nik,' came the reply.

I kept finding reasons to drink in the Mary Rose after that and chatted to Nikki a few times as she pulled pints or cleaned up the bar. Eventually, I plucked up the courage to ask her out. Maybe it was some kind of sick omen, but two of our first 'dates' were spent in court. First, her cousin was up for fighting. He was given four years – a really big sentence on the island at the time. Then, not long after, I got into a ruck and had to go to court myself. 'What you doing next week, Nik? How d'you fancy coming to court with me!' *Romantic, eh?*

A year later, we got married. I was a different person by then – thanks to her. I'd been nabbed too many times, always for laddish stuff, half pissed and fighting with nippers from other towns. That's what we did. At weekends we'd head for a nightclub somewhere on the other side of the island and half the time we'd end up in a ruck with the local lads.

Nobody got really hurt, it was all mouth and posturing, but sometimes one of us would get dragged off by the Old Bill. I got fined, then I got nicked for a more nasty punch-up. Nikki and I were serious by now, the fishing was taking over my life and I suddenly thought: *Jamie, you can either carry on getting nicked – or sort yourself out.*

So that's what I did. I grew up a bit. I realised I was happy with Nik; I didn't need to be getting pissed all the time and getting into rucks. If I'd carried on I'd have been banged up just like my old man and I didn't want that.

Nikki was a catch, all right. She wasn't tall, about 5ft 1in, with short, dark hair, and beautiful, deep eyes that melted me every time. She adored horses and had worked full-time at one of the racing stables in Newmarket before coming back to the island. Just like me, she was outdoorsy – she loved walking dogs – and, just like me, she didn't give a damn. She wore jeans and jumpers, not dresses and frills; she was her own person, bubbly, feisty, and everyone else could sod off.

We really clicked. I could talk to her, tell her everything – moan to her about the bloody crew – and it just felt natural. I'd tell her about my battles with rival fishermen and the authorities and she completely got it. She was as much anti-establishment as I was but she was no pushover, either. If she thought I was wrong, she'd say so; if she wasn't happy, I'd know.

Being with her kept me out of trouble, even slowed me down a bit until I started seeing things with a bit more perspective. I didn't go off on one all the time, and I didn't go out to get into trouble. Unless a mate was involved; if one ended up in a ruck, then we all did. Some things never changed.

It wasn't long before Nikki and I moved into a little flat in Ryde together. By the time we got married she was six months pregnant and Maisy was born in 1989. I was working flat out with the fishing, building the boats and trying to earn as much as I could to support Nik and the little 'un. We had hard times, of course, but mainly good ones. It was all part of life; I was with someone I loved, I had my first kid and every-thing was all right.

Around 1995 we moved over to West Wight where my par-ents opened a fish shop to sell the catches we were bringing back. Trade was good and customers would often say, 'Why don't you open a restaurant as well? It'd be great to eat fresh fish here.'

Eventually, that's what happened. Downstairs was the fish shop and upstairs got converted into the restaurant. The busi-ness was called Salty's, which was my old man's nickname, given to him by my sister – who insisted his goodnight kisses always tasted salty!

Our second daughter, Poppy, had now arrived and once we'd moved over to West Wight, Nikki started working in the shop. It wasn't long before our son, Jesse, was born.

Throughout it all, Nikki never lost her love of horses. As our girls grew she spent a lot of time teaching them about ponies until it eventually became serious and Poppy ended up on the UK showjumping circuit until she was about 16. We had four ponies and they'd regularly go off competing.

That's pretty much how it was – until our world suddenly capsized around us. Nikki had found a lump in her right breast and got referred to hospital, where she had a biopsy. I went with her that day and was still pretty much ignorant of where it was all heading. *My Nikki's indestructible.* There were no anxious conversations between us. I genuinely thought everything would be fine. She was in no pain, we were laughing and smiling with life, the fishing was good and Poppy was having a great time with the ponies.

Indeed, I was out fishing when Nikki went back to the hospital with her mum for the biopsy results. I'd just gone round the Needles when I gave her a call to check all was good. 'How's it gone?'

There was a short silence that told me everything. Then Nikki's voice, trying to be strong. Trying to be Stormin' Norman. 'It's not good. He's saying it's alive, the tumour is active. They'll have to go straight in and operate within two weeks.'

Oh.

'Ok, look, I've just passed the Needles, I'll be home soon.'

I put the phone down and steered the *Galwad* back into Yarmouth. *Nikki'll be all right.*

She could have had the breast removed immediately, and maybe should have done. But it was nearly Christmas and she insisted: 'I'll get it done in January. I don't want all this drama over Christmas and New Year. Let's just enjoy ourselves.'

It wasn't until a couple of weeks after the operation that we were told how long she had left to live. The results had come back and it was like being handed a sentence in court. In fact, I still wasn't taking it in, even after I'd gone back to the oncologist and asked her to repeat what she'd said.

I was hearing words but they weren't landing anywhere. Metastatic. That was one of the words. The cancer had gone metastatic.

Nik was still outside in the hospital foyer waiting for me. I was the one falling apart. I remember her saying, 'If you don't pull yourself together, Jamie, I won't have the fuckin' treatment.'

I was more angry and frustrated that something so evil had picked on her. Why the fuck did she get it when there were plenty of other bastards out there who drank and smoked all their lives yet got fuck all? That's what I was really angry about. Why were the scumbags allowed to carry on living?

We decided to tell the kids as soon as we got home. Jesse was a young teenager by then and the two girls were a bit older. We sat them round the kitchen table and repeated what the oncologist had said. There were tears and hugs and then questions. I remember Jesse kept saying, 'You'll be all right, Mum, it'll all be OK.'

Yeah, that's right, Jesse. Mum's Stormin' Norman.

The girls were a bit more subdued. I think they had a better idea of what was in store. They realised. Nik, predictably, remained her usual self. She couldn't stand people fussing over her, especially when they started asking, 'Are you all right?'

'Of course I'm all right, I'm here aren't I?'

It was her decision to fight it, not mine; her choice to have all the chemo pumped into her body. You have to be a warrior to get through stuff like that and she had the courage to take it head on. She wasn't ready to throw in the towel so, come January, the treatment began.

The hospital staff couldn't have done more but, at first, the chemo knocked the shit out of Nikki. She'd come home physically obliterated and go straight to bed, sapped of strength and energy. She lost her hair and her immune system constantly broke down, leaving her exposed to flu bugs and colds that would have bounced off her in the past.

We were worried all the time but everyone rallied round, especially her mum and dad, who'd take her to hospital for more chemo whenever I had to go out fishing. We knew she couldn't win the battle; it was all about management and trying to find the smallest thing that might give her an edge.

I threw myself into researching alternative medicines and natural remedies. I'd always believed anything natural could only do good, unlike all the processed crap we'd lived off for years.

I got Nikki taking so many pills and supplements you could practically hear her rattling. Shark fins' tablets was one of them. They're used a lot in Asian countries because sharks never get diseases so their immune systems are incredibly strong. *There must be something in this*, I reasoned. *Sharks are practically bulletproof.*

We discovered juicing, then I read about wheatgrass, which you can get in liquid form. My God, that stuff's rank! The first time Nikki tried it, she spat it right out and said: 'Urggh, that's disgusting. You try giving it a go.' So, I took one quick slug, wiped my mouth, trying desperately not to vomit, and replied, 'Mmm, lovely, that's good, you'll be all right with that.'

Next I hit on vitamins. Zinc was one. I gave her no choice: 'Come on you're having some of these now.' She was rattling all right. I'd begun to understand what metastatic meant. The cancer had spread into new areas and the only option was to bombard Nikki's entire system with anything and everything.

The question was: would any of it work? Could we find a combination of chemo and natural supplements that would knock this bastard out? Or at least give Nikki more time?

Chapter 6

HELD AT GUNPOINT

I didn't see the handgun until I jumped out of my van.

I was effing and blinding and ready to have another blazing row with the police but before my feet had even touched the ground a booming voice – just like a sergeant major's – roared, 'Armed police! Get your hands above your head! Do it … NOW!'

I stared straight in front of me and there, in front of lorries, cars and foot passengers queuing for the Lymington Pier to Yarmouth Wightlink ferry, stood three officers in full combat gear, with wide leather straps criss-crossing padded jackets and stern faces under black peaked caps.

One of them, the one in the middle, was standing slightly ahead of the others with his legs planted firmly apart, his right arm pressed tight against his torso, his hand hovering over a small black holster that dangled, almost casually, from a black belt around his waist. Inside the holster I could clearly see the handle of a gun – probably a revolver – running parallel with his belt. I watched, transfixed, as his fingers drifted dangerously close to the handle, as though he was preparing for a shoot-out at the O.K. Corral or something.

I remember thinking: *If I make one false move now, this bastard is going to do it.*

I couldn't believe or fully take in what was happening: a shooter in the car park at Lymington Pier. It was like a scene from some cheap Western movie – only this was the pay and display car park immediately next to the Brockenhurst branch line. I remember seeing the coffee sign outside the small ferry building where I'd waited many, many times before. It was surreal.

I'd just spent the entire night driving with my missus to Grimsby and back, where we'd collected our usual bulk supply of fish bait. I was weary and irritable – we'd just missed the ferry back to the island as we pulled into the car park and knew we'd have to wait an hour for the next one. I parked up the van, said to Nikki, 'let's get a tea' – when suddenly there was an almighty banging noise on each of the van's front doors, like someone was trying to batter them down with iron bars. I looked out of the driver's window, saw police uniforms and jumped out ready to give them a mouthful.

That's when I first saw the gun. As I struggled to work out what on earth was going on, one of the officers turned me round against the van and frisked me like I was a terrorist about to storm the coffee shop. As he did so, I glimpsed through the windows of my driver's cab and saw a female officer on the other side, doing the same to Nikki. That did it for me: that was my cue to give them both barrels instead.

'What the hell are you dozy bastards doing?' I demanded. 'What the fuck is this?'

Foot passengers were starting to crowd round now and windows were being wound down in cars and lorries. It must have been unbelievable entertainment for everyone there, especially the holidaymakers. I turned and the officer who had just frisked me said, 'You've got drugs on board that van, haven't you?'

'You what?'

I'd bought the freezer van about two years earlier purely so I could save time and money getting bait. Before, I'd hired lorries to traipse up and down to Grimsby where I knew a supplier who could sell it to me far cheaper than the local blokes on the island.

It was a right performance getting there and back, however. I'd have to take a car over to the mainland, park it, hire a lorry, drive it up and down the M1 to Grimsby, where I'd load it, drive it back, take it over to the island on the ferry, unload it and stick all the bait in a huge freezer at home. Then, I'd have to take the lorry back on the ferry to the mainland, return it, pick my car up – and take it back to the island on the ferry.

'There's got to be a better way,' I kept telling Nikki, who'd often come with me to share the driving. So, I decided to buy my own freezer lorry, an ex-hire one, and everything instantly became much easier: we'd take the van over on the ferry, drive up to Grimsby, load up – then come straight back home.

I was probably the only fisherman on the island doing this; the rest bought their bait locally. I was aware rumours and whispers were doing the rounds – *hello, how's Green found the money to buy his own freezer van* – the usual island jealousy. Some of my rivals would get tanked up in the pub, get a bit gobby and in voices just loud enough to be heard, slur, 'How comes you go all that way to get your bait?'

'Because it's cheaper, you knob.'

This trip had been no different from the previous ones. Nikki and I had got the midnight ferry, I'd driven up through the night – when the motorway was nice and empty – and reached the cold store in Grimsby at 7 a.m.. There, we loaded up with bait, had some breakfast and a chat with the supplier, then – around 10 a.m. – Nikki took the wheel and started to drive back.

That's when the first warning signal went up, although neither of us twigged at the time. I was getting a bit of shut-eye when Nikki suddenly started a sentence she didn't immediately finish. 'I'm not being funny …' I opened my eyes and turned, waiting for her to complete what she was about to say. I could see she was trying to peer into the wing mirror and I was thinking, *Hurry up, I want some kip*, when she added: 'But there's a helicopter following us.'

I was like, 'What, oh yeah, right, now just be quiet will you?'

Nevertheless, I tried looking out myself but couldn't see anything. Ten minutes later, though, she suddenly shouted, 'There! Look – it's back again'. This time I wound my window down and sure enough there was a helicopter hovering close by. 'It can't be following us,' I said.

'Well, it's definitely the same one.'

That was the last we saw of it. We eventually reached the M1 and carried on driving until we reached the ferry terminal. That's where the police pounced and said we'd got drugs in the back of the van. I burst out laughing. 'What do you mean "I've got drugs on board"? Are you having a laugh? I've just driven all the way to Grimsby and back.' Then it clicked. 'Oh, that's what the bloody helicopter was all about. You tossers.'

I completely lost it. 'Right, get round here.' With that, I barged past them to the back of the wagon, which had a tailgate, and yanked up the shutter door. Inside was a dense cloud of thick, white, frosty smoke, which sent an icy blast – and a rancid stench of fish bait – streaming over the officers' bemused faces as they tried to peer in. I turned the light on and said, 'Go on, get your arses in there, get the fish out, stack it on the quay, do what you want, search it all – I don't care – but when you've finished, put every fuckin' bit of it back.

'I'm going for a cup of tea.'

I was making a right performance of it. I had an audience, people were 10ft away, and I was deliberately playing up to them, cursing the police and making it embarrassing for them. 'Here you go – start with this,' and I hurled some bait boxes on to the quay floor so they'd land at their feet. 'Have a sort through them for starters.' The stench, by now, was enough to make anyone retch.

There was loads of it, too. The van was jammed with trays stacked up to the ceiling with a gap of about 3ft at the top. Even I smirked as two officers clambered in to have a look. All I could hear was them retching and groaning and going 'urrgghh'. Ha!

They came out of there like a dose of salts, trying desperately to wipe away slimy, jellified bits of fish bait that was sliding and slithering down the fronts of their black, tough-guy jackets. I was in stitches.

'Found your drugs then, have you?' I sneered.

That's when they wiped the grin off my face, though. 'Well,' they replied, 'you must have upset someone.'

I stopped clowning instantly and thought for the first time about the enormity of what I'd just experienced. They were right: a lot of time and expense would have gone into this. The helicopter, the armed police, this was heavyweight stuff.

'What do you mean?' I asked.

'You must have – we got a call saying you were bringing drugs back.'

'Don't give me that,' I replied, my mind turning over the small details of what had just unfolded. 'What, you got a random call and you went to all this trouble? You got a helicopter monitoring me down the bleeding motorway and you just took the word of someone who just called in, out of the blue? Don't give me that. Who's behind all this?'

'We'll call you over the weekend,' was their reply and, with that, they scarpered – leaving me and Nikki to pick up the boxes I'd hurled out of the van.

They never bothered calling, of course. But I was incensed and wanted an explanation. Why had they used armed police? What lies had they been told? Who had claimed I had drugs on board? And why did they believe it? Who'd done this? Who had it in for me?

I wanted an answer, so I rang Fareham police station myself two days later. 'What happened?' I asked the desk sergeant.

'Well, you've clearly upset someone but obviously they gave us false information,' he replied, picking his words very carefully, unwilling to give much away. 'Nothing further is going to happen.'

I put the phone down, explained what the police had said to Nikki and she immediately asked the million-dollar question: 'Who've you rowed with lately, then?'

Chapter 7

'YOU'RE UP TO RUNNING DRUGS'

The truth was, I had loads of enemies. We all did – the entire family – and I knew what Nikki was getting at. The police, rival fishermen, bar owners, marine authorities – anybody and everybody who'd ever tried to tell me what to do. I'd fought and cursed them all. I'd even been locked up overnight in the police cells for being pissed up and gobby, although I'd always been allowed home the following morning, nursing a hangover and ready for a bollocking.

I think I was rowing when I came out of the womb. It ran in my blood: as a family, we were always anti-establishment. When I was at school my old man was banged up for six months after fighting with the police outside a nightclub. He'd already been banned from every pub in Yarmouth by then – usually for fighting or arguing. I very quickly learned to question any form of authority and I've had a healthy contempt of petty rules and regulations ever since.

You need to be like that – a free spirit – to be a fisherman, or else you won't make it. You've got to have balls, you've got to stand your ground and stick up for yourself. Half of them – the establishment that is, the authorities and the pen-pushers – they hadn't got a clue what we went through to make a living. I had run-ins and fights with all of them and they probably all thought I was a complete gobshite. I rebelled. I didn't want them sticking their snouts in my life, my business. Looking back, I probably wound them all up the wrong way.

We worked hard, real tough graft – then we came home and drank. My bust-ups were usually after a session in the pub, and could be over stupid stuff like which match were they going to screen in the bar. But Nikki's question immediately got me thinking about two incidents with the police that had stuck in my mind.

I was in the Bugle one night when I started chatting to an ex-copper I knew. He was one of the better ones, and now that he was retired we could be a little bit more matey. I was moaning to him about the police when he leaned into me, stared straight into my eyes and said quietly, 'Listen to me: they don't like you lot. They think you're up to running drugs.' As he said it, I could see a blue vein that ran across the top of his bald head start to pulse heavily.

'You what? Where they got that from?' I snapped back. I already suspected some of my rivals, jealous of our boats, jealous of the fish restaurant, jealous of our success, jealous of bloody everything we did, would love to tell everyone we were funding it all from drug money. But I'd never heard the police – albeit an ex-policeman – say it.

'I don't know but I'm telling you the big boys have got the arse with you lot.' The vein was still pulsing. It reminded me of a blue flashing light on top of a police car.

'What do you mean "you lot"?'

I don't know why I even asked him that. I already knew the answer. They'd had it in for my dad, so they had it in for all of us. They'd even tried to screw the restaurant business by blocking our application to serve alcohol.

Because my dad had a record, my mum – who used to do social work when we lived on the other side of the island – applied for a licence in her name. The police didn't want that, so they stuck two undercover cops inside the restaurant to try to prove we were serving alcohol to customers who weren't having a meal.

This time, though, my old man properly outwitted them. He recognised the two undercover officers and plied them with complimentary drinks until they literally fell out of the restaurant pissed out of their brains! It cost my folks an absolute fortune to get the licence, but the police couldn't stop them. I'm proud to say that in the entire time Salty's has had a licence – and a separate bar below the restaurant – the police have never been called and there has never once been any trouble.

They think you're up to running drugs. That's what my ex-copper mate had said and, as the words pounded around in my head, I recalled another strange incident.

I'd been in the pub one night with a previous crew and the drunker they got, the more they started arguing and pushing and shoving one other. The mood got uglier so I waded in and sacked one of them there and then. 'I can't have you here, it's over, it's time you went.'

He wouldn't take it, though, and called the police, who eventually showed up and asked me, half-heartedly, what had gone on. They clearly weren't much interested in yet another pub brawl involving Jamie Green.

A few days later, however, another one of the crew decided to quit and headed back to his home town, Middlesbrough. Incredibly, the police followed him all the way up there but instead of quizzing him about the pub fight, asked: 'Were you on the boat when Jamie was running drugs?' I know it happened because the Middlesbrough lad phoned up my daughter and told her what the police had said.

They think you're up to running drugs.

I realised my ex-copper mate was right. There was a flag with my name on it on the police system. I was on their radar and if they could find a way to link me to a crime, they probably would. But someone must have been stirring it up in the background, passing on rumours, whispering sentences that started with the words 'Jamie Green' and ended with 'drugs'.

Who? Did people out there hate me so much they'd deliberately tell the police I was running drugs – just to get me banged up and out of the way? Is the fishing business that savage? That cut-throat?

Categorically, yes.

There may be no guns and torpedoes, but the Isle of Wight fishing business is practically a war zone. All that's missing is the bullets. Rivals will stop at nothing to destroy each other's lives and I've had long-running feuds with loads of them. I've known fishermen cut my lines or screw up my gear. I've done it to theirs. I've known rival boats go too close to mine, deliberately trying to entangle my pots so I'd have no chance of earning. I've done it to theirs.

I could name two local fishing families who detested everything I stood for. I was rucking with Geoff Blake, from the island, and Graham Butler over in Lymington, for five or six years over who had the right to fish where. One dispute, with Blake, was so bitter it ended up in crown court – the only time I'd ever been hauled in front of a judge before.

I'd gone out in lumpy weather with my crew and I was in a foul temper. I was certain Blake had been cutting my lines and I could see his boat, smaller than mine, fishing in the same area I was heading for. My catamaran was swinging from side to side, tilting and rocking us as waves crashed around. Our hands were

like human windscreen wipers, trying desperately to rub away
the wind-lashed water, yet, in the middle of this chaos, I chose –
because I was insane with anger – to steer suicidally close to him.

As far as he was concerned, I had no right to be fishing
anywhere near him. Half blinded by the sea spray, and totally
blinded by rage, I pulled the catamaran parallel to his boat and
went so close that, if I'd miscalculated the inches between us,
or misjudged the next blast of weather, we'd have collided
and either one of us, but probably him, would have capsized.
We must have looked like two pirate boats squaring up to raid
one another.

I was playing with fire, taunting, intimidating, bullying him
into backing off, letting him see what he was messing with.
I was calling him every name under the sun and I'll admit
it must have looked and sounded pretty threatening. The
next thing I knew he was on to the coastguard claiming I was
trying to ram his boat out of the water.

The pair of us ended up in Winchester Crown Court in
front of an exasperated judge who clearly thought we were
wasting his time with our island squabbles. As far as we were
concerned, it was a battle of principles, we were fighting for
our rights and we'd both been pushed to the edge. The judge
didn't see it like that and angrily kicked the case out of court.
But I'll never forget the lecture he gave us before we left.

'Let me tell you gentlemen,' – and he spat the word 'gentleman' out like it was rancid piece of crabmeat stuck in his
mouth. 'You two live on the Isle of Wight, and not in Italy.
You're not the mafia, and you're not fighting some kind of
Sicilian Crab War. Sort yourselves out.'

The judge was right but he'd also missed the point. The
hatred between me – and my rivals – was real, and it was
deep. We would never 'sort it out'. When I was next back in
court – accused of smuggling drugs – the crown prosecution

presented information about the way I set up my pots and lines, and yet nobody from the police and marine authorities ever went out to inspect my gear. Somebody who knew how I operated had told them.

In fact, I was constantly having run-ins with the Maritime Coastguard Agency (MCA) and their silly laws. In my mind, they were trying to stop me fishing wherever I wanted, no doubt because our rivals had called and begged them to do something. They even sent one of their pen-pushers around my house one day, armed with a clipboard stuffed with their pathetic rules and regulations. The more he talked, the more incensed I got until I pushed out my arms and started forcibly shovelling him back down the path until he stumbled out of our gate. 'Don't let me see your face round here ever again,' I hissed.

Was it a coincidence, then, that two years later I'd come face to face in court with a former enforcement officer for the MCA? Or were the police and all these agencies – and everyone else who seemed to hate us – simply joined at the hip?

It was obvious to me – and my family – that the more successful we became, the more boats we built, and the more we expanded our business, the nastier the relationship between us and our rivals and everyone else became. Rivals turned into enemies.

Most of them were still fishing in grounds they'd always fished in. There's a rule of thumb that if someone's fished an area for a long time then you approach that person and try to work something out. It never worked like that for me, though. This was no gentlemen's club. Instead of saying, 'I've been here for twenty years, this is where I'm fishing but you can have a turn over there,' they'd send me to an area they already knew was empty. When I came back, they'd start messing with my gear – then insist it was the sea or the tide causing the damage.

They'd had it all their own way for decades, made a fortune out of it but now they had someone they couldn't control and they didn't like it. Suddenly there was a young kid on the block, me, trying to muscle in and I'm sure their instant reaction was: *We'll get rid of him.*

As far as I was concerned, though, I didn't give a toss who'd fished where and for how long. The sea was as much mine as theirs.

I was definitely making enemies. Everyone before who'd tried to do what I was doing had encountered the same resistance and they'd all backed off. I told them to fuck off, instead. I didn't help myself; my personality put me out there, I suppose. Mind you, I wouldn't change it. I did what I had to, or else I'd have ended up like the rest of them. They were happy to spread what they caught amongst themselves, two or three of them, and try to keep everyone else out of it.

Well, sod that. We'd just moved over to the west side of the island and we were building more and more boats, each one bigger than the last. At the time, the price of boats was going up pretty rapidly, just like property, so if you built one yourself you could make good money selling it on – leaving you with enough to finance the next one. That was exactly what we did.

We were building a business empire based around the boats and the fishing – and it was working. Salty's was booming and the freezer van meant I could drive over to London twice a week and supply some high-end restaurants there. A fish shop just off the King's Road, and another in Kensington, started taking our crab and lobsters, then a couple of restaurants in Covent Garden became regular customers. It meant we could cash in on the holiday visitors to the Isle of Wight during the summer, and then sell to the London market in winter when it was seasonally flat on the island. I was getting £1,500 a week there – when our rivals were selling next to nothing.

I even had a Spanish exporter who I'd meet once a week and he'd take our fish over to the big markets in Madrid and Bilbao. It was a real family affair as well. My sister, Nicky, and my mum and dad were running Salty's, while my missus was doing some processing. We'd even set up our own business – We've Got Crabs – selling directly to local businesses and restaurants from our home, East Tapnell Cottage.

During the course of a year, I was turning over around £180,000. OK, wages and costs and mortgage repayments on our house and the boat had to come out of that, but, financially, we were making a go of it – and the *Galwad* was at the epicentre of it all. With my smaller boats, I was barely doing half that amount.

I'm pretty sure the locals saw all this and the green-eyed monster surfaced. Most of them had never changed their boat in the past twenty years. They had no way of making me brown nose to them so the old-school fishermen, who knew where and how to stir up grief, who knew which ears to bend, started spreading their poison. They made out I was trouble, up to no good. Then they embellished it.

What started as idle pub talk rapidly turned into a full-blown rumour. Then something more dangerous happened. It became a 'must-be-true' fact that, in turn, found its way to the police. It's not difficult to understand how.

'How comes the bloody Greens are building another boat? Where they getting the money from? How comes they could afford that freezer lorry? You heard the latest? They're opening a downstairs bar under their fish restaurant – how they funding that, then? Don't tell me they've earned it from fishing.

'They're up to running drugs that lot.'

There's nothing the Isle of Wight loves more than a good rumour. Life revolves around the pub – and there's no better place to spread a bit of gossip than there, where the bloke knocking back a pint at the bar is just as likely to be a copper as he is a scaffolder. Everyone knows everybody else and every little bit of chit-chat quickly becomes full-blown indisputable if it's juicy enough. *I'm telling you it's a fact.* It was bound to reach the police – they just had to be in the right bars to hear it.

I'm convinced that's what happened; a slow, insidious whispering campaign spread by fishermen who hated our operation, and our success, who let anyone willing to listen hear their theories about where we'd got our money from. In turn, people started telling the people they knew until it was no longer a rumour but a great, big, whopping fact. That's when it reached the police, who naturally listened but didn't have any actual evidence. So they went looking for it – hence the Grimsby incident …

Chapter 8

HARD LABOUR

Crew. What a gigantic ball ache. I've been through so many, I could have opened a branch of the United Nations. I've taken them from Poland, Lithuania, Estonia, the Philippines, Nigeria, Czechoslovakia – mainly Eastern Bloc countries, I guess. The Poles were probably the best, they didn't mind hard graft, but all that mattered to me was finding a reliable body for around £60 a day, cash.

Sounds easy but the only lesson I ever learned about crew was to rely on none of them.

Some never showed, some showed then realised they didn't like the look of it so fucked right off; some, who I thought might be OK, turned out to be shit and some – who I predicted would be on the first ferry back – actually stuck it out.

The exceptions were Scott Birtwistle and Daniel Payne.

I've lost count of how many I've employed over the years but Scott was the first and only one who adored fishing as much as me. In fact, he was like a mini-me when I was a nipper and I wasn't going to let him go. I had big plans for him. That's how good he was.

He was only 17 when he first came over. I got in touch after seeing his advert on the industry website, findafishingboat.com. He lived over on the mainland at Selsey, which was practically local. He wanted work, I got in touch and he came over in December. He didn't even flinch when we headed straight out into that winter's rough seas.

I could tell instantly he was made for the job. Like me, he belonged on the *Galwad*.

He was a big, strong lad, willing to tackle hard work and get his hands dirty. Yes, he was still a kid, totally hooked on his PlayStation just like all the other nippers. He had a cheeky, boyish look but his hands were already those of an experienced fisherman. He knew how to shoot strings, how to splice rope and tie proper knots and how to empty and reload pots. He understood the logic of everything; there was very little I needed to teach him.

Lads like Scott were gold dust and once you found one, you hung on. Nikki and I had a couple of caravans at the back of our house, which the local holiday parks had been getting rid of, so we put him in one of those straight away.

From then on, it was inevitable Scott would become part of our family. As much as it's a job, we couldn't just leave him in the caravan and pretend he wasn't there. So, if I went into town for a few drinks, he'd come along. I wasn't going to say, 'Sorry, this is where you stay and I won't see you again until I next need you.' As far as I was concerned, if he was working for me, I'd look after him.

Scott spent that Christmas with us – we even bought him a bloody present, a jumper I think. He became one of us and, long term, I planned to bring him through so he could take on more responsibility with the boat and even have a say in the business.

The only other crew member I stuck with was Dan. I'd known him for fifteen years at least and his parents lived just round the corner from us. He wasn't as committed to fishing as me, but he definitely enjoyed it as a hobby. His really big passion was outdoor sports – he loved keeping fit and did a lot of surfing, kick-boxing and even snowboarding. Come to think of it, he was a bit of an Action Man type, with short-cropped, jet-black hair and a permanent five o'clock shadow glued to his face and chin. I'm sure he was at his happiest climbing some snow-peaked mountain and then snowboarding right back down it.

He was actually a builder by trade but whenever work slacked off he'd give me a call, or if I bumped into him I'd say: 'What you up to, then? Need a job?' I trusted Dan; our families knew one another, we drank together and we had history. That was good enough for me.

Scott and Dan were real rarities, though. Even if I knew they were both available at the same time, I'd still need another pair of hands on deck but trying to find even one person was a nightmare.

The local lads just weren't interested – including ones from the mainland. They didn't want the sweat or the hardship; they didn't like it when you said: 'I want to go out on the tide at 4 a.m.' No, they wanted to be coming home pissed at that time, instead. God help me if they were still half cut from the night before. Yet that was the sort I often landed up with – kids in the pub who liked a beer but needed some money so they could go straight back on the piss again the next night. Waking them in the mornings was nearly impossible.

In fact, that was another reason for getting the *Galwad*. Once I'd got them on board, they couldn't get pissed because I wouldn't let them have any booze on the boat. There was never any problem getting them up the next morning then.

There were a couple of surprises, I'll admit. One weekend I noticed a young lad hanging around the town. I'd seen him in the pub as well; you clock faces, you know who's local and who's not. He was back the next day on the quay so, out of nosiness, I said: 'What you up to then?'

'Oh, I'm looking for work. Anything really, maybe a bit of labouring.'

'Well, I have some work on my boat if you're interested.'

Turned out he was sleeping in the local bus shelter, so I let him kip on the boat for a while until he could afford some proper accommodation. Unlike many, he proved to be a hard worker, reliable and he even stayed for a few months. That's how I used to get them. Completely scattergun.

I had a 16-year-old come all the way down from the top of Scotland. He surprised me: he'd only just left school, couldn't find any work but saw my ad on the website. I swear I ended up speaking more to his dad about the job than the nipper himself.

'Look, if your boy wants to come down, he's more than welcome. He can live in one of the caravans around the back. It's not an apartment but it's OK for dossing – it's got hot and cold running water, it doesn't leak or anything plus it's got heating and a telly.

'Me and the missus will keep an eye on him, don't worry.'

So the kid came all the way down on a coach and I met him at the ferry terminal. He was only a little twig of a thing, Christ knows what he was thinking, but we settled him into the caravan and Nikki cooked him some dinner.

I took him out on the boat the next day with another lad and it was a bit choppy out there. The poor little kid was so sick he couldn't stand up. He was throwing up so much, the vomit was running down him as he tried to stay on his feet. He never stopped. He couldn't have weighed more than

7 stone but he was like a ringing wet tea towel by the time we got back.

'He'll be on the next ferry out of here and back on that coach to Scotland,' I said to Nikki that evening. But you know what? He bloody stuck it out. He had more guts than I gave him credit for – and he was with me for ages after that.

In the end, he did go back in Scotland – but only so he could work on the really big boats up there. When he heard about my trial, he rang my missus and asked after our son, Jesse. 'I can get him started up here if he wants. It's a big operation, what's he got to lose?' And that's exactly what Jesse did – packed his bags and headed up to Scotland, where he is still working for one of the biggest boat operators in the country. In fact, he's just qualified to skipper a ship by himself and I can't tell you how proud that's made me.

Unfortunately, none of that was how it usually panned out. Usually, I'd organise potential crew to arrive then half wouldn't show – or I'd organise two or three in the hope one might turn up and, low and behold, they'd all be there. I couldn't win.

Then there was Vic.

Chapter 9

VIC

At first, I wished I'd never set eyes on Vic. I wished he hadn't been recommended to me. I wished I'd taken one look at him and said, 'No, fuck off, he won't cut it.'

I didn't – and, despite all the nightmares that have happened since, I don't regret that. It turns out Vic's actually all right. Just don't ever take him to sea, that's all.

At the time, he was the extra pair of hands I thought I needed and that was all that counted. I didn't care if he was illegal or what his game was. I just wanted someone to stack the bloody lobster pots once Scott and Dan had dragged them on board. Vic had 'done some fishing' – or so I was told – and when he turned up I thought: *Well, he's here, so I might as well give him a go.*

Would I be banged up right now had Vic not shown? It's hard to answer that. All I know for certain is that he's as much a victim as the rest of us.

The way I stumbled upon Vic was completely random. A one-in-a-million shot but then that's how recruiting extra crew usually went.

I'd been in one of the pubs opposite the Red Jet ferry terminal in East Cowes, just having a quiet beer. I think it was the Fountain Inn, might have been the Vectis – whichever – I was stood at the bar and chatting to a bloke I half recognised. He probably half recognised me in the same way. I knew loads of people like that and I rarely got to know their names. I'd get pissed with them in the pub and still never know who they were by the end of the night.

I probably wouldn't see them again for months on end, until suddenly they'd be stood at the bar and it'd be, 'All right, mate, all right fella, how's it going?' and we'd be chatting all over again – usually about fishing.

That's exactly how it was in the Fountain. It felt like we were picking up on a conversation from whenever the last time was we'd been stood in the same pub together. Within minutes we were taking about finding crews.

'I can get hold of casual labour now and then, if you're ever looking,' he said. 'Oh aye, what sort?' I replied.

'Eastern bloc, mainly Poles.'

I must have scribbled my number on a scrap of paper for him and said something like, 'Look if you get anything, give me a call.' I certainly wasn't going to chase – if he called, great; if not, nothing lost.

I left soon after and didn't think any more of it. I'd scrawled my number out on countless scraps of paper to people I half knew and most times nothing ever came of them. That was how it went.

I never saw that bloke I half knew again and yet, around a year later, I suddenly got a phone call out of the blue.

'You gave me your number in the pub – you still looking for crew?'

'Yeah, why? What you got?'

'There's a bloke from Montenegro, he's looking for work and he's done some fishing. Do you want me to send him over? His name's Vic Something-or-Other.'

'Great, tell him I'll meet him at the Southsea hovercraft terminal on Friday. He needs to be there for 2 p.m.. Give him my number. Thanks, mate, I owe you.' I remember ending the call and thinking: *he'll just be another tosser who doesn't show*. To be honest, I was more bothered about getting some new pots I badly needed in time for my next trip.

I always got pots from a supplier in Weymouth so Scott and I set off in the *Galwad* around midnight on the Thursday night in order to catch the ebb tide all the way down. It doesn't matter what sort of boat you've got, you always have to make the best of the tides. Even though it meant setting off in the middle of the night, I knew the *Galwad* would steam along twice as fast if the tide was with us. Meanwhile, I sent Dan off to Stafford to get a new water pump for the boat.

We arrived in Weymouth around seven in the morning and the supplier drove over with the pots, which we loaded on to the boat. Then we all had a cup of tea and a chat in a local caff, picked up some rope and headed back around 11 a.m. that morning. However, this time we were going against the tide as we came around St Albans Head, off Swanage. Suddenly the journey was taking forever. There's nothing you can do when that happens, it's just the way it is.

I realised we weren't going to get back in time to meet matey from Montenegro, so when a good pal of mine, an Isle of Wight scaffolder called Jon Beere, suddenly called me on the boat I jumped at a chance for help. I knew he wouldn't mind. 'Beerey, do us a favour, will you mate? I'm stuck on the bloody tide and I'm meant to be meeting some foreign lad off the ferry. All I know is his name's Vic. I'm definitely not going to get back in time – would you mind picking him up in Southsea for us? That's if he turns up, of course. Take him for a pint or something. Just grab him and I'll get back as quick as I can.'

Jon and I had known each other since we were young kids, playing football, going fishing down the beach, or looking for rabbits out in the fields.

We went to the same schools but we sort of lost contact during our teenage years, mainly because he lived over Ryde way and I was on the west Wight by then. It wasn't until we'd both settled down, got married and had children of our own, that our paths crossed again. He might be in Yarmouth on a scaffolding job, we'd bump into each other, go to the pub, have a laugh. Next thing, Jon and his missus, Sue, would be coming over to Salty's and suddenly we were like schoolboy pals all over again.

Beerey agreed without complaint and around 1.30 p.m. phoned back to let me know all had gone to plan – although I never expected what else he had to say. 'I've got your lad – he barely speaks a word of English, by the way – but he's got two other blokes with him as well. One of them's doing the translating and he wants to know a few things about the job before they come over.'

'You what? The cheeky bastards. What things?' I replied.

'How much he'll be paid for starters and how long he'll be out for. Stuff like that.'

Straight away, I thought: *Here we go.* 'Tell them he'll be on sixty quid a day and we'll be out for a couple of days or so. If he wants it, I'll be happy to meet up when I get back.'

Before Beerey could say another word, I then added, 'What about the other two? What do they want? I haven't got any other jobs at the moment, make sure they understand that. What's their game, then?'

He replied, 'No, they don't seem to want any work.'

I had to go to Cowes to drop some crabs off first at a local restaurant there, so I told Beerey to meet up at the Sportsman's Rest in Porchfield, halfway between Cowes and my home. They were already there by the time I turned up, sat outside in the pub garden. It was a pleasant, warm evening and there were quite a few faces I half recognised out enjoying the spring air.

'What's the score, mate – everyone happy?'

Beerey introduced me to Vic, who stood up and we shook hands.

To my surprise, I was quietly optimistic, even though he barely spoke any English, just the odd word. He was tall, well over 6ft, black haired with a strong, athletic build, like he really looked after himself, maybe did some weights. I thought that was half a result and not at all what I'd expected. He looked as though he was built right for the job and probably had a good day's work in him. Turned out he was also a family man with three kids; like so many Eastern Europeans he wanted to earn money in the UK so he could send it back home.

By then, I'd sized up the other two – although I didn't yet know their names. They were polar opposites to Vic. One was short, balding and a whole lot podgier. He was clearly out of condition and I remember thinking: *thank Christ he doesn't want to be on the crew.* The other – the translator – was tall like Vic but with a far less muscular build. He liked to be called 'Dexsa' but that was obviously just a nickname.

There was nothing smart or remotely flash about any of them. They weren't dripping in designer, or even fake, jewellery and expensive watches. They weren't blinged up and they weren't wearing any top-end clothing, either. Just jeans and bog-standard shirts that were hanging outside their trousers. I guess they looked dodgy – but only in a *we're-all-*

here-on-forged-passports kind of way. I wouldn't have been surprised if that was the case.

I asked Dexsa whether Vic had been out on boats before and was told: 'Yes, yes, of course, he loves fishing back in Montenegro.' Jon then said they wanted to know more about the work and the pay. Our conversation went like this: I'd say something, Dexsa would nod to show he understood and then repeat it to Vic. Then he'd speak back, they'd have a chat between themselves, and I'd get asked some more details. Everything they asked was pretty straightforward and normal.

I turned to Dexsa and said: 'Tell him he'll be starting on £60 a day. Depends what he's like after that. If he's a good worker and we get some decent catches, it might rise to £80 or £90. But I have to see if he likes it first.' Then I outlined what the job involved, and what I'd want Vic to do – which was pretty much stack the pots after they'd been emptied. 'That's it, take it or leave it,' I said. 'I don't know him until he's proved himself. He ain't no good to me until I know.'

I may have sounded blunt but that's how I'd got with crew. I wanted them to be sure that they couldn't muck me about.

We were only together about twenty minutes before Dexsa stood up and said they all wanted to talk about it between themselves on their way back to the hovercraft terminal. Beerey, who was probably bored out of his brains by then, agreed to take them back to Ryde.

We all shook hands but before they left I said, 'If Vic wants the job, make sure he's on Yarmouth quay around 3 p.m. tomorrow afternoon.' I didn't know enough about him to offer him overnight accommodation – that wasn't my problem. He'd have to prove himself before I'd think about putting him up in one of the caravans at our house.

Once again, Dexsa repeated what I said and they all seemed to understand. Then he asked me for my phone number in case he had any more crew in the future. I definitely remember thinking: *Yep, you're running black-market labour, ain't you matey.*

Like I said, I wasn't interested in who they were or how they operated, but I was interested in anyone who could give me reliable staff. So I let Dexsa have my mobile number and also the satellite on the *Galwad* in case he wanted to check on Vic.

I spoke to Beerey later that evening, to check everything was OK and to thank him for helping out. 'You owe me a right favour with this one,' he said. 'We got to the bloody hovercraft terminal too late and they missed the last crossing. I had to take them over to the ferry instead. Vic is staying at a B&B in Newport, by the way. By the looks of it, I'd say he's going to give it a go.'

Chapter 10

SHIPS IN THE NIGHT

We set off around 4.30 p.m. on Saturday afternoon. I was amazed Vic had even showed. You could never tell with casual labour. I'd grabbed a few swift pints down Salty's and was walking back towards the quay when I bumped into Scott and Dan heading towards me – hoping for a last pint themselves. 'You two muppets can turn round for starters,' I grinned. I needed to catch the last of the ebb tide going down the Solent, and couldn't wait for them two pissheads to have a drink. 'Has the foreign lad turned up?'

'Yep,' replied Scott. 'He's been on board for half an hour or so.'

As we climbed on to the *Galwad*, I noticed the lads had neatly stacked sixty of the new pots I'd bought in Weymouth the night before, tied them to a new string and baited them up. The other sixty were left on the quay, we didn't need them all for this trip. I quickly said hello to Vic, shook hands and tried explaining – again – what his job would be. I think he understood: Scott would be pulling in the pots already out at sea and putting them on the table in the middle of the deck;

Dan would be taking out the crab and lobsters and Vic would be putting new bait in and restacking the pots, ready to be used again.

Everything was good to go: we were fuelled up, I had plenty of bait on board and the galley was stocked with ready meals and tea and coffee. I never allowed booze on the *Galwad* if we were going out on a trip. The lads could get as pissed as they wanted on land – we all did – but not if we were working.

I'd chosen to go out that day – 29 May 2010 – because we were moving out of the winter period, which had been bleak, and starting to see the spring tides. This meant I could get out much further, beyond the eastbound shipping lane and south towards France. This was why I'd bought the *Galwad*.

I'd looked at the weather forecast, I'd be nuts not to. It was going to be a bit bumpy going out but the conditions were expected to ease. So they said.

It was definitely lumpy going round the Needles, but nothing that bothered me. We were in good time to catch the tide out and, from that point, I knew we had another three to four hours steaming ahead. I expected to arrive around 10.30 p.m. and said to the lads: 'Why don't you crash out, or get something to eat? I'll wake you when we get close.'

That's how it worked on a trip: you grabbed sleep whenever you could because you could be working all through the night without a break. Me? I'd become accustomed to not sleeping at all. Even when I had one eye open, one eye shut, I was constantly listening out for the slightest hint of trouble – maybe the engine suddenly changing pitch, or another boat appearing unexpectedly on the radar.

The others all headed down to the galley and the little bunks in the bottom of the boat, while I stuck the *Galwad* on autopilot, put my feet up and started on a crossword puzzle in the paper. The wheelhouse really was my domain, my little empire. My sister, Nicky, called it a boy's shed; she was just about right.

There were times I'd sit in there, with my radar and Olex machine and old newspapers and empty coke cans and grimy mugs – stained from infinite cups of tea – and I'd look out over the ocean, feeling like King of the Bloody Seas. I really loved those moments on my own in the wheelhouse; I defy any skipper who has bought their own boat, and poured their heart and soul into it, to feel any different.

I also loved the fact nobody knew where I was heading once I'd set off. They might see me going around the Needles but that's all. I'd never leave my course with the coastguards or anyone else for that matter. The sea belonged to me from that point and everyone else could sod off. It felt like freedom.

I was heading for a spot roughly 35 miles due south of Selsey Bill – the furthest east I'd ever go. In the winter, it's a no-go area because the weather's far too rough to get out that far. But come spring the waters are untapped because nobody else had gone there during the winter either.

We steamed out parallel to how the back of the Isle of Wight runs, past the opposite end of the island, then further out to the east, going through the westbound shipping lane first, into the 5-mile wide separation zone and finishing north of the eastbound lane.

We arrived around 10.30 p.m., as I'd anticipated, but problems had already started before we got there. Vic was in a right state.

He'd started throwing up about 8 miles out and was showing no signs of stopping. I'd seen it all before. I'd had crew members on their knees, begging me to turn back as vomit dripped down their chins. But my attitude never changed. Turning round would cost me money, and that wasn't an option.

I remember once bumping into a lad on the quay, not long after I'd bought the *Galwad*. 'Got any work going?' he asked. 'Sure,' I replied, 'but have you worked on boats before?'

'Yep – I've just had ten years in the Navy,' he answered. 'Oh Christ,' I muttered. 'Let me tell you right now, this ain't nothing like the Navy. This ain't one of your great big battleships, this is like a floating thimble compared to what you've been on.'

He wasn't put off, though, so I took him out. Once we hit some bad weather, however, he was totally screwed – to the point where he was actually hyperventilating because he was also asthmatic. That's how bad it can get. I've seen others so disorientated, they've started talking total nonsense, like they've no clue where they are any more. But my attitude never, ever changed. Once I'm out at sea, I'm staying out – otherwise, I can't earn.

It was the same with Vic. He looked queasy just going down the Solent but once we passed the Needles and the water became lumpier, he became more and more agitated. Scott and Dan had already crashed out, but Vic found the bottom of the boat – where the bunks are – too claustrophobic, even though it was probably the calmest spot to be. Instead, he was up and down, one minute lying in the galley, next sitting behind me in the wheelhouse, and then rushing off to the open platform strung along the back of the boat – where he was loudly chucking up into the Channel.

I pretty much ignored him, hoping he would somehow work through it. That can happen; in fact it's just about the only real cure. I've had nippers trying seasickness pills and magic bands – Christ, they make me laugh. Eventually the body gets used to the way the boat is rolling and pitching, and once that happens, you're usually in the clear. Unfortunately, Vic never got to that point. He wasn't the first and he won't be the last.

I was more interested in the crossword puzzle and keeping an eye on the radar as we approached the shipping lanes. I'd barely seen any boats going out, just a couple of sand dredgers 4 or 5 miles from the island, and the occasional ferry on one of their standard routes. You get so used to seeing them you can actually name which ones they are. I'm sure one was the *Commodore*. They're just like trams, going up and down, up and down.

As always, I had the VHF radio on, permanently tuned to Channel 16 where I could listen to boats calling the coast-guard, or hear any weather updates. There was certainly no improvement in the conditions; if anything, the waves were getting increasingly bulky and water was erupting constantly now over our deck. Vic was not having an easy ride for sure. I just chuckled to myself. *Fuck him, he's already a waste of space.*

The weather was coming in from the west, with the waves on my starboard side. The boat was definitely rolling around but we were running with the waves, at an angle, rather than going across them. For Vic, it probably felt like a nightmare fairground ride that never stopped. For me, it was just lumpy, nothing I hadn't encountered before. You know you are in it but it wasn't causing me any panic.

Once we approached where I wanted to shoot the new string, I gave Scott and Dan a shout. 'Lads, we'll be there in twenty, so get a cup of tea and get yer yellas on.' Yellows are what we call our oilskins; they were definitely going to need those given the amount of spray splattering the boat. Vic, on the other hand, was flat out on the small bench in the galley, groaning and whining. Just loud enough to make himself heard. I knew he'd be going nowhere.

As we slowed down, the *Galwad* started bobbing around a lot more and titling off course. Thick, white spray was now shooting up and crashing into my wheelhouse windows, to the point where it was momentarily impossible to see anything until the spray had ricocheted away and flowed back out over the deck.

I overshot my first attempt and had to turn round to take another run at it. That manoeuvre alone took at least five minutes but on the second attempt I hit the spot where I wanted the pots to go. I pulled down the wheelhouse window so I could shout over to Scott and Dan, who were now out on deck, drenched, but ready to start.

'Where's Vic?' I heard Scott yell.

'Forget him,' I replied. 'He's knackered. Let's just get on with it and get this string away. Let them go.'

That was the signal for Scott to start pushing the pots over the *Galwad*'s rail, as Dan fed them to him. Tides in the Channel basically run from east to west, so the pots have to be shot across them – north to south – or else they'd concertina and get into a right old mess on the seabed.

I was keeping the boat steady, as best I could, while at the same time watching the rope to make sure it didn't get snarled up – or wrapped around one of the lads' feet. I was basically making sure there were no screw-ups and, sure enough, fifteen minutes later, the job was done with no dramas even though it had been a tussle to keep the boat steady. I watched Scott throw over the last buoy and then had a think about what to do next, especially given the state Vic was in.

I decided to look for a couple more strings that I knew were nearby, so we could replace the big heavy buoys on them – which we use during the winter – with the smaller, much lighter ones we use in slack water. The big marker buoys have a massive amount of drag and pull on them, and they can sink right down in the spring tides – dragging and tangling your pots in the process. Worse, they could completely rip your buoy lines off, or even burst.

That's all cost to me, so now was the time of year to take them off and replace them with the much smaller buoys that are only 8in in diameter, plastic and can't get squashed.

The weather, however, was still grim and I could barely see anything outside by now. The sky and the sea had merged into a great, big, grey wall and the only break between the two was the white frothing spray that kept spewing out over the boat and, increasingly, splattering on to my wheelhouse windows.

It wasn't ideal, but it wasn't enough to turn us round. We had deck lights blazing out and I knew, if we got close enough, we could catch the buoys in the glare, and pick them out. Indeed, we eventually found a couple of strings and successfully swapped the buoys over.

I couldn't completely ignore the weather, however – or Vic's continuous groaning. I'd noticed him fumbling around with his mobile phone and thought to myself: *You dozy sod. That won't work out here. Besides, who you going to call?* Everyone knew mobiles would never connect 12 miles beyond the island. However, I decided to head towards an area where I hoped the ride might eventually get a bit more comfortable and the boat wouldn't be rolling around quite so much. Again, I told Scott and Dan to get some kip. 'I'm going to do some mapping along the way. You two might as well get some shut-eye.'

I steamed south, heading back towards the eastbound shipping lane. The weather was hitting us on the bow, which meant the boat was going up and down but not rocking and rolling quite so much. It was still pretty shitty and choppy, though.

I'd seen a ridge that looked perfect for crabs, so I decided to circle it a few times and let the plotter build up a more detailed graphic. I wanted to know how far out it stretched.

I was engrossed as a picture of the seabed and the ridge started to emerge. Vic, however, was a lost cause; within seconds he was rushing out again, heaving and retching. He was becoming a bigger problem than I'd anticipated and eventually came back into the wheelhouse, this time pointing – *the cheeky bastard* – to my satellite phone. *Really? You ain't done anything for us and now you expect me to carry the cost of using that? In any case, what you after? You want someone to get you off the boat? You havin' a laugh?*

Vic was getting more and more agitated and desperate, though, and started thrusting his mobile phone my way with a number displayed on the screen. 'Phone, phone,' he begged. I didn't want to make the situation any worse than it already was so, very reluctantly, I dialled. The line wouldn't connect at first but I persevered and eventually someone answered. I realised it was Dexsa, who I'd met at the Sportsman's the night before, although I didn't care who it was. 'Vic wants to speak to you,' I said, abruptly, handing over the receiver. I really didn't feel in the mood for chit-chat with someone I barely knew and I didn't particularly want to know. However, the weather was so bad by now, the connection wouldn't hold and the line broke within seconds. The next thing I knew, Vic was darting outside to throw up again.

Meanwhile, my attention had already shifted to a hefty cluster of huge ships that I could see on my radar heading towards us. By the looks of it, there were some slower vessels at the front, with faster ones coming up behind, like they were slaloming with one another. I could always tell – just by looking at the range rings on my radar – what type of ships they were. Each boat would be shown as a blip and by seeing how quickly those blips moved across the rings, I could judge their speed – and therefore their size. I could see some were refrigeration ships – they're the Ferraris of the shipping world; then there were some containers, the Audis, and finally came the plodding general cargo boats – the Ford Mondeos as I liked to think of them.

I had absolutely no idea what any of the boats were called, that sort of information didn't show up on my radar, but I remember chuckling to myself and thinking: *They're just like the Ant Hill Mob in Wacky Races.*

It was definitely a large group, about six or seven; I was confident they'd pick me up on their radars and plotters but, even so, I deliberately showed them *Galwad*'s rear end. I kept the navigation lights blazing as well, just to be sure they'd see me, and continued watching the ships on my radar. Given the weather, I wanted to keep a good, safe distance away, let them through and then, as the last one passed, turn and drop back to where I'd been mapping earlier on.

In the middle of managing all of that, my satellite phone started ringing. I picked up, it was Dexsa, and he was saying 'put Vic on'. I breathed in heavily – hoping he might detect some anger – put the receiver down and yelled out, 'Dexsa's on the line,' but it was a lost cause. Either Vic was too ill to stumble back into the wheelhouse or, before I knew it, the connection had broken again.

I realised this wasn't going to go away, so I waited awhile, tried at least two or three more times without any joy – and then the satellite burst into life again. I answered and said something like, 'Vic wants to go home.' I remember hearing Dexsa say, 'keep him, get him to work' but I wanted him to say that to Vic himself. Then the line broke yet again so I tried reconnecting, getting more and more pissed off with the situation.

At some point Vic stumbled back in. To be fair, he really did look a mess and kept pointing desperately at the phone. I gave it one more go – it was around 12.20 a.m. by now – we connected, and I hollered something like: 'He's no fucking use to me.' The waves were making a right old racket as they smashed against the wheelhouse windows; it was almost impossible to think, never mind hear a bloody word. I was pretty sure Dexsa said, 'Make him get through it,' but, by now, my attention had once again turned to the ships outside.

All I could see through the surrounding darkness and the incessant sea spray was a procession of gigantic outlines shuffling along. I focused on their lights – or rather the three I could see: one at the front, one on the port and finally the mast-light at the back. I envied the ships' colossal sizes; the chaotic waves drenching us and effortlessly tossing the *Galwad* around right then would simply be bouncing off the sides of those monsters.

I was also slightly jealous of their speed, too: the *Galwad* could cruise at a respectable 8 knots but these beasts were nearly three times faster.

Given the weather and the atrocious visibility, I was determined not to get caught in their wakes. You get two off vessels that size – the first off the bow, the second from the prop thrust at the back. The sea suddenly becomes like water boiling ferociously in a kettle. It's not where you want to be.

There have been times when I've steered the *Galwad* when I'd swear the boat was being physically hoisted up into the air before smashing back down into the raging water below. It felt – I imagine – like we'd been struck head on by a thunderbolt – and that was in calm weather.

With that in mind, I made sure we didn't cross behind the final ship. I didn't want the *Galwad* to get rolled over, which, in those conditions, was a real danger. As it passed by, I started to turn back round, so I could head off to where I'd been mapping earlier. I'm certain we stayed around 500m away from that last boat – whatever the distance was, I certainly couldn't see its name, its colours or anybody out on the deck. I was never close enough for that.

I do remember, though, looking up at its single rear light and thinking: *Jeez, she's nearly out of sight already and she's only just passed me. That's fast.*

The weather was definitely up to a Force Eight by now. Our bow was dipping into the water and sending gigantic showers of white foam crashing over the front of the boat that, in turn, were repeatedly thumping against my wheelhouse. All I could see were continuous blankets of white spray, one after the other, after the other. *This is really going to screw Vic.*

We were pitching up and down, dipping and plunging; one second the horizon was high, the next it had vanished and, with each giant lurch, the boat was creaking and groaning under the torrential bombardment of pounding waves.

Scott and Dan were still down below, utterly oblivious to what was going on, but the wild weather and water just pushed Vic further over the edge. He was hitting the point I'd seen before with other recruits who couldn't take it. They become totally disorientated, and start mumbling and slurring and talking gibberish. It sounds like hysteria but I guess they're just desperate to get off – right there and then. Anything, really, just to somehow end the torture they're going through. Vic wiped smears of puke away from his chin with the back of his hand and bellowed, 'Phone.' *Here we bloody go again.* I needed to calm him down, though, so – once again – I dialled his number for him.

Really, I was in no mood to help. Screw him. He wasn't up to the job. He'd left me, Scott and Dan in the lurch and now he was taking the piss, getting me to use my phone when it could barely connect to anything for more than a few seconds. Besides, what use were these calls? What was he hoping to say? 'I don't like it, please get me off.' *Well, too late for that matey. Besides, I've already told them.* By now, I was totally convinced he was black-market labour and the blokes he'd come over with were the ringleaders. I didn't want to know the details; I dialled, this time connected and bellowed, 'He wants to go home,' and hung up. It was around 12.40 a.m., I'd maybe made around nine bloody calls and he'd never managed to get to the phone once.

On top of that, the wheelhouse stank of his vomit and my mood was turning blacker than the sky outside. *What a nightmare. What a lousy waste of time. That's the last call I'm making.*

We hit the ridge soon after where I wanted to carry on mapping. I could see on the plotter this was a craggy area, but I wanted to check if the contour carried on further to the east. If it was big enough, it'd be an ideal place to return to and shoot another line of pots.

But Vic and the conditions had got to me. *Sod it*, I thought, *I've had enough.* I decided to head back up north – out of the shipping lanes – so I could get a cup of tea and some kip. I put my feet up and let the *Galwad* chug around on autopilot in a nice circle so I'd still be near some of our pots come daybreak. As far as I was concerned, Vic could throw his guts up until then. I was past caring.

The sky started to lighten a few hours later, and, thankfully, the weather began to ease. I called down to Scott and Dan and we started pulling up more pots. Vic was half comatose by now, clutching his stomach and not letting go of it; like he needed to keep what little was left in place. I heard Scott and Dan cursing as I told them, 'Just forget him.' I felt really bad for those two. They'd been left to shoulder all the heavy work themselves. I even tried to coax Vic out on deck: 'Put some yellas on.' But he wasn't having it. In fact, he just sat there, staring blankly into space. The lights were definitely out.

I even began to suspect the entire trip was cursed as we began hauling in the pots. Just about three-quarters of the string was in when it suddenly jammed. All we could do was empty the pots that were up, rebait them, and reshoot the line once I'd turned the boat back round.

We replaced some more buoys after that but all the while I was increasingly thinking: *Do I persevere, or do I go back and get shot of Vic? Maybe come back out without him, just me, Scott and Dan. He ain't no good, he ain't coming round. He ain't made for this sort of life and he's getting on our nerves.*

I decided to return home – slowly, though, because I wanted to see if I could find some old whelk pots that were about 4 miles off the island. My only hope of retrieving them would be in slack water but we'd just missed one of the tides and I'd have to wait for the next. So I carried on mapping as we headed back leisurely. At some point I vaguely remember seeing another boat way off in the distance – out on the horizon. Certainly nowhere near enough to become a problem.

I carried on, gently steaming along and messing around with my plotter – looking at different bits of ground and seeing how they showed up on my screen. We eventually got to where I'd hoped the whelk pots would be, circled round a few times, but couldn't find any sign of them. *Yep, this trip was cursed.*

At least the weather had improved by then and Dan – who liked to do a bit of fishing – said, 'Let's do some mackereling.' I knew we'd be passing a stretch of coast on the Isle of Wight called The Caves, which was a popular spot for mackerel. Once there, I let the *Galwad* drift up and down a few times on the tide, parallel to Tennyson Downs, staying at least a quarter of a mile from the shore. I knew the seabed rose steeply soon after that, with plenty of jagged edges that could tear open the bottom of the boat. I kept well clear of them.

By now it was time to get home so I told the lads to clear up our rubbish, bag it – and chuck it overboard.

This ritual happened on every trip before we got back to Yarmouth. The *Galwad* didn't have a toilet, so we had to use a bucket at the back of the boat instead. The contents of that would be poured into regular black bin bags, along with everything else that had been swept onboard, or any bits of unused food and rubbish from the galley. I think Scott chucked them over before hosing down the deck.

There was definitely nothing left on the boat when we headed towards the Needles and into the Solent. Helped by the tide, we were motoring along at a good 11 knots as we passed Fort Victoria and on into Yarmouth harbour, where we tied up on the pontoon.

Oh, yes. There was something else. As we came round the Needles – around 7 p.m., I'd say – I spotted a small plane through the gaps in the rocks. I remember thinking it was close to where my sister, Nicky, lived. It was flying extremely low over Freshwater Bay, where we'd just been mackereling, and I continued seeing it as we came down the Solent and pulled into Yarmouth.

It had been a shitty trip. We'd got some bits and pieces but, as far as I was concerned, certainly not enough to cover my expenses. We maybe had thirty or forty crab and around ten lobsters. I asked the lads to stick it all in the fish pens, and said, 'I'm shooting off but I'll meet you down the road later, alright?' Meaning the pub.

I wanted to get home to see the missus, and then I planned to meet a mate at the Fat Cat bar over in Freshwater. He wasn't there when I arrived and then I suddenly got a call from my sister, saying they needed some lobsters in the restaurant. I phoned Scotty – who was still sorting the catch with Dan on the *Galwad* – and asked him to pick out the best ones from the pens we had dangling in the water at Yarmouth.

I headed back, chatted with Nikki for a while, and then returned to the quay to check Scott had sorted the lobsters for Salty's. That's where I met Dan and that's when we were jumped on.

Nothing in my mind could explain why on earth I was now being accused of importing cocaine. How and when? At what point in the last thirty hours had I done something, anything, that might make these idiots suspect I was up to something?

Chapter 11

BLACK OBJECTS

The police changed their story slap bang in the middle of my first interrogation. The tragedy was, I never clocked the significance – until it was too late.

First, I was told the *Galwad* had been 'observed' dropping 'holdalls attached to a red buoy' into the sea near Freshwater. Seconds later, I was told it was actually 'black objects' that had gone into the water. 'You've been seen to throw black items over the side,' I was informed. 'What were they?'

If only I'd realised just how critical that discrepancy would prove to be. *Holdalls attached to a red buoy v. black objects.* I mean, they're two totally different things, aren't they? They couldn't possibly look the same, their colours are worlds apart, they bear no obvious similarities. Hell, their descriptive names don't even sound the same. You couldn't possibly confuse one for the other. It wasn't 'black, rucksack-shaped items attached to a brightly coloured beacon', for example.

In fact, they were asking me outright what the black items were, presumably because they didn't know themselves. By doing that, they were effectively saying: *We know they're not holdalls attached to a red buoy – so what were they?*

We were sat in an interview room at Fareham police station, where I'd already been held for over nineteen hours. I genuinely hadn't got a clue what was going on or why I'd been dragged over to the mainland.

After we'd been arrested on Yarmouth quay – and I'd been shovelled into the back of a police car – I'd been made to sit and wait while police and frogmen dived all over and under the *Galwad*.

There were two officers sat in the car with me. One was DI Gary Breen, the other was SOCA officer Oladele Thomas. The three of us sat there for what felt like hours. I had a hoodie on, some black leggings and my rigger boots as I call them. I just pulled my hood up and closed my eyes, trying to blank everything out. I couldn't stand watching those guerrillas leaping all over my boat. But Breen and Thomas wanted to get me talking, like they wanted to be new best mates. 'How long you been in the fishing game then, Jamie? You live near here, how long you had that boat then?'

Don't call me Jamie. We're not mates.

I was eventually told we'd all be going over to the mainland on the midnight Wightlink ferry. I wasn't even allowed out of the car and stayed cuffed throughout the crossing. Forty-five minutes later I was being driven through the New Forest to Fareham police station, where the custody sergeant seemed to take great delight in telling me I was being arrested. Then I went through all the usual routines: fingerprints, mugshot, confirm ID, name and address – as if they didn't know already. Throughout, I was kept well separated from Dan and Vic; they clearly didn't want us talking to one another.

Next, I was charged with the 'importation of Class-A drugs'. I remember looking at the custody sergeant as he said 'importation' – he enjoyed that word, I could tell. The smirk was still lingering, his lips were still rolling as if they were savouring each individual letter. He was feeling big and important and I could imagine him going home and telling his wife all about it.

He was a proper jobsworth, too, doing everything by the book, making sure every line and every box on his paperwork was filled in immaculately. What I didn't know at that stage was that he'd also written on the charge sheet that the drugs I'd allegedly imported had all been found stashed on the *Galwad*.

'What the hell's this all about?' I protested.

'We'll get you a solicitor in the morning,' he said, like he was reading the words straight off an autocue. 'Oh – and we've rung home and told your family you're here, Jamie.'

Don't call me Jamie. We're not mates.

I wanted to speak to Nikki myself, though. 'Can I call my missus?' The desk sergeant nodded and even though it was around 3 a.m. by now, she answered almost immediately.

'It's me, luv, sorry it's late, I'm at Fareham.'

'Yeah, I know, you OK? It's another screw up, ain't it.' I could hear the anger and frustration in Nikki's voice but her tone remained calm, like she'd experienced all this before and, like me, was sure it would blow over.

'The dozy sods think I've stashed drugs on the *Galwad*,' I said.

'Don't worry, Jamie, it'll get sorted. It's just like Grimsby – someone upstairs has got the right hump with you and they're trying to stitch you up like last time. It isn't going to be anything. We'll see you back here later on.'

'Yeah, you're right. Goodnight, luv, tell the kids I'll see them later.'

I was handed a blanket and taken to a cell – although first I had to hand over my clothes, just in case I planned to use them to top myself. Even as the door closed behind me and

I looked down at my regulation blue prison gear, I was sure Nikki was correct. I'd be kicked out later on because that's what always happened. They'd done this to me before: I'd even been to Fareham a couple of times when I was younger and pissed up. They'd ask me over for a 'chat', then – as soon as I showed – they'd say, 'By the way, we're arresting you. Go sit in the cell.' Hours later I'd be back home. I had no time for any of them.

This night had felt different, though. Everyone had been rushing around like blue-arsed flies at the police station, the desk sergeant was showing off, phones were ringing non-stop, little groups of plain-clothes detectives were standing in huddles deep in whispered conversation, glances were being exchanged – most of them aimed at me. My head was spinning as I sprawled out on the cell's whitewashed concrete bed. I closed my eyes and, as I drifted towards sleep, the last thing I remembered rattling through my brain was one single word.

Importation.

The following morning I was told a duty solicitor had already been appointed. I still hadn't been questioned and I still had no idea what evidence the police thought they had.

In fact, the questioning didn't begin until much later that afternoon, around 5.15 p.m., with Thomas and DI Richard Crouch. We were sat round a tatty office table with a fake melamine top covered in scratches and make-believe wood grain. Next to me was the duty solicitor – young and blatantly out of his depth judging by the permanently startled expression on his face. I don't think he spoke a single word throughout the entire process. I didn't care, I had nothing to hide.

In front of us was an old-style recorder taping the conversation as we spoke. They asked me really basic stuff like what was the name of my boat, did I own it, who was working for me, how did I know them? They asked me how I'd come across Vic, so I told them I'd met a guy in a pub in Cowes who said he knew someone looking for work.

I didn't go into any great details – in fact, I told them I only met Vic when he turned up in Yarmouth on the day we set off. What was the point of telling them I'd run late coming back from Weymouth and had asked Beerey to go pick him up and, oh, he was with two strangers as well. They were probably running a black-market labour scam. Maybe I should have told them all that but it just didn't seem relevant to anything. The only thought going through my head was: *when can I go home?*

The questioning carried on in the same vein – a lot of gentle stuff about how I shot strings, how many did I have out at sea, how many pots were attached to them, how often would I go out, how long would each trip last? I remember Crouch kept saying 'pods' instead of pots. I don't think he understood a word I was saying.

I couldn't tell if I was annoying them, giving them what they wanted or whether they didn't know where on earth any of this was heading any more than me. They just carried on asking for more details about the trip, often repeating the same questions in slightly different packaging – like where I'd been and why I'd gone there.

I explained that Vic had been violently ill and I wished he'd never turned up. The trip had been lousy and I think I told them we hadn't caught a thing. That wasn't strictly true, either, but in my book we'd not caught anywhere near enough to make any money, so it all amounted to nothing to me.

The only time they got arsey was when they kept pressing me for the name of the pub in Cowes where Vic had been recommended to me. I genuinely couldn't remember, other than it was the one next to the Red Jet ferry terminal. Crouch didn't like that answer and said, quite seriously, 'Surely you know the name of every pub on the island?' I remember replying, 'Well, do you know the names of every pub in Essex?'

The interview lasted around forty-five minutes and I went back to my cell utterly confused and none the wiser. *You holding something back – or can I go home now?*

I was called back for a second interview around two hours later and straight away I told a lie. It was such a dumb thing to do, although it was quickly overshadowed by a bombshell I never saw coming.

I decided to lie to spare Scott. I thought I was being smart but once I'd done it there was no turning back. Once I realised I shouldn't have done it, it was too late to press rewind.

Thomas and Crouch had asked me about Dan and Vic, but never once mentioned Scott. I suspected they didn't know he was on the *Galwad* with us, so why drag him into this farce when it was all bound to disintegrate? I'd been hauled off to the cells before, pissed up and argumentative and every time it had ended the same way. I'd be kicked out the following morning with no further action.

Then there was the time armed police had jumped me and Nikki at the ferry port. Another gigantic police cock-up. Everything told me this would be the same. These idiots would realise they'd dropped another clanger and that Jamie Green would have to be let out, just like he always was.

Why tell them about Scott? He was only 17, for Christ's sake. I'd even met his parents and they were thoroughly decent people. We'd got on. Why get Scott dragged into this nonsense when every bone in my body, every instinct and every bit of experience I'd ever had with the police told me the whole thing would end at any moment?

So, when Thomas asked: 'Can you tell me how many people were on board', I took a punt, 'There were three of us.' He didn't blink, and nor did I. But it was a lie that would well and truly screw me.

They then asked what we did when we got back to Yarmouth, so I explained I tied the boat up, called in back home then went off to meet a mate in a pub at Freshwater. He wasn't there but the restaurant called and said they needed some lobsters. So I headed back to our storage pens at the quay. I didn't mention that Scott had been told to get them. That was part of the lie getting out of control.

Then came the bombshell I never saw coming. Everything had been reasonably matey-matey – until, suddenly, Thomas's tone changed completely. 'For the purposes of the tape,' he announced in a solemn, officious voice, 'the *Galwad* was observed dropping holdalls attached to a red buoy into the sea in the vicinity of the Needles and Freshwater Bay.

'The holdalls are believed to contain Class-A drugs.'

A crushing silence instantly fell over the room, carrying all the weight of an anchor crashing over the side of the *Galwad* and plummeting into the depths below. My mind frantically tried to repeat the key words ... observed ... holdalls ... red buoy ... Freshwater ... Class-A drugs ... and then I heard his voice once again. 'Do you understand? Have you any comments?'

Any comments? I looked blankly into his face. My brain felt like the insides of an asylum, shouting and screaming and exploding hysterically. *Observed ... holdalls ... red buoy ...*

I don't know how long my silence lasted but I swear I can still hear it today. All I know is I reacted. I didn't scamper away and say something like 'no comment'. I didn't look nervously at my duty lawyer – fat load of use he was, by the way – I just did what any innocent person would have done in a situation like that.

'It's ridiculous.'

I'm glad I said that because it set my marker straight away, but my brain was in complete overdrive, barely able to concentrate on anything else I was being asked as it tried to compute everything it had just heard.

Observed? Was someone 'observing' us? If so, who – and where from? And what's all this crap about 'holdalls attached to a red buoy'? What holdalls? *What's going on?*

Maybe I should have said: 'Can I just have a quick chat in private with my lawyer? That's a hell of a loaded statement you've just thrown at me and I need to work out what on earth you're talking about.'

Needless to say, I didn't – and, in any case, there was no stopping Thomas. He was going for it. 'Did you stop in that area, then?'

'Yep, to do some mackereling.'

'Some what?'

I looked at him. Maybe he didn't understand. 'Some fishing,' I explained. 'I just had a couple of drifts, you go up with the tide, drift down, go up, come down.'

I really couldn't focus on a word I was saying.

Observed.

Holdalls.

Red buoy.

Freshwater.

Class-A drugs.

He asked more about Vic, and what experience he had, and I tried explaining he barely spoke a word of English and he was throwing up all the time and that I could never predict whether casual labour would be any good, or even turn up. It was all just words pouring out of my mouth. All I could think about was the holdalls and the drugs and suddenly, out of the blue, I heard myself saying, 'We never chucked nothing in the sea.'

Thomas ignored that, though, and asked whether Freshwater was a good spot for mackerel fishing. Then Crouch said something about, 'You just throw a line over with some hooks on, don't you?' and I remember looking at him, then Thomas, and seeing their eyes drilling into me like a pair of wolves waiting to leap, and my brain was totally frazzled. Those same words kept churning over and over – only now they were interrogating me over what sort of rod and line I used to go mackerel fishing.

Is this for real? Is this some sort of dream?

Then came the moment when their story changed and I just didn't twig how important that was. Crouch suddenly said, 'Like my colleague said, you've been seen to throw black objects over the side.'

Something instantly resonated, though. 'Black objects?' *What on earth? You said holdalls with a red buoy a few moments ago. What's the black objects all about?*

Maybe my face looked quizzical because he then repeated it, 'You've been seen to throw black items over the side. What were they?'

I didn't have a clue what they were talking about but they kept on hammering home the point. Black objects. Black items. 'Have you got anything on your boat that could be black that you would've thrown over?'

Observations … Holdalls … Red buoy … Freshwater … Class-A drugs … Black Objects.

'No … no … no.'

None of it was making any kind of sense. Why was it, 'You've been observed dropping holdalls on a red buoy,' one second, then 'throwing black items' the next? Something inside me should have screamed 'pause' but it didn't. I might then have remembered the bleedin' obvious – the 'black items' were obviously the rubbish bags Scott had chucked overboard. Only I couldn't mention Scott and, in any case, my head was totally scrambled by trying to work out what the holdalls and red buoy were all about.

I just wasn't thinking straight. I didn't know all the facts; I didn't know what the background was or why there was such a confusing mix-up. Besides, they suddenly started grilling me about my mobile phone. Had I used it to call Vic – 'no'; had I used it to call Dan – 'yes, all the time'; what was Dan's number stored under – 'Dan or Danny, I think'; did Dan have my number on his phone – 'I've no idea.'

Next, they wanted to talk about Vic again and whether he'd perked up at all on the way back to Yarmouth, so I told them he was less sick once the weather improved.

Then, out of the blue, came, 'Have you got any money issues and that's why you've done it?'

'No … no … I haven't done it.' *Whatever it is.*

That interview lasted around thirty minutes and then I was interviewed for a third and final time an hour later, around 10.15 p.m. Crouch was no longer there – in his place was SOCA officer James Ellice, along with Thomas. They wanted to know more about where I went on the night, and opened a map of the island so I could show them where we'd gone mackereling.

Then they started grilling me about how many cars I owned, which one had I taken to the quay and whether I owned a trailer. *What's all this about?*

He eventually got to the point. The holdalls had apparently been tied together in the same way lobster pots would be attached to a string and they'd found a piece of rope in my trailer. 'Matches the rope which the bags were attached to,' he said, almost triumphantly.

I explained that the rope I used was commonplace but he wasn't finished. 'Also, on the boat, was exactly a similar colour rope.'

I thought about that one for a while, especially the words 'exactly similar'. Doesn't that mean almost identical, but, actually, not identical? Why didn't he say 'exactly the same'?

I'd no idea what had been used to tie these holdalls and whether it matched my rope. 'These companies must sell the same rope to loads of people,' I pointed out.

Thomas wasn't finished, though. He clearly felt he was on to something and said they were going to do a 'mechanical-fit test' that would examine the way the rope on the holdalls had been cut. They would then establish whether the cuts matched the cuts on the bits of rope they'd found in my trailer.

He fixed me with a steely stare, no doubt hoping I might crack under its intensity, and said, 'Is there any chance we will find out the ropes are the same ones?'

There was only one answer to that. 'No.

'No. No. No'

I thought that'd be the end of it and, as the third interview came to a close and the tape recorder clicked off, I looked at them and said: 'Come on, what's happening here? Can I go home now?'

Their reply left me speechless. 'You'll continue to be held on remand overnight and tomorrow morning you'll be going straight to court.'

You what?

Sure enough, the following day – 2 June 2010 – the three of us were driven off to Portsmouth Magistrates' Court, charged with conspiracy to import cocaine and held on remand until the case could be heard at a crown court.

My first thought was Nikki. *You can't keep me locked up, my wife is battling cancer. I need to help her. You've got to let me go.*

Chapter 12

PRISON

It's amazing how a television explodes when it slams into a 3 inch-thick steel door. The sides burst outwards, the screen splinters and crumbles but the circuit board inside stays pretty much in one piece. Until, that is, a prisoner – on the edge of a breakdown – starts tearing it apart, jumping up and down on it, tugging out strands of multi-coloured wiring and hurling bits of soldered chips and fuses into the solid brick walls of his cell.

Nothing prepares you for a shithole like Winchester Prison.

Nothing prepared me for my first afternoon as I lay on my top bunk wondering what the hell had happened and how on earth I was going to look after Nikki.

Suddenly, my silence was shattered, the cell door was pushed open and a prisoner was forcibly shoved in, his arms flailing around as he tried to keep his balance. He was shouting and yelling in a foreign language – an avalanche of words spewing out, none of them making any sense to me, except the word 'fuck', which I guess is universal. Turned out he was Polish and he was clearly insane with anger but the screw who'd just shovelled him in wasn't interested. 'Yeah, yeah, you go have a lie down.' The door slammed shut, leaving me alone with what I assumed was my new cellmate.

I don't even think he saw me. Instead he saw a television on a shelf, grabbed it on each side, raised it above his head and hurled it straight at the cell's solid steel door. Then he marched over and started jumping up and down on the shattered casing, bending down to pull and tug at its innards. Once it was pulverised, he started grabbing anything that could be picked up whole, or snapped in half – bits of shelves, a bedside table – and hurled them at the door, laughing and cursing as they splintered and fell apart.

The funny thing was, the bloody telly wasn't even working – but right then didn't seem the ideal moment to tell him. He was about to single-handedly smash the entire cell to pieces while I just lay there. I didn't give a monkey's to be honest. I had problems of my own. I didn't care what he did.

Besides, it was vaguely entertaining: my own one-man prison riot on my very first day in jail. Except the show couldn't last. The cell door opened again, a couple of screws came in, grabbed him roughly under each arm and dragged him out. Just as they were leaving one of them looked up at me and said, 'Do us a favour – tidy this place up, will you?'

'You what?'

Nothing prepares you for a shithole like Winchester Prison. The Victorians must have been evil bastards because it crushes you the moment you see it.

Inside and out, it's a soul-destroying monstrosity. Huge, imposing brick walls tower over rolls of barbed wire and mesh fencing. It's bleak and horrible and fit only for horror movies with five drab cell blocks spread out like spokes in a gigantic wheel.

I was put on A Wing: to get in I had to walk through a double layer of ugly, iron-grille gates that rose through three more floors all the way up to the roof. I shivered as I stood on the main ground-floor hallway: on my left and right, running the entire length of the corridor in front of me, were rows of heavy steel doors studded with massive rivets and set at regular intervals within thickly painted cream brick walls.

I shivered again as I looked up and saw the other three floors, each with their own lines of cell doors opening on to suspended narrow landings that seemed to be stacked on top of one another along either side of the block. Metal hand rails ran the length of each landing – presumably to stop inmates either falling or being pushed into the great cathedral-like void that filled the centre of the entire building. The only way of entering the upper floors was via a central staircase that began just ahead of me. This, too, was caged in by metal mesh fencing – it looked like every picture of death row I'd ever seen, or imagined. I was well and truly submerged inside a brick, steel and wire fortress.

Even bits of windows were barred as if someone was saying, 'You've lost the right to daylight in here, son. Welcome to hell.'

Every bit of me ached to be back on the *Galwad*, sat in my wheelhouse mapping new stretches of the seabed or instructing the nippers to shoot new lines of pots. What the hell was I doing shut away in this Victorian shithole? Christ, I hadn't even been to trial, I hadn't been found guilty of anything – I didn't even know what the police had against me. Why was I here? Way more importantly, what would happen now to Nikki? How on earth would she cope?

Me, Dan and Vic had been driven straight to Winchester from the magistrates' court. Dan and I chatted on the way. 'What the hell's going on? This'll sort itself, don't worry,' but I don't think we said a word to Vic. It felt like we were in this mess because of him, even if we didn't understand how or why.

I remember Dan leaning forwards and mouthing: 'Who is this bloke?'

'You know as much as me Dan,' I replied. 'He's a foreigner, I was told he was looking for work, you know what it's like.'

'I don't believe this. What a nightmare. Still, it'll all come out in the wash, won't it, Jamie?'

'Yeah, sure, course it will. It'll all come out in the wash, Dan.'

Even then I was thinking: *any minute now, someone's going to fling open the doors of this police van and say, 'Right, you three, that's it, it's all been a misunderstanding, you can all go home now.'*

That little fantasy was quickly shattered, though, as the van came to a halt, the doors flung open and the bleak walls of Winchester Prison loomed in front of us. Although I'd spent nights in a police cell, I'd never been inside a prison before. Talk about steep learning curve. We were put in a holding room, where we waited for a medical. That included stripping off, bending over, coughing, then seeing some woman who wanted to know whether I had any suicidal thoughts. *You what?*

The only thing on my mind was phoning Nikki. I'd been allowed to make a very quick call as soon as I'd arrived: 'I'm in Winchester, luv' – 'yeah, I know, I'll get a visit booked in' – and that was it. I assumed I'd be allowed to make more calls for longer once I was in my cell.

Then I was told how everything would work: when I'd get my meals, when we had to get up, when we'd be locked up for the night. 'You'll have a TV and your own kettle.' Then I was given a rolled up blanket, some tea bags, an ID card with my mugshot and prison number on it, and taken to my cell, up on the first floor. As we walked up the stairs, other inmates started leaning over their balcony railings to take a look at the new suckers coming in. I was with a screw who stopped outside one of the steel doors, pushed it open with his shoulder, and said, 'Right, you're in here, in you go.'

As I walked in, I couldn't help noticing that the walls either side of the door must have been at least 12in thick. It felt more like the entrance to a huge underground vault stashed with priceless jewels. Instead, I stepped into a dark, pokey room, barely 8ft deep by 6ft wide. The second I walked in, the door behind me slammed shut, sending an echo shuddering through the tiny cell that seemed to say, 'You're screwed, Jamie Green.'

There was a metal-framed bunk to the left with a couple of blue plastic mattresses, while on the right was a bit of a desk, a plastic folding chair and a couple of tatty MDF cabinets. Right at the end – facing straight at me – was an old porcelain sink, discoloured and chipped and barely clinging to the wall. On its right, side on to me, was a toilet basin with no seat and a rag of a curtain dangling waist high along its left side – presumably to give you a scrap of privacy when you sat on the bog. *Jesus.*

That's when I saw the telly on a shelf above the desk. I tried switching it on to cheer myself up but the screen stayed blank.

I blinked in disbelief at the brick walls surrounding me, thick with Christ knows how many layers of more cream paint. 'Come on, Jamie,' I said to myself, 'let's have a cup of tea.' There was a kettle on the desk top, so I went over to the sink, filled it with water, and plugged it in. Nothing happened, no little red light came on, the slow murmur of it kicking into life never started. I opened the lid: the filament inside was missing; the damned thing had been cannibalised. *Bastards.*

So I climbed up on the top bunk, my mind and imagination racing away with itself. I couldn't get Nikki and the kids out of my head, they'd be worried sick. Then I started thinking about what I needed to do to get out of this mess. *You've got to tell them about Nikki. You've got to get bail. She's dying of cancer for Christ's sake. Surely they'll listen.*

I took another look round the cell, trying to find something to lift my spirits. Slowly it dawned on me, in a perverted yet wonderful way, that the space wasn't entirely different from the wheelhouse on the *Galwad*. Everything was compact – the sleeping area, the narrow shelves – all I had to do was close my eyes and imagine the rolling waves outside and the lads out on deck. In that moment I discovered a survival mechanism I have clung to ever since: whenever I'm low, I lie on my bed and imagine I'm back on the *Galwad*, king of the bloody seas. The only bit I never get used to, though, is the moment when they slam the door shut.

The following morning, at 8 a.m., I was taken to an 'induction meeting' for new arrivals where we were given a rundown on how everything worked. What we were told, however, bore no resemblance to the realities of what goes on at Winchester. The only way to find out anything was by talking to the other inmates.

I couldn't phone home because I hadn't been allocated a PIN, which would take twenty-four hours to be activated. Nobody had told me that. The kettle hadn't worked because the other prisoners in the block are like bleedin' seagulls and when there's a cell waiting to be filled, they dive in there, nicking anything that's in working order. Nobody had told me that.

The missus had been waiting for days on end to be granted permission to visit when it was actually her right to see me every day if she wanted because I was only on remand. Nobody had told me that.

I was spending just about every day banged up in my cell. However, if I went to the gym, or the chapel, or volunteered for some cleaning jobs, then I'd be allowed out. Nobody told me that.

Then there was the battle to be granted bail. Nobody told me how to go about that, either. The other inmates told Dan and I to see the prison chaplain and ask him for help – first to get transferred to Parkhurst, so at least we'd be back on the island and it'd be easier for our families to visit. He was incredibly sympathetic when I told him about Nikki and, after countless trips back to the magistrates' court to state our case, we were eventually allowed to move.

The next step was to get out on bail. It took nearly two months to persuade them and the sole reason it was eventually granted was Nikki's health, and certainly not because someone thought I might actually be innocent. None of the others were allowed out, only me – and, boy, did they make me suffer for it.

There were loads of restrictions: my parents had to put up a surety, I had to wear a tag round my ankle and was ordered to sign on at midday, every day, at Newport police station. I was banned from working and wasn't allowed to go anywhere near the *Galwad* – and certainly not on it.

I wasn't even allowed out of my house before seven in the morning and had to be home by seven at night. All my bank accounts, business and personal, were frozen – they even came round to our house to check we hadn't got a safe or buried treasure stashed away somewhere. I couldn't use a cash machine and in the end needed a solicitor to persuade the Old Bill to let me have £250 a week to live off.

Inevitably, I messed up one day. I'd overslept and it was gone midday by the time I'd got out of the house. I phoned the station and said, 'I'm sorry, I'm on my way, I'm just running late.'

'Oh, right,' was the reply but the damage had already been done. I'd phoned around 12.10 p.m. – just ten minutes after I was meant to sign in – and they already thought I'd done a runner off the island. The alarm had been raised, the mainland police informed – even the bloody coastguard in case I'd jumped on the *Galwad*.

Luckily, the girl on duty was my sister Nicky's pal and she managed to convince everyone upstairs that it had been a genuine mistake. I made damned sure I never ran late again though. Bail felt like 'wow, I'm out, I can breathe.' I was desperate to never go back inside again, especially to Winchester.

Despite all the hardship and the injustice and the uncertainty and the restrictions, Nikki was taking everything in her stride. Her mum and dad were incredibly supportive, helping her get to chemo sessions and bringing her back home afterwards. I didn't call her Stormin' Norman for nothing: she never complained or moaned, even when the chemo was knocking her for six. Instead she turned her attention to me and how we could set about proving my innocence.

Chapter 13

TORN APART

I only really saw what they'd done to the *Galwad* once I was out on bail. The bastards ripped it to shreds.

It had been bad enough watching them crawl over my boat when we were first arrested and I'd been forced to sit in the back of a police car at the quay. The fire brigade had appeared from nowhere and attempted to drain out the water tanks; then I saw black cases being gingerly lifted on board, opened, and all sorts of electrical gadgetry being pulled out – presumably to test the *Galwad*'s surfaces, inside and out.

It had been agonising to watch and I'd desperately wanted to yell: *For Christ's sake, it's not the* QE2. *There's only three spaces – one at the front, where the engine is, the vivier tank in the middle and our accommodation at the back. Two blokes can go right through it in forty minutes.*

They wouldn't have listened, of course. They were too busy throwing everything at my boat, men and machines. They had frogmen going round the outside and then underneath the water line, clearly desperate to find something. They even brought sniffer dogs on board but when men, machines and dogs failed to find the faintest whiff of anything, they decided to haul the *Galwad* off to Portsmouth's marine docks.

That's where I lost sight of it — and that's where they really tore it apart, murderous hands clenching hammers and wrenches and heavy iron claws, gleefully plunging them into anything that would splinter and shatter and capsize.

I often lie awake at night and imagine their frenzied destruction. What they did was so violent I swear I can feel my body flinching at the thought of each blow. They didn't just tear my boat apart, they tore me apart at the same time. The *Galwad* was my life and they ripped it from me.

They had it for two months and they trashed it. Vandals couldn't have done a better job.

It was deliberate, too. They wrenched locker doors off and mindlessly tossed them into the bilge — then dumped lifejackets and bedding down there as well. Everything was upended and then hurled away until it became mangled and clogged up inside the *Galwad*'s vital organs.

They pulled wiring out of sockets and left it dangling like entrails; they dragged the tops off water tanks and randomly chucked stuff around, not caring where it landed because they had no intention of putting it back. It's not hard to imagine the bastards laughing and smiling as they warmed to the rampage, either. 'We're pulling this apart because we can and you can't do nothing about it.' Every distorted and disfigured part told me they'd got a kick out of it. It was a jolly, and they were laughing.

They didn't care if I was innocent or guilty. They just obliterated me — and then, no doubt, went down the pub to tell their mates what a craic it had been at work that day.

The first time I saw the *Galwad*'s broken carcass was when it limped back in to Yarmouth. It was heartbreaking. The people who'd disfigured and maimed my boat must have been the sort of people who'd never sweated in their lives; they'd never experienced days and nights out at sea in a raging Force Eight storm with no sleep and precious little money to show for it because a member of crew was puking up and begging to go home.

There was no reason to throw all the stuff into the bottom of the bloody bilge. You bastards.

I remember staring at the murky outline of oversized footprints where Doc Martin boots had jumped up and down and bounced around the white surfaces of my precious boat like it was a trampoline. I looked despairingly for missing lids on tanks in the forlorn hope someone had maybe stacked them securely somewhere. When I clambered inside I stared blankly at a remaining cupboard door, dangling desperately on one remaining hinge, trying lamely to hide the smashed up MDF skeleton it was barely clinging on to.

There was no reason to yank the cupboard doors off. Why couldn't you have just opened them? You bastards.

The bruises and gashes on the *Galwad*'s bodywork told a similar destructive story and I could instantly see where it had been deliberately left to smash against a concrete quay wall. Metal stripping was bent and buckled from the relentless clouting; the catcher, the iron framework at the back of the boat, was caved in – and that's a tough piece of kit. You could smash it with a sledgehammer and it wouldn't dent. They'd obviously let it whack against the quay instead. Each clout had also torn open paintwork, revealing telltale cracks along the seams where the *Galwad*'s planks had once been tightly joined.

All the *Galwad*'s paperwork – like the registration documents and licence – were either torn up or thrown overboard. When my old man went to get the boat back from Portsmouth it wouldn't even start because the batteries had been flattened.

They didn't give a fuck about the *Galwad*. In their eyes it was a drugs boat. They just wrecked it. He's not getting this back in one piece, that was their attitude. They were called the 'rummage team' and they were desperate, of course, to find some minuscule trace, anything to prove cocaine had once been on board. They didn't.

There was never any cocaine on the *Galwad*.

Chapter 14

DID YOU DO IT?

Five months later, we finally found out what it was all about. Our solicitor phoned; I can still remember word-for-word what he said: 'This is how it is, this is what they are saying.

'You went out there, had a "rendezvous" with a container ship and within a space of three and a half minutes you picked up eleven bags, which were packed with cocaine, from the sea.

'You then threw the bags overboard near Freshwater Bay, intending to pick them up later on, under the cover of darkness.'

I must have fallen silent. I was at home and Nikki had just returned from another chemo session. She was flaked out on our sofa, drifting in and out of sleep.

I looked over at her; her skin was unnaturally white, like the porcelain sink at Winchester, no longer the healthy shade it used to be. She was vaguely aware the phone had rung and I could hear her weakly whispering: 'Who is it? Who's calling, Jamie?'

'Get some sleep, luv, don't worry, it's just the bloody solicitor.'

I'd almost forgotten he was still on the line until I faintly heard a disembodied voice calling 'Jamie? Jamie, are you still there?'

'Yeah, yeah, I'm listening, sorry, I was just talking to the missus.'

'Well?' he responded.

'Well, what? Did you just say "rendezvous"? Did you just say I had a fuckin' "rendezvous" with a container ship? Is that what you just said?'

There was something about our solicitor, Julian Hardy, that made me uncomfortable. He felt like one of them, part of the system, one of the establishment – someone who always played by the rules. The sort of bloke I instinctively rebelled against. I wasn't sure he believed us, or that he was willing to go the extra mile to prove our innocence. If he had friends in high places, I was sure he wouldn't want to step on their toes to help us out.

'Just tell me, Jamie. Did you do it?'

I pulled the phone back from my ear and looked at it in my hand as if, in some way, the manoeuvre would help me imagine I was actually looking straight into his face.

I paused once again, this time so I would get my words right, then placed the receiver back to my ear. 'Did I do it? Of course I didn't do it. It's fuckin' impossible. It's ludicrous. It's not even feasible. What do you mean, "I picked up the bags in three and a half minutes"? Are you having a laugh? Think about it man, we were in a Force Eight, rolling all over the place. How the hell could I have possibly done that?

'Which idiot has come up with this nonsense?'

I must have been shouting. Nikki was trying to sit back up. 'What's up, Jamie? What's going on?' she asked.

'It's all right, luv, don't worry. I'm just getting some more details from Hardy. Please lie down, you've got to take it easy.'

Hardy had been recommended to my sister Nicky after we'd all been banged up. I'd lost all confidence in the duty solicitors provided by the police and needed someone with more experience, given the mess we were all suddenly in. He wore black, thick-framed spectacles when we first met, and I thought he looked serious, experienced, like he knew how the system worked and wouldn't put up with any shit. What really set him apart, though, was that he lived on a houseboat in London's St Katharine's Dock. I liked that. *At least he'll know something about boats.*

To be fair, Hardy was as much in the dark as we all were at the beginning. We were simply waiting for the police to reveal what they had because it was impossible to believe they had any kind of case at that stage.

Those details didn't start to emerge until February 2011, when information was painstakingly drip fed to Hardy. Each week seemed to bring another phone call from him until, slowly, a picture emerged. 'The cargo ship was called the *Oriane*,' he said in one call. That was the first time we'd heard that name and my sister Nicky and I started hitting the internet to find out whatever we could.

The MSC *Oriane* had only been built three years earlier and sailed under the Panamanian flag. It was one of the big ones, weighing in at 66,399 tonnes and measuring 277m in length by 40m wide. It could carry 5,762 of those giant corrugated metal box containers you always see stacked up alongside docks, or at railway sidings – the ones that usually have Maersk stamped along their sides. It was operated by a real global giant, the Mediterranean Shipping Company (hence MSC), and could steam along at well over 20 knots. *It'd leave the* Galwad *for dead if we were in a race.*

I started looking at pictures but didn't recognise anything unusual or peculiar about its markings. In other words, it looked like every giant cargo ship I'd ever seen. It was painted black with huge, white initials, MSC, along either side, plumb in the middle. I'd seen that many times before, but it was only visible once you were side on to the ship. In much smaller lettering and high up on either side of the bow was the name MSC *Oriane*, practically invisible if you were facing the ship head on. I remember thinking: *There's no way I could have seen that name in the middle of the night. It's too high up and too small.* Besides, why would I have even been looking? It was just another giant cargo ship I wanted to steer well clear of.

On the night that concerned me, it had been travelling from Brazil, heading towards Rotterdam. A couple of days later Hardy rang again and said, 'The police's marine expert has analysed the radar readings off the *Galwad* and says your paths must have crossed at around 12.31 p.m. He reckons you then had three and a half minutes to scoop the bags out of the water.'

Hardy's next call was to inform me the United Kingdom Border Agency (UKBA) had a surveillance boat out in the Channel that night, the cutter *Vigilant*. A sort of police spy boat, if you like. The UKBA had apparently received a tip-off that a drug exchange might be happening and they were specifically watching the *Oriane* to see if any boats went anywhere near it.

'Well, bingo,' I said. 'Surely, if they were watching the *Oriane*, they must have photographs or video of me caught in the act,' I argued. 'Where's that evidence, Julian? Have you asked for it? If their boat was watching the *Oriane*, they've got me red-handed and bang to rights. End of. So let's see the pictures of me scooping up these bloody bags.'

He fell silent. I could hear the cogs turning round in his brain.

'Please tell me you're not just believing every single word they're telling you? Please, Julian.'

At the time I was furious and frustrated that all this information was coming over in scraps. Looking back, I realise that's how it was being deliberately fed to Hardy. It was a tactic to cloud the waters; it stopped us getting an instantly clear picture of what we were being accused of. I was getting bits and bobs of information from Hardy; most likely he was getting out-of-the-blue phone calls and listening to someone read incomplete fragments of information to him.

I didn't see it quite as calmly or rationally back then, though. I'd often lose my temper over the phone as Hardy read out more unexpected details. I remember him saying to me, 'I haven't got a PA you know, I have to do all the paperwork and the photocopying myself.'

That was like a red rag to me. 'What the hell are you bleating about?' I replied, entirely unsympathetic. 'You want to change places with me, eh? You're supposed to be a heavyweight, a big practice, yet everything's all over the place and you're just sat there waiting for the next piece of the jigsaw to land. They're pissing all over you man.'

'This is what they're telling me,' he'd argue. 'I can only pass it on once I get to know it myself.'

'Well, you're the so-called expert, you've got to find a way of rectifying this because it's just absurd. Jesus, you even live on a boat, you've done a bit of boating yourself, surely you can see this whole thing is ludicrous. Surely.'

'Yeah, well, maybe it is, but it's what they are telling me.'

'For Christ's sake, Julian, just ask anyone with boating experience and they'd tell you this is impossible. Why the hell aren't you getting angry and fighting my corner? It's complete nonsense, man. Surely you've told them that? Haven't you?'

I didn't know any better at the time. I was blinded by frustration, by anger, by a crushing sense of injustice and by the fear that I was being sucked into something that was out of my control. On top of all that, I had Nikki to worry about. She was having chemo sessions practically every day by then.

Eventually, we were handed paperwork: witness statements, our own statements and the police marine expert's report. Like everything else, it was drip fed: it never came to us in one full bundle. We only had the tip of the iceberg, and no idea how huge and crushing it might become. All I could do was wait for the next instalments and give Hardy as many answers as I could as the allegations dribbled in.

I couldn't get my head around the three and a half minutes and the sheer impossibility of the logistics. To me, it was blindingly obvious: nobody could go perilously close to a monstrous cargo ship in a Force Eight storm and somehow scoop up bags of drugs from a raging sea – all inside three and a half minutes. Surely nobody could actually give it credibility? Could they?

The other bone of contention was the terminologies beginning to emerge in the statements and how they made completely normal, logical and correct boat manoeuvres seem dodgy.

It was how I imagined an out-of-body experience to feel like. Suddenly I was reading statements that bore no resemblance to my reality: I'd been moving the *Galwad* in an 'erratic way', I was doing something abnormal, not what proper fishermen might be expected to do. I remember staring at those two words – erratic way – and my mind drifted back out to sea, searching for something that might make me think: *Oh, yeah, erratic, they're right. That'd be when I weaved backwards and forwards around that cargo ship and got the*

nippers to lean over and pick up all those bags. Only nothing like
that had happened.

How could someone who wasn't out on the *Galwad* that
night, who wasn't experiencing the tug and pull of engorged
waves as they smashed into us and over us, how could they
talk with any profound understanding about the way I was
handling my boat? How could they seriously imagine I would
risk my boat and my crew by going so close to a container
ship that could crush us to pieces if we were bounced against
it by the weather? I consider myself a good, experienced skipper and if there's one thing all my knowledge has taught me
it's this: you don't fuck about with a 66,300-tonne container
ship in a raging storm. If I had truly gone out on a drug-
smuggling operation that night, I'd have cancelled it long
before 12.31 a.m.

I know with complete certainty that I was handling the
Galwad the right way, the only way, the way I'd been taught
and the way I had learned over years of sheer hard and relentless experience. The more I stared at 'erratic way', the more
I knew there was absolutely nothing erratic at all. Jesus. Those
words annoyed me. They went straight to the core of my
professionalism. 'Are you listening to me Julian? Are you getting this down? What they're saying is impossible. They're
making it up.'

Eventually we received a printout showing the lines of
where the *Oriane* allegedly went and where the police reckoned I steered the *Galwad*. This was meant to show my
'erratic' movements and yet, when I looked at it, all it showed
was the *Galwad* steaming along in one straight line, bar some
tiny dog-legs due to the weather. Then we turned and headed
back to the area where I wanted to do my mapping.

If I had been steering erratically, I would have expected
the printout to be a jumble of zigzag lines, showing me

inexplicably going one way, back another, then maybe coming back on myself and twisting round – in other words, going all over the show as I tried to tap dance round a cargo ship while scooping up bags of drugs from the water. If anything, the printout showed the polar opposite: the *Galwad*'s movements were totally consistent with a boat changing direction in terrible weather conditions.

And yet there was something about the word 'erratic' that worried me. *That word is going to stick with people who know nothing about boats and fishing.*

Two police officers had apparently been positioned on the cliff tops at Tennyson Downs, near Freshwater, and they'd seen us throwing 'dark bags' into the water there as we came back to the island. That struck a chord. That explained the contradictory questions at Fareham police station and why I'd been asked about 'black objects'.

Even those officers were claiming the *Galwad* had been making 'erratic manoeuvres'. Yet all we were doing was drifting up and down with the tide. How was that erratic? Was it erratic because it's a clever word to use and would resonate with a jury? Did someone tell them to stick the word 'erratic' into their statement because they knew it'd cause havoc? Or did it simply seem erratic to them because they knew nothing about tides, and how a boat is steered to work with them? *Fuck that word erratic.*

Another statement claimed we crossed the path of the *Oriane* four or five times that night when it was at least 10 miles away – maybe even further. That might have been true, I just don't know. The point is I couldn't know: I could never have seen it that far away and it wouldn't have shown on my radar. Even if it had, it would only have been a small blip: my radar didn't flash up the names of boats as they came into range. There were loads of big cargo ships in the Channel that night and I didn't know the names of any of them. Nor was I interested.

Admittedly, my Olex machine did have an Automatic Identification System (AIS) installed and I guess that might have made the blips more identifiable. But I'd only got the Olex for the mapping; I had absolutely no idea how to operate the AIS and I wasn't even sure if it worked. I had nobody to show me and I didn't see the need; I was far happier using my trusty radar because that did the job and it was what I was used to.

Then came the police marine expert's report. Paul Davidson certainly had the right credentials: he'd worked for all the major marine and coastguard agencies – in fact, all the ones I'd clashed with over the years. The bastards who tried telling me my boat was the wrong size. Was that a coincidence? He was widely regarded as an authority and his report clearly stated the *Galwad* crossed paths with the *Oriane*. Even though I'd absolutely no memory of that, it never occurred to me he could be wrong. If he said we'd crossed paths, then we must have crossed paths. *Strange I never saw it, though.*

I had no way of contradicting him. It didn't even occur to me to think like that. It didn't dawn on me – then – that the AIS machine I didn't know how to operate would have logged my exact route throughout the night. I was naive. 'If that's what Davidson said I did, he must be right,' I said to Julian.

The next bombshell came some *eight* months after I was nabbed. First, Beerey was arrested – followed shortly afterwards by Scott. I wasn't allowed to go anywhere near the *Galwad* while I was out on bail, so Scott and another lad had been fishing it themselves to keep the business ticking over. Why not? OK, the police hadn't realised he'd gone out with us that night but he'd done nothing wrong, he had nothing to hide, so why on earth shouldn't he carry on working – even if I couldn't?

The police had even returned to the *Galwad* to check it out in September. Scott was on board when they turned up and still they didn't think anything was wrong. Four months later, though, he was arrested – 'we think you were on the boat that night' – put on bail and ordered to stay away from the Isle of Wight. He didn't get charged until February 2011.

While I was devastated for Scott – and realised my 'lie' would come back to haunt me – it was Beerey's arrest that was the most shocking and significant. I never saw that coming, none of us did. He wasn't even on the *Galwad*. So what on earth was his crime?

Again, we had to wait an eternity before that bit of information was fed our way. In fact, we didn't get to know until shortly before the court case – giving us hardly any time at all to deal with the specific allegations. Until this point there'd been a gaping hole in the police's case against us: who was the mastermind behind this alleged operation and what was the link between them and me?

Jon Beere was their answer. Without him, they couldn't square the circle. They needed to find a go-between: someone who was both liaising with the masterminds and then with me. So the police declared Beerey had been in contact with a mysterious 'Balkan Gang' who needed a man with a boat, someone mug enough to go out and do their dirty work in the middle of the Channel.

'Why do they think Jon did that?' I asked Julian.

'Well, you got him to meet Vic at the ferry terminal, didn't you? Then he brought those other two guys over with him.'

'That was because I was stuck on the bleeding tide coming back from Weymouth. How many more times must I tell you? I couldn't get back in time so I asked Beerey for a favour. How does that make him a go-between? What's this "Balkan Gang" stuff all about, in any case? Are you telling me it was those other two muppets?

'How on earth were Jon and I to know they'd turn up with Vic? We'd never met Vic or any of them before. We didn't know who they were, or what their game was; for God's sake, I didn't even know Vic's real name. In any case, they left a few hours later. Why would they do that if they were a Balkan Gang pulling off some massive drugs operation? Surely they'd hang around to check it all went well. Why didn't they wait so they could take the drugs off us when we got back?

'What proof have they got? If Beerey's a go-between, then the police must have phone records or emails off his computer showing he was in touch with this Balkan lot. It must have all been planned in advance. Where's that evidence? If they've got emails or texts then they've got us bang to rights, haven't they? He couldn't possibly have organised a great big international operation like this without talking to someone beforehand. What a load of bollocks.

'Tell me, Julian. Where's the bloody proof?'

Julian Hardy and I were rowing constantly by now; I lost count of how many times I yelled down the phone, 'I want the phone records of those two officers on Tennyson Downs who reckon they saw us dumping bags overboard. Why the hell haven't we got them? The police have got all our phone records, so why can't we have theirs? I want to see who they phoned when they saw us – and at what time. Jesus. How do we even know they were there? We've only got their lousy word for it.'

'This is not how it works,' was always his reply. 'The judge won't like it if we question the police's honesty and integrity.'

'Oh, please, Julian – give me a break.'

Then I got to hear about the aeroplane.

Chapter 15

GHOST PLANE

When is a plane not a plane? Simple: when the police say it's not.

That pretty much sums up the mystery of the surveillance plane I saw just as we were passing the Needles on our way back to Yarmouth. The sort of small, twin-engined plane you often see parked outside giant hangars at provincial airports like Exeter or Newquay. The sort of plane the Ministry of Agriculture and Fisheries would often fly low over the island.

I saw that plane flying over Tennyson Down with my own eyes; it was so low I could have shaken hands with the bloody pilot. Except the police say that's impossible. They say I couldn't have seen it. They say it was never there.

So what did I see? An apparition? A trick of the light?

We didn't know anything about the phantom plane until late February, after the police produced Davidson's radar analysis claiming the *Galwad* and *Oriane* definitely crossed paths. They then produced aerial photographs – clearly taken from a plane – that showed us legitimately fishing out in the Channel around 4 a.m., and then making our way back along the Solent into Yarmouth harbour much later the following evening.

Something was missing, though. I'd definitely seen it flying over Tennyson Downs, roughly where we'd drifted with the tide to do the mackereling and where the police spotters allegedly saw us dumping bags.

I remember it so clearly because it was a beautiful, clear blue sky that evening and my sister Nicky used to live in a flat close to that spot. I recall thinking: *That's passing right over Nicky's place right now.* I'd just come round the Needles and could see it through the gaps in the rocks: the plane had come round over the south side of the cliffs and was almost skimming the open fields below. It was clearly looking for something and I carried on watching it as it flew over Tennyson Monument – a tall, solitary marble cross that stands on top of the cliffs and can be seen from miles around just like a lighthouse.

Then I thought no more of it. We were used to seeing low-flying planes. Most of them were either doing surveillance for the coastal or agricultural agencies.

The moment we first saw the photographs taken from the plane I realised the timings weren't complete. First, there were pictures of us potting in the early hours of 30 May (0342 hrs). I had no idea a plane was overhead at this point but the pictures looked accurate and there was no doubt we were all busy fishing as usual.

Then came an almighty gap of at least fifteen and a half hours before more pictures were taken around 1930 hrs (still 30 May) – this time of us heading down the Solent.

'Why's there such a huge gap?' I asked Julian. I could imagine him shrugging his shoulders on the other end of the line, so I carried on talking. 'If a plane had been following us at 0342, why didn't it carry on taking photographs of everything we did right up to the moment we docked back in Yarmouth?'

I got my sister, Nicky, on the case and she came back with the answer – although there was still a gap. 'The crew are only allowed to fly for a set amount of time then they have to come back in for a break. The plane had to be grounded for twelve hours before it could take off again,' she said. 'They weren't allowed to go back out again until 6.30 p.m. that evening.'

We knew the plane was based in Bournemouth and could reach the Isle of Wight comfortably within five minutes. Still something gnawed away in my mind. 'I'm telling you, Nicky, I saw that plane coming over your place and Tennyson. I'm certain it was around 7 p.m..'

The two of us were sat in my home with Nikki, who – despite her own battles – was making sure she knew every twist and turn of the case against me. 'What time did those two coppers on the cliff claim they saw you dumping the bags?' she asked.

I fell silent and sifted through the paperwork strewn across our dining table until I finally unearthed their statement. They'd reported seeing us at 6.45 p.m. 'Surely the police would have called in the surveillance plane at that moment,' said Nikki. 'They'd want to fly over as soon as they could and get a good look at whatever you'd chucked in the water. They'd want photos of everything.'

'That means your timings are bang on, Jamie,' said my sister. 'The plane could take off any time after 6.30 p.m. The spotters reckon they saw you at 6.45 p.m., they raised the alarm and the plane would get to Tennyson by 7 p.m. easy.'

That was definitely it. The girls had found the missing link. Of course, the police would get that plane in the air as quickly as flight regulations would allow them. They'd just been told by two of their own officers that we'd dumped bags around Tennyson and they'd be itching to get aerial photos of whatever they could see, ideally bags floating around in the water. Suddenly all the timings made sense.

Except. Except the police statements told a different story. They said the plane didn't fly over Tennyson around 7 p.m. that evening and that I definitely hadn't seen it flying over my sister's flat. In fact, they claimed it didn't even take off from Bournemouth until 7 p.m. and then first saw me east of the Needles. They never said what time that was. They then followed me as we came down the Solent, eventually filming the *Galwad* as we came into the harbour at 7.39 p.m.

'The bastards are covering something up,' I screamed down the phone at Hardy the next morning. 'And I can tell you why they're denying it, as well. That plane went to Freshwater all right, it took loads of photos and you know what – it found sweet Fanny Adams. No bags, no cocaine, no nothing.

'They can't admit that, though, can they? That would totally screw their case.

'So you know what they've done? I'll tell you what they've done, Julian. They've made out the plane never went there, so they don't have to admit it didn't find anything. That's what they've done.

'There's only one way to resolve this. You've got to demand the flightpath of that plane.'

That was greeted by a hefty sigh. 'Yeah, well, I'll see what I can do'.

The more I thought about that phantom plane, the more light it cast on what the police had been doing. Although I didn't know it at the time, when we were first arrested the police inexplicably wrote on my charge sheet that the drugs had been physically found on board the *Galwad*. Now

I realised why. The plane had checked out the area, reported there were no bags in the water, so where else could they be – other than on my boat. It also explained why they tore it apart in such a frenzy.

I was also puzzled why the police had never swarmed all over Tennyson as soon as the spotters reported seeing the bags. Why didn't they zoom in and pick up what was allegedly in the water? More, why didn't they hide in the bushes and long grass and wait for one of us mugs to come along and retrieve our multi-million pound haul? Then there was the surveillance cutter, the spy boat *Vigilant*. That had remained close by throughout, barely a mile away – so why hadn't that come haring in like a dog off the leash? None of it made sense.

The missing plane explained everything. The plane had effectively said: 'Don't bother. There's nothing down there. The drugs must be on their boat.'

So, to cover a huge hole in their case, they simply hid the plane. They provided irrelevant video footage of us coming into Yarmouth; they insisted they'd only taken off at 7 p.m. and they'd stayed to the east of the island throughout – never once circling Tennyson.

Chapter 16

DON'T UPSET THE POLICE

What chance did I stand?

The highly respected Queen's Counsel meant to represent me in court dropped out at the last minute because she had a murder trial to defend instead.

What chance did I stand?

I only met her replacement *once* before my trial started.

What chance did I stand?

None of the stuff I'd begged Hardy to get – phone and flight records, surveillance reports – was handed over.

What chance did I stand?

Despite my pleas, the case was heard in leafy Surrey and not on the coast where a jury might have known something about boats and the sea.

I didn't stand a cat in hell's chance, did I?

I'll never forget Hardy's words when he first introduced me to my new barrister. I was meant to be represented by Miranda Moore QC – she was a high-brow operator used to defending heavy-duty criminal cases with bags of experience and contacts. There was something matriarchal about her,

I felt I was in safe hands so when Hardy suddenly told me she was no longer available it didn't feel like good news.

'There's been an error and she's double booked,' he said, like that was perfectly normal and what else could I expect.

'What do you mean, she's double booked?'

'She's got a murder case to deal with and she didn't realise your case was at the same time.'

'Really?!'

My replacement was Julian Christopher, QC. 'Who's he then?' I asked. 'What's he done?'

'He's done a lot of work for the other side, so he'll know how they think and what tricks they like to pull in court.' Hardy then told me Christopher had prosecuted cases for the Serious Organised Crime Agency (SOCA) – in other words, the mob trying to screw me.

'Won't that compromise him, though?' I replied. 'Won't he have mates on the other side who he won't want to piss off?'

'It doesn't work like that, Jamie. He's one of the good guys, trust me.'

I didn't get to meet him, though, until one month before my trial and even then it was only for a few minutes. There was barely time for a quick handshake and some quick 'we'll do everything we can for you' bullshit.

He was younger than I'd imagined: tall, thin and immaculately groomed with closely cropped hair that looked like it'd been styled at a gentleman's barber just seconds earlier. There was barely a single strand out of place. He was wearing a razor-sharp white shirt with a silk tie, fastened high in an old-school Windsor knot. Thinking about it now, he physically looked every inch like a young Nigel Farage and, just like any party political leader, I sensed he was driven, passionate and extremely devoted to a cause he truly believed in – the fairness and beauty of the English Judicial System and the implicit and unwavering sincerity all those who served within it.

We met at his chambers at 5 Paper Buildings, just off the Strand. I'll never forget the way Hardy introduced me: 'Julian, this is Jamie Green. Jamie has an issue with the police.'

Christopher stretched out his arm and, as we shook hands, exclaimed: 'Really?' as if the very idea shocked him to the core. 'And what issue is that?'

I couldn't be arsed with pleasantries: 'They are stitching me up and I want their phone records.' It was like I'd said something blasphemous; I could literally hear the combined intake of breath from both Christopher and Hardy.

We all sat down round one of those huge, deep mahogany office tables with lots of dangling gold antique handles and a vast inlaid leather writing surface. Just like Hardy, Christopher didn't favour upsetting the police or anyone else for that matter.

'We can't really go into court and ask a judge for something like that,' he responded, in a very grave, serious tone. 'It's not a good idea for me to go in accusing the police before the case has even started. No judge would want that.'

That pretty much signalled the end of our meeting. Jesus. Thinking about it now, I should have said: 'It's my life on the line here, my freedom at stake. I want to see you for a week solid, matey. I want to go through absolutely everything with you, right down to the tiniest details and I want you to get all those phone records you say the judge won't like me asking for. Just do it. If you're too busy, then I want someone else to represent me.'

I didn't do that, though. I didn't know how to, or whether I even could. Besides, the clock was ticking: there was only four more weeks until my trial. I couldn't have another last-minute change of legal representatives.

Hardy and I sat in a nearby park once we'd left Christopher's building and – once again – he told me I was 'in the best of hands. You've just got to trust us, Jamie, we know how this works.' How could I argue? I'd been sucked into the legal system and my own teammates were ordering me to play by the rules.

That didn't stop the rows over the phone between Hardy and me, though. In fact they became more and more heated as the trial inched closer. I'd be bawling, 'What about doing this? Have we spoken to such and such? Have we asked for this? For that?' I'd be on his case 24/7, demanding answers. 'Why aren't we doing this?'

I remember being shown paperwork that categorised the evidence against us. For the first time I saw the words 'undisclosed schedule' and I remember saying to Hardy: 'What's on that, then?' He simply replied: 'We don't know, it's all covered up'.

'Well, challenge them for it. Find out what it is and challenge it.' He wasn't interested.

I wanted Hardy to dig and find our own expert witnesses, rather than simply accept whoever and whatever the police threw at us. I expected him, and Christopher, to microscopically analyse and then challenge statements and information – particularly what the marine expert Davidson had said about the two boats crossing paths.

'I'm telling you, Julian, I don't recall a great, big, dirty cargo ship thundering right across my path. Please tell me why I don't remember something like that? I've been doing this job since I was a teenager and, forgive me, I reckon I know a 66,300-tonne container ship when I see one. Why are we just accepting every bloody word Davidson says? What does he know? He wasn't even there.'

I might as well have been rowing with myself. Nothing I asked for, or suggested, was picked up on. Hardy's attitude was: 'Look, I'm running this case and I know what I'm doing. It'll get done when I want it done.'

I couldn't help thinking my side was happier to take the words from the other side of the wall rather than go to the judge and say, 'What's going on here, what's all this undisclosed stuff, we need to know.' They seemed more worried about their own credibility than defending us.

A classic example of this came when I decided to contact the local Maritime and Coastguard Agency (MCA) to see what other boats – besides us and the *Oriane* – had been out in the Channel that night. I remember saying to Nikki, 'The MCA keep all the data on everything that moves in the Channel. They'll have a record of exactly which boats were where, and at what time, on the night we went out. That might throw something interesting our way.'

I called them a couple of times but was flat batted. 'Can you leave us your contact details, Mr Green? We will need to do some research. We'll get back to you' – that sort of shit. Next thing I knew, I got a phone call from Hardy, saying: 'Er, what've you been doing, Jamie? Why have you been intimidating police witnesses?'

'What you on about?'

'You've been on the phone,' but before he could continue I snapped back, 'All I've done is rung the national coastguard agency. Since when did they become police witnesses? They hold all the official information on boats out in the Channel – surely that's public record. How can the police claim ownership of that?'

Hardy wasn't having it, though. 'We will get into serious trouble if you keep going on like this, Jamie.'

You what?

'How the hell was I to know the MCA are in bed with the police? Nobody's told me that. There were other boats in the

Channel that night and we know nothing about any of them. We don't know their bloody names, where they were heading, how fast they were going or what their courses were. We don't know anything yet now you're telling me I'm not allowed to even ask for the information.

'Isn't this what you should be doing, Julian? Isn't this sort of stuff important?'

I've no doubt money was one of the root causes of the problem. I'd ask for something that might take time and resources and would be told: 'We won't get any funding to do that. There's no money available.'

It was a wake-up call, I guess. I'd always assumed legal aid meant access to whatever it might cost to help prove my innocence. I soon realised that wasn't the reality. My legal team were dragging their heels and waiting for the next police bombshell to land because they weren't being paid to go out and look for evidence themselves. Their attitude seemed to be: 'We can't do that, we don't get paid enough.'

For the record, Hardy pocketed £45,000 for his efforts while Christopher earned sixty grand. I don't think it was all down to a lack of money, though. I was desperate for them to get the phone records of the two spotters who allegedly saw us dumping bags. I wanted to prove whether they were actually on Tennyson Down when they said, because I had my doubts.

More importantly, the phone records would show who they called, and when, to raise the alarm. This had become critically important; as inconceivable as it sounds, the police were claiming neither of them had spoken directly to their superiors.

'They're trying to tell us two police officers, specifically watching the *Galwad*, saw us throw black objects overboard – then never bothered to tell their own bosses what they'd just seen. If we got their phone records, it'd prove they're lying.'

Hardy and Christopher didn't want to know. They didn't want to 'upset' the judge; they didn't want to accuse the police of anything sinister or underhand. What was all that about? Were they just all too matey with one another across both sides of the court room? Was there a gentleman's code of conduct so the likes of Christopher could comfortably prosecute on behalf of SOCA on one case – and then defend against them on another?

What chance did I stand?

They wouldn't even battle to get the trial heard at a different court. The last place I thought it should be was in Kingston upon Thames, or Nappy Valley as I called it, where the police are always goodies and never told a lie. Very conveniently, it was also where SOCA was based at the time.

I'd begged and begged Hardy to get the trial moved to a coastal town, so at least some of the jury might have a better understanding of boats, weather conditions – heaven forbid, even fishing. Maybe a couple of them would have walked the cliff tops in wild weather and watched how boats manoeuvre when they're being battered by the waves. Was that an unreasonable request? Should it not have been my right?

Then the penny dropped. The prosecution had to convince a jury we were guilty. They'd stand a far better chance of doing that in leafy Surrey than they would on the south coast, where the jurors just might know something about the sea. The prosecution would have way more sway with a land-locked person.

Then there was that ugly issue of cost again. All the legal teams were based in London: they wouldn't want the expense and hassle of travelling to a coastal town every day. Much better to let us suffer that. If Jamie's family wanted to come over each day from the Isle of Wight to support him, then fine. They'd just have to fork out for it themselves.

Like I said:

What chance did I stand?

Chapter 17

ALTERED STATEMENTS

It was 9.45am on 26 April 2011 when I suspect the awful truth dawned on Julian Christopher, QC. That was the precise moment when he just might have realised I was right.

The police were lying bastards.

Not that he would have used those words. Ever. Let's be honest, Christopher came from a different planet to the one I inhabited, one of jolly fine fellows who all got on tremendously well with each another, who obeyed the rules because they genuinely believed in the pureness and inherent honour within the justice system – and who shared a powerful common denominator: the police were always on the side of good. I'd never seen the world like that. It was easy for me to think badly of the police because that's all I'd ever experienced.

It must have been hard for Christopher to wake up to my reality.

I'd arrived at the court building for the first day of our trial around 9 a.m., an hour before kick-off. My family had decided to rent a flat close by in Kingston; I'd spent the previous evening munching pizza and going over the case with my mum and dad, sister Nicky and my daughter Maisy. Nikki was still having chemo. It would have been impossible for her to make the 200-mile round trip and then get back to the island in time for her next day's appointment.

The trial should have been held on the coast, somewhere like Bournemouth or Portsmouth.

I missed her badly, but we were all relaxed that evening, reasonably confident the entire case was too unbelievable to be treated seriously. We even laughed at the absurdity. How on earth could we have picked up bags of drugs in a fierce Force Eight storm inside three and a half minutes? Nobody would believe that. Impossible.

I was definitely apprehensive the following morning, though, as I walked up the short flight of steps that lead from the street pavement to the main court entrance. Kingston isn't a particularly foreboding building from the outside – it's modern with lots of glass within a greyish-white concrete frame – but the two words 'crown court' written in sombre-black capital letters above the main doors certainly focused my mind.

It took forever to get through all the security at check-in and I remember thinking, *This is worse than an airport.* Julian Hardy was already waiting for me – one of the very few occasions I actually saw him during the trial. We shook hands and he said, 'Right. We must be quick. Julian Christopher wants to speak to you. Follow me.'

He led me to a small room where my QC was waiting with a pile of folders, stacked haphazardly on top of one another – like they would collapse at any moment. Christopher held out an arm to shake hands as we entered the room, looked me straight in the eyes and, to my complete amazement, said, 'You'll be pleased to know I've changed my opinion about the police.'

He looked embarrassed, though, like he didn't feel comfortable saying something so treacherous. I didn't know whether to laugh out loud or hug him and say, 'Hallelujah, welcome to my world.'

'Oh, why's that then?' I asked suspiciously.

I'll never forget his reply. He was too establishment to say something like 'they're a bunch of lying bastards.' Instead, he said, 'I'm afraid there are one or two coppers who have been a bit naughty.'

Did you just say 'a bit naughty'?

Despite his upper-crust way of talking, I was taken aback. 'What do you mean? What's happened? Why are you suddenly telling me this?'

I looked at my watch – it was 9.45 a.m. and the trial was due to start at 10 a.m. 'Come on, what is it?'

That's when he looked away. Instead of holding my gaze, like he had when I first walked in, he turned and, almost apologetically, mumbled, 'They've changed their statement.'

'Who's changed what statement?' I snapped back instantly. What was Christopher talking about? His mood had swung, though. He wasn't comfortable with this conversation. It was like he didn't want to tell me because it undermined his faith and belief in the justice system.

'The two policemen who saw you throwing bags overboard at Tennyson. They've changed their story.'

My body seemed to react quicker than my brain in that moment. It wanted to explode; it was like all the stress and anxiety and worry and frustration and disbelief and everything I'd ever felt since the moment we were arrested wanted to spew out of me in one foul torrent. 'What do you mean they've changed their story? They can't do that, surely? How's that allowed? What the hell are they saying now?'

Christopher fell silent, still not looking directly at me. He explained how he'd been asking for logs and statements from the police for days on end but very few had actually been handed over. Now I understood why he was being so sheepish: he'd only just found out himself about the altered statements. He was as much in the dark as I was, presented with paperwork that he should have been given weeks earlier. He'd barely had time to get his own brain around it and, to his credit I suppose, now he was smelling a rat.

The trouble was, it cut to the core of how he believed the police operated. Worse, it was too late for him to react. He'd already prepared our defence and was mentally focused on sticking to the format he'd mapped out. Now he was being told information that could take weeks to unravel and totally alter the entire structure of how he planned to defend us.

Christopher grabbed the pile of files on his desk and, as we walked towards courtroom 10, explained that the two spotters had met with their boss in a car park the following day. Instead of saying they had seen us throwing 'six or seven dark objects' overboard – which is what they originally stated and what I'd been asked about in my interview at Fareham – they'd now changed it to:

> Holdalls tied together on a line were dispatched from the boat one after another, totalling 10 to 12. They were thrown in a controlled deployment with the aid of a rope and an orange fishing buoy.

The bags themselves couldn't possibly be confused for 'dark items' or the 'black objects' I'd been quizzed about at Fareham police station. These bags were the exact opposite: they carried the Brazilian brand name 'Mochila Wind' and five were silver, three were green and three red.

Unbelievably, there was more. The police had kept a comprehensive log of everything that happened, as it happened, during their operation that entire weekend. Officers would radio in to report what they'd seen, or what was going on, and their information would be written down by a loggist, Louise Parry, who would also note the time of each call. It was an open radio link, meaning everyone on the operation could listen in each time someone added extra information.

However, at the moment we were arrested on Yarmouth Harbour – and for the following hour and a half when all hell was breaking loose – Parry's radio apparently broke down without her realising. With no radio messages coming in, no official contemporaneous log was being kept to accurately record what had happened, when it had happened, who'd done what, what was said, or what was found. Nothing. There was zero accountability.

My head was spinning. I was about to step into a court room and fight for my freedom and suddenly everything I'd half prepared in my own mind was being blown apart. It must have felt the same for Christopher as well. And that wasn't all.

The police spy boat *Vigilant* – which had been watching the *Oriane* all night long – had no entries in its logbook either for the period when we were meant to have crossed paths and scooped up the drugs. Instead, the word 'SPOILT' had been scrawled across the pages where a record of what they'd observed should have been written.

You what?

My liberty, my life, was on the line and suddenly I was being swamped with an avalanche of unknown material there simply wasn't any time to research or question.

I looked at Christopher. I was furious but he simply seemed conflicted. Why wasn't he swearing and cursing and, like me, calling the police every name under the sun?

Naughty was as strong as it could get for him. Maybe he was on a back foot, trying to play catch up. Maybe his head was spinning as much as mine, maybe he just had a different way of dealing with it.

His attitude remained the same and his final words to me before the trial started were: 'Don't upset the court, don't upset the jury and don't be nasty to the prosecution.' It was like he was saying, 'Be nice to them all and it'll be all right.' I think he actually believed that.

'Oh … and one more thing, Jamie. Don't look any of the jurors directly in the eyes.'

Which is exactly what I did the moment they all filed into the courtroom and sat down. Who were these people? They all looked prim and proper in ties and jackets and buttoned up blouses. I could feel my stomach churning: these were ladies who lunched and men who downed G&Ts at private clubs. They didn't get pissed down the pub. How could they possibly understand my life?

I was supposed to be judged by my peers yet just one look told me this lot weren't from my world, any more than Christopher was. If they came to see how we lived on the Isle of Wight, they'd either laugh and find it charmingly quaint or they'd turn their noses up in horror.

'Darling, they don't even lock their doors at night.' No, we don't – and we leave our car keys in the ignition 24/7 and the dog wanders in and out whenever it wants because the back door's open as well. Even the front sometimes. That's what it's like on the island, that's our lives.

They didn't have a Scooby Doo. They'd have their houses with security boxes that flash in the night and gates that automatically close and shut as the company car goes in and out. Their biggest worry would be whether there were enough bobbies on the beat down their leafy lanes.

These were people who relied on the police to make them feel safe and secure and protect them. They didn't mistrust the police. They didn't think the police might be capable of lying. I've never relied once on the police in my entire life because, in my world, I never expected anything off them. Least of all, protection.

You're God damned right I looked at the jurors. Fuck the rules.

The court room was modern and functional. It wasn't like walking into a scene from *Rumpole of the Bailey*, there wasn't any history or age in there. Instead, it was overwhelmingly clad in high-gloss light wood panelling, with large cream and brown tiles covering an entire wall as if someone had reluctantly thought, *Well, we'd better decorate it with something.*

We were sat at the back, effectively inside a self-contained glass box within the court. Our view of everything was from behind floor-to-ceiling thick glass panels, separated by tiny slits just large enough to slip hastily written notes to our legal team, who were directly in front of us. Opposite and raised above everyone else, sat His Honour Judge Paul Dodgson, perched on a velvety throne with a thumping big crown on the wall immediately above his head.

The witness box was on our far right, just below the judge, while the jury sat to our left in two parallel rows, directly facing the witnesses. The public gallery was at the back as we looked at the judge, level with us on our right-hand side but hidden behind a wall of obscured glass that made it almost impossible for us to see who was there.

I wasn't intimated, although I'll admit, when H.H.J. Dodgson walked in with his wig on and sat on his throne with an air of grandeur, I definitely thought, *Yeah, we're getting down to the nitty gritty now.*

Scott and I were the only ones not in custody, so we always walked in together. Jon, Dan and Vic would come up from the cells below and the five of us would sit in a line, side by side, in our own self-contained world behind glass panels and locked doors.

Let's get this show on the road.

Chapter 18

COOPERING

Twenty minutes. That's all it took. That's all I needed to stop being a fisherman, a father, a husband with a wife dying from cancer. Twenty minutes was all I needed to ditch all of that and become an international drugs smuggler instead. Twenty bloody minutes.

I could barely comprehend what I was hearing as the prosecution explained how I'd got involved in a plot to import £53 million worth of drugs into the UK. There were 255 packages in total, each containing 1kg (2.205lb) of high-purity powder cocaine. Their total weight came to 255kg or 562lb.

The prosecution case was presented by Tanya Woolls, a 'mere' barrister and therefore not as senior as Julian Christopher. Woolls cut a sharp contrast to my defence team: her vivid, blonde hair seemed to be a statement in itself, standing out amongst all the dull, grey wigs that surrounded her. You instantly knew she was in the room and yet she didn't carry the seniority or gravitas Christopher was meant to have. You'd have never known.

There were times when I'd look at my lot, lofty QCs with junior barristers clutching piles of paperwork and endlessly looking hassled as they scribbled notes to one another, and think, *How come she's more forceful?* She wasn't meant to have reached their heights and yet she seemed more combative, more hardened, more snappy. *She must have some balls.*

Her case revolved around the following:

1   I lied about Scott not being on the boat. Boy, did she make a big deal of that.
2   The two spotters who claimed they saw us chucking bags overboard.
3   The *Galwad*'s 'erratic movements'.
4   Davidson's radar evidence.
5   The 'dirty phones' and the calls from the *Galwad* when Vic was throwing up and pleading to go home.
6   Jon Beere's alleged role in the operation.

She opened the prosecution case by explaining that the Serious Organised Crime Agency (SOCA) and the Middle Market Drugs Partnership (MMDP) had been working together on a drugs bust they'd called 'Operation Disorient'.

They'd received 'intelligence' that a container ship from Brazil was carrying drugs that, at some point, would be dumped into the Channel and picked up by a waiting boat. Interestingly, she never mentioned the *Oriane* by name, even though it was being trailed and watched microscopically by the UKBA cutter, *Vigilant*.

She then outlined the main allegations against us. We'd not gone out on a routine fishing trip, all our movements and routes that night were not what proper fishermen would have done. Instead, we had gone out specifically on a 'coopering' exercise.

That was a new word on me. *Coopering.*

She managed to put enough bite into the way she pronounced it that it automatically sounded sinister and illegal even if nobody knew what the hell it meant. One thing was sure, the way she spat it out left little doubt we'd gone into the Channel for cocaine – not crabs.

She saved her real bite for the fact I'd lied about Scott. That made me a deceitful person and therefore nothing I said could ever be believed again. She never let go of that throughout the trial. 'Mr Green is a liar, he lies, they all lie.' Her voice seemed to reverberate round and round and round the courtroom until it, no doubt, embedded in the jurors' brains.

Her stock phrase was *we believe*. 'We believe' Mr Green was on a coopering exercise. 'We believe' he waited to cross paths with the cargo ship. 'We believe' he was able to pull the bags out of the water within three and a half minutes of the boats crossing each other. 'We believe' he then jettisoned the bags below Tennyson cliffs and was planning to return to that spot later in the night to retrieve them. 'We believe' Zoran Dresic (Vic's real name) was part of a Balkan Gang who masterminded the entire operation. 'We believe' he placed calls in the middle of the night to liaise with the gang and to tell them the operation had been a success.

We believe. Is that all you've got, Tanya? *We believe* isn't exactly proof, is it? I looked at my crew, sat alongside me in the dock – Beerey with his gigantic palms tightly clutching either side of his head; Scott, wide eyed in disbelief staring directly at Woolls; Dan silently shaking his head from side to side – and I instinctively knew they were all thinking the same as me: *This woman doesn't give a shit about the actual evidence.*

It was hard to listen to, although Christopher had warned me this would happen. 'You're going to hear statements from the prosecution that will make your blood boil,' he'd said. 'You mustn't react under any circumstances. Do not' – and he'd said the word 'not' like an army sergeant bollocking a recruit – 'do *not* shout out, do *not* swear, do *not* show any anger at all. You'll get your chance to talk.'

It was difficult, though. Woolls was pissing me off, making stuff up and nobody was stopping her. 'They headed for areas they wouldn't usually go; their movements that night were erratic and not at all consistent with a normal fishing trip.' I wanted to scream, 'Yes they were. I'd fished round there before. Besides, what do you know about bloody fishing? You ever been out in a Force Eight, Tanya? How do you know what the boat's movements should have been in that sort of weather?' I was spitting feathers but, rightly or wrongly, Christopher's words kept me in check.

Instead, I reluctantly acknowledged the cunning way Woolls was laying out her case. She did it with such a silky tongue, repeatedly emphasising key words like 'liar', 'coopering' and 'erratic'. I lost count how many times she used them and I could easily imagine the jurors talking about the case during their breaks and using those very words themselves, like they were regular parts of their normal vocabulary. Like they now knew everything they needed to know about fishing and were suddenly sufficiently qualified to judge whether we were proper fishermen or drug mules.

I'd always known the Scott lie would come back to haunt me. I thought I was being honourable at the time, a skipper trying to make sure the youngest member of his crew – in fact the best and a possible future partner in the business – didn't get dragged into this baloney. I was certain everything would blow over and I'd be sent home with no charges, so why tell them Scott was also on the *Galwad* that night when it made no difference to their drummed-up case?

Woolls made me pay for that, practically telling the court, 'Whatever Mr Green tries to tell you cannot be treated as fact. He is a liar and everything he says is a lie.' That was her mantra and I'm certain it stuck.

One thing Woolls never spelt out, though, was our motive. If I was to gamble my entire livelihood and freedom on something so insane, surely there would've had to be a pretty convincing pay day waiting for me?

Woolls made no attempt to tackle this. She never said, 'Green was promised many hundreds of thousands of pounds, which he was planning to divide among his crew.' In fact, no attempt was made to explain who on earth would be paying us. The police had raided and closed down all our bank accounts and there was no huge windfall in any of them. In fact, it could all be accounted for.

They never said we had any debts – because we hadn't, other than an overdraft that went up and down according to the fishing, and the mortgages I'd taken out to buy the *Galwad* and our home. All of which were being paid on time with no problems.

Instead, she tried to imply I had an 'expensive lifestyle' that fishing couldn't fund. Her sole evidence for this was the ponies we owned – and my wife's love of personalised car number plates. We'd had lo55ter (lobster), another one that spelt Green and some with the kids' names on them. Nikki paid no more than £200 or £300 for them; it was something she did for fun and it certainly didn't break the bank. We even kept the receipts for them.

As for the ponies – we'd had them since Maisy and Poppy were youngsters, 6 or 7 years old, and continued with them when Poppy was doing junior showjumping on the mainland. That was our choice, it was what we enjoyed as a family. We never went on holidays, couldn't give a damn about them.

We preferred to have long weekends at the showjumping instead and we'd take the horsebox all over the country doing it. It certainly wasn't the millionaire lifestyle.

Besides, the ponies were worth pennies at best, although Woolls tried to suggest they were practically Royal Ascot winners.

I went straight back to the flat after the court session and remember saying to my old man, 'These sods haven't even explained what our motive was for all this. They haven't said who was meant to be paying us, or how much we stood to earn. They haven't found a single penny in any of our bank accounts – so please, tell me, how can this case stand a cat in hell's chance?' He nodded and trundled off to the fridge to get a couple of lagers.

Then came the twenty minutes moment; the moment in court when Woolls explained when and how I'd got roped into this plot. When she attempted to answer the gaping questions that hung all over the prosecution case – like who were the masterminds and how on earth did Jamie Green come across them?

That came, she said, when I met Vic for the first time at the Sportsman's Rest in Porchfield. Jon Beere had taken him there – along with the other two mugs who'd unexpectedly shown up.

According to Woolls, we didn't talk about the job I needed Vic to do, or how much he'd earn and how long he'd be out for. Instead, the others spent twenty minutes persuading me to take part in the biggest drugs-smuggling operation ever mounted in this country.

Twenty minutes. Don't you think I'd need a little bit longer to think it over, Tanya?

'Jon Beere is the link between the Isle of Wight and the mainland conspirators,' she announced. 'He is there so he can introduce them to Jamie the Skipper – the man with a boat who will go out to collect the cocaine for them.

'Beere was the go-between to oversee the safe collection of that cocaine.'

You what? International drugs baron? Beerey? The same Jon Beere who idolised Formula 1 racing and would make us sit with him in the pub and actually get excited as the cars went round and round and round in bleedin' circles. Drove me mental. That Jon Beere? Father of three kids he absolutely idolised – and who loved him back in equal measure? Are we actually talking about the same Jon Beere here? Great, big soft lump of a bloke with a baby face who loved collecting mussels and cooking them outdoors on a camping stove. Is this for real?

Tanya, you've got this spectacularly wrong. Beerey only came into contact with Vic because I asked him to do me a favour. 'I'm stuck on the *Galwad*. Could you go collect him from Southsea for me? Thanks mate.' I knew he'd say yes because that was the sort of stuff we'd do for each other. I'd return the favour by putting clients his way if I heard someone was looking for scaffolding.

I was speechless. We hadn't even sat in a private room at the Sportsman's – we were outside on one of the table and bench sets, surrounded by families and regulars, and people enjoying an early evening drink. Absolutely anyone could have overheard what we'd been talking about. I sat behind our glass petition and started to imagine the scene:

Me: *So, let me get this straight. You want me to take the* Galwad *into the Channel, wait for a cargo ship to turn up around half past midnight and someone on board will chuck over eleven holdalls with the cocaine stashed inside. Our job will be to pick up the bags, dump them back in the water at Tennyson, then go back later and pick them up again. Is that right?*

Bloke on Table Next to Me (whispering to pals): *Hey, you lot, be quiet. That's Jamie Green sat behind me – he sells crabs in here sometimes. He's just said he's going to be picking up bags of cocaine off some cargo boat out in the Channel then dumping them back in the water at Freshwater. Shut up, let me carry on listening.*

I was known to loads of people in the Sportsman's. Like all the island's pubs, it's where everyone knew everyone else's business and a whisper suddenly becomes a full-blown rumour in the blink of an eye. It would literally be the last place on the planet where I'd have a conversation like that.

Yet again, my defence simply sat back and let Woolls set the scene as she wanted to.

Nobody said, 'Hang on, a plot this enormous would have surely taken months to plan. You're not seriously saying Jamie Green was talked into it within twenty minutes at a busy local pub – and then actually went out the next day to do it. Are you?'

It defied all logic, yet all Christopher said was that I'd gone to the pub to meet a crew member. He never clearly spelt out how ridiculous Woolls was being. My entire life revolved around fishing, I'd owned and built seven boats, my missus had just been given six months to live and we had three kids to look after, and yet the prosecution was claiming I'd agreed to put everything on the line within twenty minutes to people I'd never met in my life before.

Why didn't you say that, Julian? Why didn't you turn to the jury and say, 'Hang on, take a step back and actually think about what the prosecution are asking you to believe.'

Woolls' first major witnesses were the two spotters, Jeans and Dunne. I was looking forward to hearing them. *How are these mugs going to explain changing their statements?* I was confident Christopher would be able to rip them to shreds after they'd first claimed we'd thrown six dark bags overboard – then changed it to eleven brightly coloured holdalls.

Instead, I got my first glimpse of what really goes on behind the scenes. The deals within deals, the handshakes and the nods between the prosecutors and the defence that never come to light in court.

I'd been banging on to Christopher that Jeans and Dunne's version of events was a physical impossibility. 'Why? What do you mean?' he asked.

I explained there was a fence that ran all the way along the cliff top at Tennyson but it was set back to stop idiots going too close to the edge. 'They say in their statements they were standing behind that fence at the time.

'If that's true, then there's no way they could have seen us. The fence is too far back, and the cliff top slopes in such a way that you can't possibly see anything in the water below. So how could they possibly see us?'

I thought this was a huge point and one Christopher could hurl right at them in court. Make them squirm and expose their bullshit. In fact, I wanted the jurors to be sent over to the island, so they could see the lay of the land for themselves. 'Surely you can demand that, can't you?'

Christopher just shook his head despairingly from side to side and then – to my horror – told Woolls in advance that he would be raising my point about the fence being too far back to see our boat. In other words, Jeans and Dunne would be pre-warned and therefore have a chance to come up with a different version of events.

Which is exactly what happened. Once again I had to sit in stony silence while they told the court a completely unrecognisable story to the one they'd put in their statements. 'How did you manage to see the *Galwad* from where you were standing on the cliff top?' they were asked.

Jeans replied, saying something like, 'I climbed over a stile and then slid *snake-like on my stomach* to the cliff edge so I could peer over the edge.'

You what?

I glared at Christopher, thinking, *This is your fault. If you hadn't warned them, they'd have never come up with that pile of shit.*

I tried to console myself with the thought of what was to come. *How are these mugs going to explain changing their statements?*

Paul Jeans kicked off by explaining that he and Andy Dunne – bog-standard Hampshire constabulary officers – had been seconded to work with SOCA and the MMDP on Operation Disorient. They were on the Isle of Wight to be lookouts if required.

Sure enough, nearly eighteen hours after we'd allegedly picked up the drugs, Jeans got a call from SOCA superintendent DI Dave Storey telling him to drive out to St Catherine's Point – on the island's most south-western tip – because the *Galwad* was heading back to the island. Some old pictures of my boat were sent to his iPhone so he'd know what it looked like.

Inexplicably, Jeans ignored his superior officer's instructions and unilaterally decided to drive with Dunne to Tennyson Down instead because he knew that area and felt he'd get a better view from there.

Hang on, this is already sounding dodgy. Your boss has ordered you to go to St Catherine's Point but you've decided to go somewhere totally different – 15 miles away. Are you making this up?

As that thought raced through my mind, I remember also thinking, *I never saw anyone on Tennyson. I'd no idea we were being watched from the cliffs. Were those two even there?*

Suddenly there was a clear vision in my mind of that moment: we were poodling back, the weather had turned, we had blue skies and even the sun had come out. All I wanted was to let Scott and Dan do a bit of mackereling – and then get Vic off the boat ASAP. He was still sat with me in the wheelhouse, white as a sheet, head down, saying nothing. At least he wasn't throwing up any more or begging me to make stupid satellite calls.

Jeans and Dunne claimed they first saw us 3 miles out, south of Tennyson. They then had to run back to their car to get a spare battery for their communications radio and by the time they returned, they reckoned we were heading in.

As we approached, they walked alongside the cliff-top fence, away from the Tennyson monument towards the Needles, so they could monitor our positions and estimate how far we were from the shore. They carried on walking up the hill there and marked on a chart three points where they claimed they could see us from – A, B and C.

There's no way you could see us from Point B.

Then, at 6.50 p.m., they allegedly saw us throwing bags overboard and Dunne radioed the police loggist, Louise Parry, to tell her they'd just seen: 'Six or seven black items thrown at intervals from the boat.'

After that, they waited for us to leave before Jeans walked along the cliff top to get a better view of the water below. The bags – he said – had clearly drifted in a straight line from where he'd seen us chuck them and were now floating in a U-shape, close to the shore, with the bottom of the U facing Freshwater.

I remember my bottom lip dropping instantly like it had a mind of its own and had just independently digested what Jeans was claiming. God knows what I looked like; I knew my mouth was wide open like it wanted to release a torrent of words and yet I remained totally mute. I wanted to scream to the entire courtroom: 'What he's just said, that stuff about drifting in a straight line, it's, well, it's … *it's impossible.*'

My brain was in overdrive. I couldn't believe what I'd just heard and I was certain nobody else could believe it, either. Surely?

Let's get this straight. You're basically saying the bags defied the laws of physics and somehow miraculously floated in a completely straight line – across the flood tide.

I was bursting to talk to Christopher about this. After each day's session, we'd have a fifteen-minute debrief to discuss what had been said and as soon as I saw him, I launched into one.

'Look, it's basic common sense. For those bags to end up where he said they were, I'd have to steer the *Galwad* much, much closer in to the shore – and that would have been suicidal. Jeans wouldn't know this, but the seabed rises sharply at Tennyson and is covered in huge, jagged rocks. They'd have ripped the bottom of the *Galwad* to shreds if I'd gone anywhere near them.

'You don't have to take my word for it, either.

'The plotter will have recorded exactly where we went. That will prove we were never in the position we'd have needed to be for Jeans to be right. If I'd really thrown them overboard where he says I did, they'd have shot off down the coast and be six hours away.

'Think about it. Once they've gone, the ebb tide's nowhere near strong enough to bring them back to the same spot.

'What he's saying could never, ever happen. Not only would the bags have had to cut miraculously across the tide – impossible – they'd have to climb a steep seabed, dodge rocks sharp enough to tear them apart, and then nestle all neat and tidy in a nice little U shape.

'Oh, and by the way, there wasn't one single mark on them. Not even a scratch.

'Surely that's enough to prove they're making this entire case up?'

My heart was pounding. It felt to me like I was proving my innocence; years and years of experience out on the water, building boats, steering them, studying fishing, shooting strings – all of it had taught me intimately how tides worked. I also knew what Jeans could have never seen with his own eyes: what lay beneath the waters at Tennyson. He didn't know the seabed was smothered in razor-sharp rocks. I did.

Christopher started shuffling his feet from side to side, like he was agitating to go somewhere else. In that moment, I knew I was wasting my breath. The glazed look in his eyes told me he was either bored of me rattling on – or just didn't believe the points I was making mattered very much. I realised my allotted fifteen minutes were up, let out an exasperated sigh and headed for the nearest pub with my old man and Nicky.

'Don't worry,' said my sister as she wrapped a consoling arm round my shoulder. 'How are these mugs going to explain changing their statements?'

Chapter 19

THEY'D NEVER LIE

The police would never lie in court to frame five innocent men for a crime they hadn't committed.

They would never deliberately doctor logs and records in order to make a case stick. They wouldn't sign documents knowing them to be false – unless they did it by mistake, of course. They wouldn't cynically and dramatically alter their own evidence.

How are these mugs going to explain changing their statements?

They couldn't. Surely.

It was obvious to me then – and it remains obvious to me now – that Jeans and Dunne were a big problem for the police. Dunne had radioed in to tell Parry they'd seen six or seven black items coming off the back of the *Galwad*. They said my boat was a quarter of a mile from the coastline and that's what she wrote down in her official log book.

They then phoned their own bosses back at mainland headquarters to report what they'd seen. Soon after that, they left the scene, seemingly without a care in the world – leaving absolutely nobody to watch over the bags, or to see if anyone came along to pick them up. Why would anyone be interested in bags full of rubbish, after all?

Two hours later, we were arrested and the *Galwad* was torn inside out as the police tried and failed to find evidence of drugs on board.

It wasn't until the following morning, around 9 a.m., that local fisherman Simon Hutchinson found eleven holdalls – attached to a rope and bright red buoy – tangled up in his own lobster pots at Freshwater. He called the coastguard, the police were alerted and around 9.40 a.m. they discovered £53 million of cocaine.

The man in charge of Operation Disorient on the Isle of Wight, SOCA's Gary Breen – he was one of the two officers sat with me in the car at Yarmouth immediately after my arrest – suddenly had a dilemma. He had us banged up in Fareham, £53 million worth of coke at Freshwater – but sweet Fanny Adams to link the *Galwad* to any of it. Other than Jeans and Dunne.

Breen also had to hold a meeting with all the officers who'd taken part in the operation over the weekend, so they could analyse what they'd recorded and logged seeing – and compare notes with one another. This 'debrief' – held in a local hotel – is a critical police procedure, allowing alterations and corrections to be made but only within strict guidelines that dictate how changes must be dated and signed off.

Inexplicably, Jeans and Dunne were not invited to the debrief – even though their eyewitness reports from the Tennyson cliffs were central to what would be discussed. In fact, fourteen of the twenty-one log entries (66 per cent) written down by Parry – before her radio mysteriously stopped working – were from Jeans and Dunne. Realising they weren't required, they started to make their way to the East Cowes ferry port, expecting to be on the 10 a.m. back to the mainland.

However, once the drugs were discovered close to where we'd been mackereling, Breen suddenly realised Jeans and Dunne might be key players. At around 10 a.m. he called them, told them drugs had been found at Tennyson, and said something like, 'Meet me at East Cowes in a couple of hours. We need to talk.'

The debrief went ahead – still without them – then, around 11.45 that morning, Breen met Jeans and Dunne in a side street close to the chain-link ferry between East and West Cowes. In his hands was the surveillance management record – an ultimate account of everything that had happened, signed by everyone who'd attended the debrief. The three sat in the back of his car for fifteen minutes and inserted two addenda, which they labelled W and X.

Amendment W stated the *Galwad* wasn't where Jeans and Dunne had originally reported seeing it. Instead of being a quarter of a mile away, it was just 100m from the cliffs.

Similarly, amendment X made it clear they hadn't seen six or seven bags being dumped after all. Instead it was ten to twelve holdalls attached to a rope and a bright red buoy.

How are these mugs going to explain changing their statements?

Jeans was nonplussed in court, like he couldn't understand what all the fuss was about. 'Amendment X was made because when I made the original entry it did not correspond with what I had seen on Tennyson Down,' he calmly told the jurors.

'There could be a number of reasons why it wasn't written down correctly – I didn't personally write it. Dunne was holding the radio.'

He continued, 'It's not the case that I only saw what was originally put in the log.

'Packages were coming off the port side at the back. A line was at an angle sloping down into the sea so I could see each package as it hit the water. The last item I saw going in was a red and orange marker buoy as if to locate the items in the sea.

'I saw the bags dropping into the water. It seemed like they were on some sort of reel. They went in one after another quite quickly, disembarking as though they were on a winch.

'Dunne was on the radio and I was relaying this to him.'

Bloody hell.

I glanced towards the jury but they just seemed impassive. Like the addenda were no big deal. Jeans had just found a way of changing the entire contents of his original report and making it sound completely acceptable. Page two of the original log had stated:

> SU116 now stationary, about quarter of a mile from the coast, facing east.
> 1853: 6–7 items overboard at intervals.

Now it was:

> In relation to location, it was about 100 metres from the coast cliff line and approximately half a mile west from the Tennyson monument.

While addendum X added:

> Items tied together on a line and dispatched one after another 10/12 – the last with a red buoy. Items appear to be dark in colour and the approximate size of a large holdall.

Dunne was happy to back it all up. The original log had stated the six to seven bags were almost submerged in the water – suddenly he was saying, 'When we went back the next day, they were floating in the water with a red colour around them.'

In fact, the recovery of the bags at Freshwater was delayed for three hours so Dunne and Jeans could allegedly observe them being pulled out of the water. Jeans told the court they were still – inconceivably – in exactly the same U-shape they'd been in the previous night.

You couldn't make it up. Could you?

I clung to the belief that the loggist, Louise Parry, couldn't possibly talk her way out of this. Surely she had to agree she'd written down 'six to seven items' as Dunne had told her over the radio. I should have known better. 'I may have misheard it,' she said.

'Seven and ten can sound the same on a fuzzy radio.'

You what? Seven and ten? Sound the same? No they bloody don't.

Parry had even more surprises to explain. After 7.56 p.m. no more calls came over her radio, even though all the officers were tuned in to it and were meant to carry on updating her throughout the evening. Apparently she hadn't realised her radio had mysteriously broken down.

'I don't know what prompted me to check my radio – I just did.

'I received no calls for one hour and forty-five minutes so we missed all the arrests.'

So there is no official log of why we were arrested and who did what.

Parry then explained that James McMorrow, SOCA's bronze surveillance commander on the mainland, declared all the missing entries that officers would have radioed over during the lost hour and three-quarters would have to be added by addendum.

'I was pretty concerned,' she admitted.

So was I. The police now had an excuse to add whatever they wanted at the debrief and stick it all under the word 'addendum'.

Unlike Dunne and Jeans, Parry said she attended the debrief the following morning. Nearly everyone present already knew her phone had gone down and a staggering twenty-four addenda were made. 'There were more addenda than I would normally expect,' she conceded and admitted the addenda written by Jeans and Dunne were not what she was used to seeing.

'That is not proper procedure … there shouldn't be a debrief written after the event.'

The best was yet to come, though. Once Jeans and Dunne had finished their addenda, they were asked to sign the management surveillance record Breen had brought with him. Their signatures simply appeared alongside the officers who'd actually attended the debrief and therefore created the false impression they'd attended alongside everyone else.

Of course, Christopher went to town with all of them – first of all, Jeans: 'You were describing in the back of Breen's car something you had learnt but had not actually seen,' he proclaimed loud and clear.

Then he tore into the fact Jeans and Dunne had simply left the scene instead of watching over the bags once they'd allegedly seen us throw them into the water.

'Come on, you must have known the significance of what you say you saw,' he said. 'It would have been entirely your fault if the packages you say you saw disappeared that night and you'd left them unwatched and unguarded.

'The truth is you don't say any of that until you're in the back of Breen's car.'

I was now beginning to think Christopher was getting the upper hand. He was showing some bite and, in my mind, scoring points that would surely register with the jurors.

Then he pointed out that neither Jeans nor Dunne had made any mention of the thumping big anchor that was attached to the bags when they were found. It was so big and heavy, it would have needed at least two of us to lift it over the side of the *Galwad* – and yet the spotters seemingly never saw that happen – or heard the gigantic splash it would have made as it hit the water.

'You describe the sound of bags splashing into the water – yet you never once mention the noise of a huge anchor as it went in.'

And he continued: 'You never even said to the loggist "holdall-size items".'

To be fair, Christopher was making them squirm, especially when he grilled Jeans over the fact he hadn't taken any pictures on his iPhone of us dumping bags.

'You had a smart phone, surely you would have used it to photograph such a vital piece of evidence?'

I'll never forget his ludicrous answer: 'I didn't take any pictures because there was no zoom function on my mobile phone camera – or if there was, I didn't know how to use it.' He said it with such a deadpan face as well, like it was a perfectly plausible explanation. *I'm just a police officer, I don't understand phone cameras.*

Christopher is romping this.

Next up was Breen, who laughingly claimed Jeans and Dunne hadn't been asked to attend the debrief because he thought they needed a lie-in after working such long hours on the operation.

Nine officers had attended but when it came to Jeans and Dunne, Breen said, 'You have to be mindful of the well-being of the officers deployed. I was aware they needed a rest.'

Then came the final straw as far as I was concerned. Christopher demanded to know why Jeans and Dunne had signed the surveillance record alongside everyone else's names – creating the impression they'd physically attended the debrief when they hadn't.

Breen replied, 'They incorrectly signed it on the wrong page. There is a separate page they should have signed to confirm they hadn't been there. I didn't notice this error.'

Even Christopher saw through that and snapped back, 'You needed Jeans and Dunne to provide a link between the *Galwad* and the drugs and that's what you did.'

Breen paused and simply replied, 'They added the addenda of their own volition.'

There was more. As well as radioing Louise Parry, Jeans and Dunne also phoned their bosses – Breen and DI Storey – the moment they allegedly saw us dumping bags at Freshwater. It would be an obvious thing for them to do. However, unlike radio calls – which everyone could listen in to – phone calls remained private between the individuals. Both Breen and Storey completely denied ever receiving such calls; there was no way of knowing who was telling the truth. Christopher wasn't having that and grilled Breen.

Question: 'You received phone calls from Dunne, telling you they'd seen bags being thrown off the *Galwad*?'

Answer: 'No, I didn't. I never received any phone call.'

Question: 'Let me get this straight. Are you telling the court that you received no phone communication whatsoever from the two men you instructed to be lookouts? Are you saying they never directly told you they'd just seen bags – possibly the very bags of drugs you were after – being jettisoned off the boat you'd specifically asked them to watch?'

Answer: 'That's correct. I never had direct contact with them.'

Question: 'But what about the plane? Mr Green specifically recalls seeing a plane flying low over Tennyson. You did send an observation plane up, didn't you?'

Answer: Yes, we did, but not until later. It never flew over Tennyson. The plane just observed the *Galwad* returning to Yarmouth and took photographs and video of it coming along the Solent.

By this point I really was thinking *there's no way they can prosecute us.* The lies are so transparent. OK, I'd gone mackereling at Tennyson but my plotter clearly showed I never stopped and I certainly didn't steer the *Galwad* up a rock-strewn seabed that would have cut us to ribbons.

Then there was the sheer absurdity of the loggist claiming she mistakenly thought Dunne had said 'six or seven dark bags' when he phoned in − plus the clumsy amateurism of the statements being altered the following morning. The changes weren't even subtle. The descriptions defied all plausible belief.

And would anyone really believe Jeans and Dunne hadn't called their bosses, and that nobody had called in a surveillance plane to check out the area?

Once again, I was desperate to speak to Christopher at the end of that day's session. 'Dunne must have called his bosses. He'd have been in deep shit if he hadn't. We need all their phone records and we need the official flightpath of that plane. I'm telling you, their records will prove I am right.

'This is all bullshit. Woolls is constantly telling the court I'm a liar − now it's our chance to prove she's wrong.'

This was a step too far for Christopher, though. 'We can't do that,' he protested. 'The judge won't like us asking for police phone records. No. That's not going to happen.'

I never slept that night. I went back to our flat and tried to untangle all the altered evidence. 'This is all about the plane,' I said to Nicky. 'Of course they phoned in and of course it wasn't ignored. They sent the plane in straight away to check out the area. I saw it flying right above Tennyson, right over your flat, Nicky. I know it was there.

'They're denying it, though, because the plane destroys their case. It clearly saw nothing – not even the rubbish bags. That explains why nobody stayed at Tennyson to keep a look out.

'If they admit the plane flew over and saw nothing, just us heading back to Yarmouth, then that's it. Case over. Or rather no case at all. It also explains why they tore the *Galwad* apart when we got back to Yarmouth. They thought we had drugs on the boat – in fact, that's what they wrote on my charge sheet that night.'

Then Nicky added something else that made me even more hopeful. 'What about the customs cutter, the *Vigilant*?' she asked.

'That was out on the water watching you as well and nobody can deny that. In fact, it trailed you all the way back to Tennyson. It had a high-powered, fast inflatable on board – how come that didn't zoom out as soon as you started dumping bags? They'd got their binoculars on you the entire time, so why didn't they swoop straight away?

'It doesn't make any sense, Jamie. This is meant to be a massive drugs operation and yet everybody has completely ignored you at the exact moments when it might have looked like you were doing something bad.'

Yep.

The police would never lie in court to frame five innocent men for a crime they hadn't committed.

They would never deliberately doctor logs and records in order to make a case stick. They wouldn't sign documents knowing them to be false – unless they did it by mistake, of course. They wouldn't cynically and dramatically alter their own evidence.

Chapter 20

MR ANYTHING-IS-POSSIBLE

I've been out in the Channel when the water's been so smooth and turquoise it's looked like the baize on a gigantic snooker table, perfectly level, not a ripple in sight. In those moments, the *Galwad* has felt like one of the balls gliding sweetly across its surface.

Paul Davidson was smooth like that. Gliding across the court room, dressed immaculately, not a ripple in sight: suit, tie, shirt – sharp, crisp, no creases.

I'd guess he was in his early 50s with an uncomfortably high forehead that suggested he had more grey matter in there than most people carry. He was a 'master mariner' after all, lofty, with a naval sort of build: solid, square shoulders and when he spoke – even if what he said was bollocks – he sounded commanding and very believable. 'I'm very knowl-edgeable. You can completely trust what I'm saying.' One of those types.

When he smiled and nodded at the jury he might as well have been shaking each and every one of them by the hand. I could imagine him saying, 'I know you, don't I? Haven't

I met your charming wife? We all met at a recent social function. Didn't we?'

They lapped him up. He was one of them. He was among friends and I suspect they simply adored his huge CV with loads of initials attached to it. He'd had more jobs than I'd caught lobsters: his background was Merchant Navy, then passenger boats, then government agencies such as enforcement and the MCA (the mob I clashed with over the length of the *Galwad*). At the time of our trial he was working for the huge marine consultants, Brookes Bell.

He really was the prosecution's dream witness: an eminent private-sector bigwig who was now gracing the establishment with his considerable experience. Even though he was meant to be an impartial expert, he never conceded any point that might have made us appear innocent. Instead, his stock answer to just about everything would always be the same: 'Well, it could have been possible.' Nothing was ever impossible; black or white. Just lots of grey.

'Mr Davidson, would you say the bags could have defied the laws of physics and drifted across the flood tide in a perfectly straight line?'

Pause for thought. 'Well,' more silent musing for the benefit of the court room, 'there's more than one way to skin a cat.'

Or: 'Mr Davidson, is there actually any proof that these bags could have been picked up in a Force Eight gale inside three and a half minutes?'

'No ... but ... anything is possible.'

Then: 'Would it really be possible for the bags to be thrown, from a considerable height, off the back of a huge container ship into storm-lashed waters below, and remain in immaculate condition, not split or disfigured in any way?'

'I can't comment on how they've come off the boat but, as I've said, it's not impossible.' In fact, he said it so often it became a standing joke for our defence team and Davidson was duly dubbed 'Mr Anything is Possible'.

The problem was, there was nothing remotely funny about Mr Anything is Possible from our perspective. His evidence, more than anybody else's, was instrumental in swaying the jury, especially when he picked up the baton from Woolls and used the expression 'erratic manoeuvres'. That stuck.

So, too, did his opinion of mapping and whether that was a legitimate exercise for me to be doing out in the Channel. 'Gathering information on the seabed is not fishing,' he proclaimed with all the authority of a school master at morning assembly.

Significantly, he'd never worked on small boats like the *Galwad*. All his experience had come from working with huge ships, yet he made out he was still perfectly qualified to comment on how our boat would handle bad weather.

The police brought in Davidson almost immediately after they'd arrested us. They wanted him to advise them on what electronic and radar evidence they needed to get from both the *Galwad* and the *Oriane* to be able to prove we crossed paths. We know what they took from us and we know they eventually went to Tilbury when the *Oriane* docked there. As far as we know, though, nothing was ever taken off the cargo ship; the only evidence he studied was the data that came off the *Galwad*.

Davidson used a second marine electronics specialist, William Smith, from another marine company called Ambex. Smith's job was to take all the radar and electronic units off the *Galwad* with a police officer, download the information and pass it on to Davidson – who would then use the positions and co-ordinates to chart what happened in the Channel that night.

Although Smith was heralded as an expert, he struggled to extract and unravel all the data stored inside my Olex unit – which took its information from a GPS signal. Instead of simply downloading the digital readings, he physically wrote down 1,300 complex latitude and longitude co-ordinates by hand, and then tried to work out our path on a tiny 3in screen that was way too small for piecing together an accurate track of where we'd gone. To say he made a complete hash of it would be an understatement: at one point he had us going round the Needles, then backwards under the cliffs, before heading out into the Channel again.

I remember thinking, *This bloke hasn't got a clue*. But I was underestimating Mr Anything is Possible. When Davidson was asked to explain why Smith had completely misinterpreted the Olex data, he coolly responded, 'I think we can safely ignore the GPS signals.'

What the hell? How could he possibly ignore the GPS? It fed *all* the positional data into the Olex. Because Smith had spectacularly cocked up downloading that data, Davidson was now telling the court, 'We won't take any notice any more of the GPS.'

I knew this was crucial and collared Christopher during a lunch break. 'If these bastards are saying "take no notice of the GPS", it follows they can't possibly say where on earth the *Galwad* was. All their information about our position has come from the Olex – and all its data has come from GPS.

'They're totally discrediting the source of their own evidence.'

Again, Christopher wasn't convinced and my legal team never grilled Davidson over this point. They just didn't think it was relevant. As much as I screamed and shouted at them and told them it was critical, their attitude was, 'We're in charge of this case.'

'H.H.J. Dodgson won't thank us for raising this,' they insisted. 'He'll think we are splitting hairs and therefore wasting court time. We mustn't get on his wrong side.'

I was gobsmacked and remember saying to my sister that evening, 'If we can't explain stuff like this to our own legal team and get them to realise why it's so important, what chance have we got of defending ourselves in court?' Like me, she had no answer.

I knew I was right: Davidson commanded the court room the next day and the jury were hanging on every word he told them. Nobody was challenging him. Mr Anything-is-Possible was beyond reproach and when he said, 'You can ignore the GPS', well, that was accepted without a murmur. As for William Smith, the jury very quickly forgot all about him.

Davidson simply stuck resolutely to his story: 'The *Galwad* crossed paths with the *Oriane*, they had three and a half minutes to pick up the bags and I know all of this because I've accurately interpreted all the available radar information.'

He even had the nerve, or maybe it was confidence, to admit there was some guesswork involved. Imagine how I felt when he conceded: 'Position dots have been connected to each other using straight lines. The boat may not have gone in these lines – there could have been a curve.'

You what? Are you saying, then, that you've simply connected the dots and don't actually know for sure that's the route we took?

I was going ape behind the glass petition while all this was being said without so much as a raised eyebrow out in the court room.

I desperately wanted to slam my fists into the glass and scream, 'No. This is all wrong. He's just told you to ignore the

GPS and yet he's using it himself to say we crossed paths with the *Oriane*. He can't get away with that – our lives are at stake.'

I didn't, solely because my legal team had ordered me not to. They still had that power over me. I had to trust someone, so I had to trust them. I couldn't defend myself, I didn't look the part, sound the part or have any understanding of all the dos and don'ts. I'd have pissed the judge off within seconds, that's for sure.

Davidson also kept very quiet about how he worked out the *Oriane*'s track. He'd gone to a marine company in Holland, QPS, which keeps records of ships' movements around the world, and got them to supply details of every boat that had started a journey from Brazil and passed through the Channel within the previous six months.

QPS found ten ships, including the *Oriane*, by using the Automatic Identification System (AIS) – a satellite tracking system that uses, you guessed it, GPS receivers to monitor position, course and speed.

We never saw this data, though. It was never disclosed in court, yet my legal team simply accepted the *Oriane* went where Davidson said it went. Even when he was asked what information was used to help him establish this, he never once mentioned GPS. Once again, no attempt was made to double-check his accuracy. My defence didn't want to 'upset the judge', so everything Davidson said, or did, was taken as gospel.

Even when he was asked if one of the other nine boats from Brazil could have been carrying the drugs, instead of replying 'anything's possible' – as we'd come to expect – this time he actually got off the fence and insisted the *Oriane* was the only one the *Galwad* had gone close to.

In fact, he confidently announced the closest AIS fix for the *Oriane* had been 0026.56 with the next one logged at

0038.39. That left an eleven-minute gap during which, he stated, we must have crossed each other's paths.

The fact remains, he had no way of knowing that for sure.

According to Davidson, the *Oriane* got to the 'rendezvous' point at 12.30 a.m. and we arrived at the same position at 12.34 a.m. My Olex unit had shown we also crossed the paths of other boats that night but they could all be ignored, Davidson told the court, because I'd kept my speed at 5 knots. 'That would have been too fast to pick up anything from the water,' he explained.

However, the Olex also revealed we had slowed down for about two and a half minutes. According to Davidson, that had to be when we crossed the *Oriane*'s path.

> **Question:** 'Are you saying, despite the atrocious conditions, they could have picked up eleven holdalls at that moment?'
>
> **Answer:** 'Anything is possible. I would agree it's a difficult task.'

My mind was struggling to sift through all the contradictions. Nothing he said remotely resembled my memory of the night. I recalled slowing down to turn, and I definitely remembered keeping far enough away from the container ships that I wouldn't be clattered by their wakes. That would have been like smashing against a brick wall.

Davidson provided his own chart to illustrate what had happened – yet, when I looked closely, it bore no resemblance to what he was saying from the witness box. His chart had us crossing the back of the *Oriane* at a speed of 5 knots – which, by his own admission, was too fast for any pick-up. It then showed us carrying on to the south for a further minute. It definitely didn't show us coming to a stop immediately behind the *Oriane*.

I turned to Scott, sat on my right, and whispered, 'Look, even his own chart proves we didn't get behind the *Oriane*'s line and track. In fact, it even claims we steamed right across its stern at 5 knots. Why's he not explaining that to the jury – and why's our defence not asking him about it?'

Scott nodded. He understood the significance of this in the blink of an eye – as anyone with just the slightest knowledge of boats would. 'Davidson's own chart completely contradicts what he's telling everyone,' I added. 'The *Oriane*'s going east to west, we're coming north to south, and – according to his bloody chart – we carry on for another minute. So, if he's right – which we know he isn't – how come he's also claiming we stopped directly on the *Oriane*'s line? In that fucking sea? We were up and down all over the place, how could we have stopped dead like that in a force eight?'

The jurors had all been handed a copy of Davidson's chart; the evidence was right there in front of their noses. But would they see it? Would they even bother to look?

Scott looked as exasperated as me. He was just a kid, what on earth was he doing wrapped up in this nightmare? I looked as his face. Instead of the baby-faced teenager full of jokes and life that I knew, his eyes looked like the lights had suddenly been switched off. *That's why I lied about him being on the boat, Tanya.*

I looked away, weary and frustrated. Once again, what was being said in court was being completely contradicted by the evidence and yet nobody was challenging it – or even pointing it out.

I never heard these words: 'Mr Davidson, could you please explain why your own charts show the *Galwad* steaming past the *Oriane* at 5 knots – which you've already told the court is too fast for a pick-up – yet you are now saying the *Galwad* actually stopped dead in the *Oriane*'s track. Which are we to believe …?'

Instead, Davidson announced my manoeuvres at the 'rendezvous' moment were 'erratic'. Maybe he'd already heard
Woolls using that word and seen the impact it had on a
Kingston upon Thames jury. It was like the whole room took
a collective and colossal intake of breath.

*Did you hear that? Davidson's just said 'erratic'. Real fishermen
aren't erratic; this lot must be shady. Erratic practically proves they're
guilty. Green's clearly weaving in and out, picking up drugs. He could
do that within three and a half minutes, easy. Don't you reckon?*

Nobody corrected the jurors, or prevented them thinking
like that. Nobody said to Mr Davidson, 'Isn't it actually the
case that the *Galwad* never went behind the *Oriane*? In fact, it
had turned away when the two boats were at least 500m apart
from one another.

'Please, tell us Mr Davidson, what's erratic about that?'

Instead, I had another showdown with Christopher during
our debrief. 'All this shit about erratic manoeuvres – it's terminology that suits them and makes it sound like we were up
to no good. It needs stamping out. The jury needs to understand I was on a perfectly normal course.'

He wasn't having it, of course, and reassured me everything
was going to plan and under control. I was left clinging to the
hope that he was the legal expert and maybe I was being over-
sensitive. I phoned Nikki to tell her what had gone on and
remember saying, 'Maybe I'm missing something but I can't
help thinking the defence isn't jumping all over the stuff that's
just plain wrong. Nobody seems to be screaming: "Where's
the evidence to back all that up?"'

I was about to launch into a Force Eight rant when I was
suddenly interrupted. Nikki was coughing. That stopped me
in my tracks: there was something infinitely more important
to worry about.

Jamie Green out fishing before he had the *Galwd Y Mor.*

The *Galwad*'s deck while it was moored at its home in Yarmouth

The *Galwad* rusting away after the trial at its current home in Cowes. On the left is the men's lawyer, Emily Bolton, with a law student alongside her

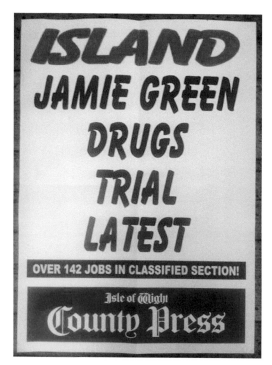

Local Isle of Wight newspaper poster during the trial

Dan Payne.

Jamie Green in the days when he could still raise a smile.

Scott Birtwistle – still a teenager when he was arrested.

Jon Beere – the alleged mastermind of the plot.

Strands of rope on board the *Galwad*. The police claimed the rope was similar to the rope attached to the 11 holdalls packed with cocaine that were found at Freshwater.

The *Galwad Y Mor* at Portsmouth naval dock before it was stripped apart and searched.

Artwork used on the 5men, 104years website.

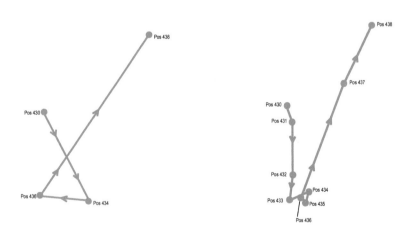

Prosecution Expert

New Evidence

The first chart shows the route the prosecution claim the *Galwad* took. The *Oriane* passed through the triangle and it was at this point that the drugs were dropped into the sea.

Appeared in the *Mail* and helps set location.

Another from *Mail on Sunday*.

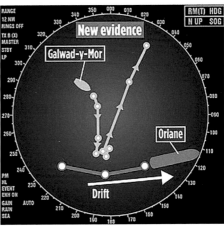

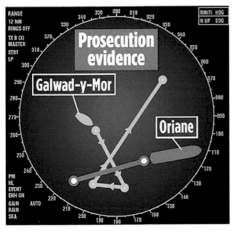

What the prosecution claimed happened.

MSC *Oriane.*

Jamie Green with his wife Nikki, who tragically died
while he was in prison.

Chapter 21

TIED UP IN KNOTS

Someone asked me, 'How high were the waves?'

I looked up to the court ceiling, which was pretty lofty, and pointed. 'About the height of this room,' I answered, glancing over to the jury to see if that had registered in any way. It was maybe twice the height of an average lounge. They looked at me like I was an idiot.

The fact we'd have had to somehow scoop up eleven holdalls in waves as high as that, with the water tossing and submerging the bags relentlessly, and our boat flopping around like a bloody rag doll, was utterly lost on them. They weren't imagining the impossibility of it. They weren't buying into the fact it simply couldn't be done.

Worse, I was beginning to suspect they didn't even want to understand. Believing we were innocent required effort on their behalf and I don't think they wanted to waste that energy on us. It was far easier to believe everything that nice Mr Davidson had said, return a verdict and get on with their lives.

To get people from the middle of Kingston and London on the same wavelength as a bunch of fishermen or scaffolders from Yarmouth – with our lifestyles – well, it'd be like trying to keep a phone connection in a Force Eight storm.

They probably took sideways glances at us and shivered. We were their worst nightmare: a bunch of scags from the neighbouring council estate who were lowering their property values. We were meant to be judged by our peers, weren't we? Well, I didn't see any bloody fishermen on that jury. We didn't act like them or live like them or share their values. We were worlds apart.

Maybe I'm being bitter. Maybe I expected too much of the jurors. They weren't even shown a video of what a Force Eight storm looks like. I wanted them to be hauled off to Tennyson Down so they could at least see the area for themselves; judge first-hand if Jeans and Dunne could have been lying. But no.

We needed them to understand our world. To be fair, H.H.J. Dodgson seemed to have the best grip of how bad conditions could be: after I'd tried explaining what makes people seasick and how violent the waves can be, the judge chipped in with, 'Let me tell you members of the jury. A Force Eight is rough and I would be amazed if most people weren't sick in that sort of weather.

'If you were on a cross-Channel ferry, even in a force four or five gale, most people would be sick. So, being on Mr Green's boat, which is a lot smaller, it's no surprise someone was sick.'

I was startled to hear him volunteer all that. *Christ, that's positive for us, coming from the judge. Are you taking that in, jury?*

When my moment came to stand in the witness box and give evidence, I was racked with nerves. Why wouldn't I be? I had little faith in the jury, little faith in my own defence counsel and zero faith in the prosecution to play fairly. Besides, I wasn't a public speaker, I didn't have the fancy lingo, the sharp turn of phrase, the polished look. Nothing about me said, 'Come on, I'm one of you.'

I'm sure Woolls sensed all this. She saw my weaknesses and she attacked, like she was holding a machine gun, rat-a-tat-tat, firing bursts of questions from all angles, barely letting me draw breath, unleashing round after round until I was barely able to remember which question I was meant to be answering. That was her job, she was a professional and I was in her line of fire.

Looking back, I can see she was aiming to prove I either didn't know what I was talking about, or I was simply a liar. I lost counts of the number of times she referred to Scott. The mapping was also one of her big targets: this, she insisted, had nothing to do with fishing.

I tried to counter. I tried to explain that fishing is simply the catch-all term for everything we do that is connected with our business. Mapping is an essential part of it because it helps me decide where best to fish. But, yes, Ms Woolls, technically you are right. 'I was never fishing, like you understand it to mean, I've never said I was,' I admitted.

Only that wasn't quite what I meant to say, it was the way it simply came out. I was trying to talk her talk but I could never hope to do that. I couldn't say it quite so confidently or coherently. I wasn't an orator, I didn't have a silky vocabulary, I knew what I meant but I didn't know how to say it with court-room eloquence. Everything seemed to sound tongue-tied. I couldn't explain in their terminology why a 3D image of a seabed was so crucial to someone like me.

'The slower you go, the better the definition of what's below,' I volunteered. *Jesus.*

Woolls questioned the way I'd come across Vic and wouldn't accept he'd simply been recommended to me by someone I'd been chatting to in a local pub. 'It's a lie,' she proclaimed. 'He does not exist, you're not able to locate him.'

Reluctantly, I had to concede that I couldn't find the man who had recommended Vic, although God knows I'd tried. The problem, I told the court, was that everyone on the island had seen what had happened to us. 'I can't find him because all the publicity about this case has scared him off,' I said. I still believe that to be true.

Her next target was where we went that night. Woolls was adamant we'd gone to places we'd never been before – and where no proper fishermen would ever go.

I tried explaining that I'd gone in to the shipping lanes many times before. I always wanted to explore areas other fishing boats couldn't reach. In fact, that was the main reason why I'd bought the *Galwad* – it gave me the range to do that.

The data in my Olex proved that I'd been in similar areas before, I said. We were moving out of the winter season so it was time to push out further. Then I got tangled up, trying to appease her, trying to be reasonable and not simply dogmatic. 'You are right,' I said – *why did I say that* – 'I do try to avoid the shipping lanes because it costs me a fortune if one of the big boats runs over and smashes our marker buoys.'

I was suddenly wide open.

Question: 'Well, if you try to avoid them, how come you went back to them?'

Suddenly I was backtracking, trying to convince a sceptical court that – overriding everything else – was my determination to fish in areas that might give me a great return. I needed to earn around £400 just to break even – and that meant pulling in 150kg of crabs and around forty lobsters. That was my target: I had the *Galwad*, I had my Olex to map the seabed, so the shipping lanes were a legitimate place to go.

'Yes, it's more dangerous than anywhere else,' I conceded. 'But I fish wherever I can get a return. I can get a better return in the shipping lanes because they're not so well fished.' *Am I digging a hole?*

I felt I somehow had to prove that I was a genuine fishermen, and not some sort of imposter. I even tried explaining how I set about shooting and retrieving strings. *Why did I bother?*

We use GPS, I told the jurors, so we can track where the strings are on the *Galwad*'s plotter. When the first pot goes overboard, I look at the GPS navigator and write down the co-ordinates. I'll have two co-ordinates for each end of the string so when we go back, I can use those figures like a grid reference.

When I go back to look for the ends, I'll go up and down in an imaginary grid on the surface of the water. That way I'm not just going round in a circle. Instead, I steam up and down the grid until I find the buoys. If the ends are not where I think they are, nine times out of ten I'll know the direction they've moved to. I've been doing it for such a long time, it's just experience.

This is what I call fishing.

I swear I could see a fog, a real Channel pea-souper, descend over the jury box. Were they getting this, were they interested? Did it even matter?

Come on, Jamie. This is your life, this is your bread and butter, this is what you do. Tell them who you are.

Then came the heavyweight accusations, starting with the satellite phone calls. Rat-a-tat-tat. Why did Dugic (aka Dexsa) have my phone number? Why were there nine calls inside two hours? Why did you lie, lie, lie?

I explained that Dexsa had asked for my mobile and satellite number at the Sportsman's Rest on the night we met so he could keep in touch with Vic, or let me know if he ever had more crew looking for shifts. I never took his number, though.

Shit, did that sound weak? Was I sinking?

I carried on. At some point in the night, when Vic was throwing up and desperate, he showed me a number on his mobile and begged me to call it. I tried, it didn't connect, then I'd try again and someone would answer. 'Vic wants to speak to you,' I would say but either the line would go dead or Vic would be back outside throwing up.

Then my satellite phone would ring, I'd answer and the same voice, which I realised was Dexsa, would ask for Vic. So I'd put the phone down and call out, 'Dexsa's on the line.' The reaction was always the same: Vic was still incapable outside – or, by the time he stumbled back in to the wheelhouse, the line would be lost in the weather.

'Vic still wanted me to ring again,' I told the court. So I tried calling back but, by then, we were probably calling against one other and nobody got through. Then my phone would suddenly burst into life again and I'd say, 'Vic wants to come home, he's all over the place.' Even when the line did connect, and we managed to talk, it was always brief and limited. I remember hearing, 'Can't you keep him, get him to work,' to which I replied, 'Hold on, I'll get him … tell him yourself.'

Another time, Dexsa said, 'Make him get through it.' At some point I definitely said down the phone, 'He's no fuckin' use to me.'

At 12.38 I called for the last time to try to finish off yet another interrupted call. We connected and I simply said, 'He wants to go home.'

'Ironically,' I told the court, 'Vic never spoke to anyone. He was too busy being sick.'

Woolls wasn't having any of this, of course. 'Why did it take two hours and nine calls to establish all this?' she snapped.

'You lied because the calls coincide with the moment the *Galwad* crossed paths with the *Oriane*.' The calls, she insisted, weren't to tell Vic's mates he was ill and wanted to come home – they were to tell the ringleaders that we were close to the *Oriane*, we were in position and, finally, that we'd completed the mission.

I could hear a gigantic intake of breath across the courtroom. The jury had understood that statement, all right. The fog had lifted.

Thinking about it now, I should have said, 'But we didn't cross paths, so the calls are completely innocent.'

I should have said, 'If you're right, Ms Woolls, how come there were no calls when it really mattered – when, you say, I was trying to locate and pick up the bags? There's a call made nine minutes before, and there's another one five minutes after – but absolutely nothing when you, Ms Woolls, claim this operation was taking place.

'Surely I'd have wanted to be on the line constantly with whoever was on the *Oriane*, making sure he knew where we were, making sure he could see us, making sure he threw the bags overboard at the exact moment I needed him to.

'You'd think there'd be a running commentary between us – right, I'm edging in, can you see me, could you wave your torch – OK, I see you – now, wait, wait – OK, let it go …

'How could I have done this without liaising directly with that bloke on the *Oriane*? Instead, all I've done is phone Vic's mate back on the mainland, he's tried phoning me and between us we've barely managed to say two words because my crappy satellite phone kept breaking down.'

Yep, that's what I should have said.

I didn't because I wasn't composed enough in that moment to think like that. When you're stood in the dock, and the questions are coming at you rat-a-tat-tat, and you're trying to keep up with them and you know your freedom is hanging on every word, and you look at your mates sat behind a glass screen and your family in the public gallery and you see your teenage daughter and wonder, *Shit, will I ever see her grow to become a woman* and then you realise the jury is staring *into* you and not just *at* you, well, it's a bit like being in a perfect storm. It's fuckin' hard. The pressure is seismic.

Woolls knew exactly the right words and terminologies; the prosecution was like a well-oiled operation. I was more like a diesel motor with loads of oil leaks and water sloshing around the engine.

I persevered. I had to. 'The phone calls were so brief,' I said. 'The boat was rocking and rolling, I was trying to get Vic from wherever he was, keep the *Galwad* steady, deal with the shipping lane. We just kept losing the connections.'

Then Woolls tried a different line of attack: 'You did not set out to catch lobsters at all.'

I shook my head from side to side and reminded the court I'd gone all the way to Weymouth just twenty-four hours earlier solely to collect new pots for the trip. 'The bait went on board on Saturday morning,' I said. 'Sixty of the new pots were baited.'

Also, I added, if I wasn't lobster fishing, how come I headed off for some slack water and pulled up thirty-five to forty pots around four in the morning? Those were emptied and then put back with new bait. *Why would I bother doing all that if I'd just reeled in £53 million worth of drugs?*

Next, Woolls focused on the moment we returned to Yarmouth and moored up. Our plan, she said, was to get back on to the *Galwad* under the cover of darkness and go back to Freshwater to recover the drugs we'd dumped by Tennyson cliffs. We hadn't chucked black bags crammed with rubbish there at all.

I explained that once we returned to Yarmouth I jumped in my van, went back home and then headed off to Freshwater to see a mate. At some point I got a phone call from Salty's asking for lobsters. I knew my daughter was taking her boyfriend's parents to the restaurant so I tried calling Scott to make sure he picked out some of the best ones from the pens we had at the quayside. Just like the satellite on the *Galwad*, our mobile phone signals kept breaking down, though – *ask the locals, that's extremely common on the island* – so I went back myself to check he'd picked out good ones.

Woolls wasn't happy with that explanation. I'd gone back to the quay, she said, to get back on the *Galwad*. Yet even the police admitted they later saw Scott walking away with the lobsters – and when they arrested Dan and me, we were walking along the pontoon away from the boat.

'All you have to do is look at the CCTV footage of the top of the *Galwad*'s mast,' I said. 'As soon as one person steps foot on board the mast will move 6in to a foot straight away. It's like a pendulum up there but it clearly doesn't move.'

Then Woolls moved on to the rope that had been used to tie the bags of drugs together at Freshwater. The way they had been attached was exactly how a professional fisherman would tie lobster pots together, she claimed. The rope itself was made by the same manufacturer – Euronets – that I used on the *Galwad*.

I took a deep breath. This really was my subject. Yes, I use Euronets because they are one of the biggest manufacturers in the business, but no, the bags absolutely weren't tied together in the way a professional fisherman would have done it.

The main back line was entirely the wrong type of rope – I would only ever use 16mm leaded rope because it would sink once weights were attached at either end. The rope holding the bags together was a floaty rope and I never used those on the *Galwad*.

I was on a roll now. Everything else about the way the bags were tied was wrong: there were eleven of them attached to eleven individual legs, which, in turn, were tethered to the back line. If they were going to be winched into the water – which is what Jeans and Dunne claimed they saw us doing in their amended statements – the legs would *have* to be identical lengths to one another. *They weren't.* Some were way too short for the *Galwad*. Their ends needed to be burned to prevent the rope fraying. *They weren't.* The legs needed to be 12m apart from one another – the length of my boat. *They weren't.* They were 16m.

These weren't minor inconsistencies or errors, or me trying to be a clever sod. This cut to the core of being a true lobster fisherman: legs have to be the same lengths to guarantee they run smoothly through the winch and not fly out and hit someone on deck. I would *never* tie them any differently – out of sheer habit. No professional would. Ever.

It flashed through my mind that Woolls had forgotten the 'mechanical-fit test' DI Thomas had got so excited about during my Fareham interview. The one that would prove the strands of rope in my trailer would match the cuts on the rope attached to the holdalls.

What's up, Tanya, didn't the cuts match up? Shall we not mention that, then?

There was another thing. The weights attached to the back line also bore no resemblance to any of the anchors I'd ever used. In fact, I'd never seen anything like them before: great clumps of iron off an old railway track – old couplings, I think. More tellingly, only one end of the back line was attached to the anchor. I would always weight both ends.

This is what I call fishing, Ms Woolls. This is my bread and butter, this is what my life is all about. This is my territory.

It goes back to when I was on the pier fishing with my grandad, it spans my time at college studying fishing and knots and boats and tides and nets and pots, and it tugs on everything I know – and everything I've learned – through sheer hard graft as a working, professional fisherman.

It's stuff I could do in my sleep – or blindfolded – and, every time, it'd never come out any differently. Even the knots used to tie the holdalls bore no resemblance to knots I'd ever used.

'Knots to me are like riding a bike,' I told the court. 'I've been using the same knot for twenty-five years.'

This is what I do.

Chapter 22

IT'S IMPOSSIBLE

Are you listening to this?

'It's impossible for all the bags to have been picked up in those conditions in three and a half minutes. It's virtually impossible to collect even one rucksack in that time, never mind eleven.'

Are you listening to this?

'If the holdalls had been thrown off the *Oriane* individually, or on a line, they would have been ripped apart as soon as they hit the water.'

Are you listening to this?

'If they were tied together in one big bundle, the *Galwad*'s lifting gear wouldn't have been strong enough to haul such a huge weight out of the water. This idea is not worth considering.'

Are you listening to this?

'The *Galwad* could never have got close enough to the shoreline to dump the bags where they were discovered at Freshwater. The depth was too shallow.'

Are you listening to this?

'The weight attached to the bags at Freshwater was not heavy enough. They would have bounced along with the tide.'

The court was told the truth, all right. Instead of everything being grey – a 'possibility' as the prosecution's expert witness Davidson kept insisting – the truth was spelt out for the jurors in black and white.

The truth used unambiguous words such as 'impossible', 'not' and 'never'; the allegations were 'not worthy of consideration'. There was no room for doubt. The jurors were not asked to fill in the blanks for themselves.

Imaginary question to the prosecution expert witness: 'Could there be life on Mars?'

Answer: 'It's a possibility.'

Same question to our expert witness: 'No. Never.'

And that was the fundamental difference between master mariner Paul Davidson and our man, Mik Chinery. As far as Chinery was concerned, the entire mission could never have taken place – he said that loud and clear – and he had all the credentials needed to make his verdict matter.

His marine expertise and knowledge was beyond reproach: forty-five years training coastguards, customs officers, security forces. He even specialised in night-time searches and rescue training and – get this – *intercepting vessels in the dark.*

It wasn't until he was stood on the witness stand, though, that an awful truth dawned on me. As he spoke, I looked at the faces in the jury box and knew instinctively what they were thinking: *this man isn't one of us.*

Chinery wasn't refined. He didn't ooze class. Davidson was snooker-table smooth and polished, a member of the right clubs and societies. He spoke with eloquence and authority and he exuded the kind of lifestyle that I suspect most of the jurors enjoyed – or aspired to.

Chinery was far more salt of the earth, the Antichrist to Davidson. You could smell the sea on Chinery; he was choppier, unpredictable, a bit dishevelled – much more like the sea we were in that night than the confines of a gentleman's club. Those jurors couldn't identify with a man like that: they'd much prefer the clean cut of Davidson's suit.

I genuinely can't think of any other reason why they'd choose to trust and believe Davidson more than Chinery. Whenever I analyse what Chinery said in court, the more unequivocal, clear, straight and bang-on plain correct it seems.

He didn't leave doubt about anything – his answers were confident, they were yes or no, black or white. He did what you'd hope an expert would do. He gave the court the benefit of his forty-five years in the marine business and made it clear for them to understand in simple terms what would have been possible that night – and what wouldn't.

How much clearer can a man be: 'One rucksack in three and a half minutes is virtually impossible. It simply cannot be done.'

'It simply cannot be done' versus 'it's a possibility'. You must choose, members of the jury.

He painted a scene of what happened that night – and the following day – which, for the first time in the entire trial, I actually recognised. Davidson had said all he could to back up the prosecution case, and when he wasn't sure, he hid behind the words 'it's possible'.

Chinery did the opposite and challenged everything – but not in vague language. For example, everyone took it for granted when Davidson – and Woolls – said our behaviour, our route and our destinations that night were not consistent with previous trips. After analysing the Olex data from our previous sixty-nine trips, Chinery reported, 'There are plenty of examples of almost the exact same pattern in and around the mid-Channel area. They deploy, they sit around, they go to sleep – while someone else is in the wheelhouse mapping the seabed.'

Similarly, everybody seemed to simply accept that we threw the bags off the *Galwad* from our port side at Freshwater because that's what Jeans and Dunne claimed they saw.

Chinery saw the flaw in that, too. Our winching gear was at the opposite end of the boat. 'It makes no sense,' he told the court. 'The starboard side is the one designed to deploy and retrieve lobster pots. All they had to do was turn the boat around and then nobody could have seen them because the *Galwad*'s high side would have been facing the cliffs and blocking out the view.

'In any case, The *Galwad* needed to be in at least 3m of water but it was low tide then and the depth would have been 2.2m. There would not have been enough water to float the boat. It would have been impossible for the boat to have been there at that time.'

There's that word again. *Impossible.*

Woolls confirmed that Chinery and Davidson had met before the trial, spending an entire day trying to agree some common ground. They both accepted the bags couldn't have been thrown over on a line because it would have been ripped apart in that weather. In all likelihood, they must have been jettisoned in one large bundle – probably from the aft mooring deck, which was 20ft above sea level.

Again, Chinery analysed what that would actually mean. How would we be able to physically haul on board such a massive load – which he estimated to be around a quarter of a ton? 'The *Galwad*'s lifting gear couldn't handle that weight,' he declared. 'The lifting gear was in very poor condition; personally I wouldn't have lifted anything on it.'

The only possibility would have been to separate the bags individually before they were lifted on to the *Galwad*. But, as Chinery, pointed out, how on earth could we have done all that in three and a half minutes?

'The boat would have had to somehow remain totally stationary – that's perfectly still in a Force Eight sea – and that didn't happen,' he said. 'The GPS system is extremely accurate and consistent about that.'

Was anyone listening?

Chapter 23

SPOILT

In the dead of night, when we're in the middle of the Channel and it's pitch-black outside, the *Galwad* lights up like one of Blackpool's gigantic illuminations, casting a dazzling white glow across the water. It's probably quite a spooky sight, but we need powerful lights to see what we're doing – and to make sure we can be seen from far and wide.

I've got deck lights everywhere, then strip lights on the railings and a thumping big spotlight aimed directly at the deck floor. On top of all that, my five wheelhouse windows each throw out their own brilliant white glows and we have a huge, cylindrical search light with white sides. That's aimed straight into the water to help us locate our buoys.

It's quite a light show – and yet a UK border control cutter, out that night specifically to look for a boat just like the *Galwad*, couldn't see us even with all their hi-tech equipment and binoculars. Even though we were practically ablaze with light.

The *Vigilant* had its sights glued to the *Oriane*, looking and waiting specifically for a boat like mine to approach. At the exact moment the prosecution claimed we would have been scooping up bags of drugs, the *Vigilant* saw absolutely nothing – even though the *Galwad* must have stood out like a sore thumb.

How is that possible?

In fact, the *Vigilant* didn't officially spot us until four hours later. We were 7 miles away from them by then, yet they clearly saw us reeling in lobster pots and working on deck. So there was certainly nothing wrong with their state-of-the-art binoculars.

There can only be one legitimate reason why they never saw us when it mattered most. We simply weren't there. We never went close to the *Oriane*. Which means we couldn't possibly have picked up any bags. We were never in their field of vision and that's why they never saw us.

I still don't understand why that alone didn't bring the case to an end.

Then we come to the 'spoilt' log.

The last written entry in the *Vigilant*'s logbook was made at 0030 hrs. After that, there was nothing recorded for a further four hours and eighteen minutes – which was when they finally saw us … lobster fishing. Where there should have been pages of entries, especially as this covered the critical moment we were meant to be picking up the bags, there was simply one word – handwritten across a blank log page – in small ballpoint-pen lettering: 'Spoilt'.

There was nothing to explain why or how the log was spoilt. No entries had been written down and then blacked over or hastily crossed out. There were no dull stains to suggest a pot of tea had tumbled over and soaked the pages.

Not even any jagged edges stuck in the spine to show pages had been ripped out.

Just that one, small – yet hugely shattering – word, floating in oceans of emptiness where you would have expected to see a deluge of words painstakingly recording every tiny detail of our crime. Excuse my fantasy, but maybe something like:

> 00.31: *Galwad*, brightly lit and clearly visible, turning and approaching rear of passing *Oriane*.
>
> 00.32: *Galwad* slowing down, almost to a standstill.
>
> 00.33: Huge object, possibly holdalls tied together, thrown from *Oriane*'s rear upper deck. Can't see how. Object floating towards *Galwad*.
>
> 00.34: *Galwad* still stationary despite ferocious battering from *Oriane*'s prop thrust and estimated 20-foot, force eight waves.
>
> 00.35: Men seen leaning over side and hauling huge, dark object – believed to be the one thrown off Oriane – out of storm-lashed water and on to *Galwad*'s deck.
>
> 00.36: Object successfully dragged on board inside three minutes.
>
> 00.37: *Galwad* heading back towards Isle of Wight.
>
> 00.38: *Vigilant* RIB zooming over to board *Galwad* and catch men red-handed.
>
> 00.48: Eleven brightly coloured holdalls seized, each containing high-purity powder cocaine inside 255 packages. Possible street value estimated £53 million.
>
> 00.53: *Vigilant* heading home with suspects. Operation Disorient huge success.

OK, maybe not those very words. But surely not one solitary word either. A word that is left to cover off the entire expanse of when we were allegedly pulling off the UK's biggest drug-smuggling operation.

Spoilt. A word that tells you nothing but lets you imagine anything you want.

What makes it even more baffling is that, up to that moment, the log was in pristine condition and showed the *Vigilant* crew were certainly keeping a close eye on all the *Oriane*'s manoeuvres – and writing them down in precise detail.

The log noted the *Oriane*'s range (i.e. its distance from the *Vigilant*), its bearing (the compass direction it was from the *Vigilant*), its course (the route it was taking) and its speed in knots. This information was regularly updated; someone was doing a thorough job, for sure.

Then came the entry that surely proved we were never there. At 0030 GMT – when the prosecution insists we were manoeuvring into position – the *Vigilant* simply recorded the *Oriane* was 7.7 miles away, its bearing was 109, course 081 and it was travelling at 17.6 knots. That was it, end of entry.

There was no mention of a fishing boat – us – moving alongside. There was no mention of the *Galwad* at all. Even the distance of 7.7 miles is significant. The *Vigilant* was often watching the *Oriane* from 19 miles away, so at 0030 hrs it had one of the closest views of the cargo ship that it had enjoyed all night. Yet it never saw us.

Nothing else was written in the log again until 0448. Other than the word 'spoilt'.

I was praying Christopher would make a huge song and dance about this in court. Perhaps I should have known better.

The *Vigilant*'s skipper, Antony Tucker, gave evidence but Christopher simply let him off the hook. To this day, I don't know why. He admitted he was responsible for keeping the log and told the court, 'I'd make entries about what I saw. I was in charge of the boat. If someone saw something I'd go take a look and then make an entry.'

So tell us why the word spoilt appears in the log? Who wrote 'spoilt' – you, or someone else on board? Why was nothing logged for another four hours after that? What happened?

Instead, Christopher just asked some gentle questions about what the *Vigilant* did after it spotted us, and who else was on board. Tucker explained there was a crew of nine, along with a watch keeper and two SOCO officers. One of them was Andy Marwick, who was also keeping in contact with a surveillance plane, he said.

Interestingly, Marwick later denied he'd ever been on the *Vigilant*, which I thought was strange. *Why's that then? Surely the skipper knew who was on his own boat?*

Tucker confirmed the *Vigilant* carried on tracking us from then on, and never let us out of its sights. Which meant it was still watching us when we went mackereling off Tennyson.

Hang on. If the *Vigilant* was watching us intensely at Tennyson, why did nobody see us throwing bags overboard? Why didn't it zoom in there and then and nab us red-handed? Why wasn't anything written down in the log about that?

How come the only two times in the entire night when we were meant to be doing something dodgy, the Vigilant *– a spy boat, for God's sake – saw absolutely nothing?*

The cutter wasn't the only one watching us, either. After the *Vigilant* first spotted us at 0448 hrs, a surveillance plane was sent over and videoed us out on deck. We were shown some still photos from the video and it clearly showed us hauling in pots. I'd no idea the plane was up there.

The only plane I was ever aware of was the one I clearly saw flying low over Tennyson at 7 p.m. The one the police claim I never saw because it was still at Bournemouth airport at that time.

I'd begged Christopher and Hardy to get that plane's flight-path and force the pilots to give evidence. Neither happened. The only witness called was the photographer on board, Andrew Whittall. 'I was operating surveillance equipment and was in radio contact with the *Vigilant*,' he told the court. He was adamant they hadn't left Bournemouth until 7 p.m. and they didn't see us until we were heading down the Solent towards Yarmouth.

Once again, I was left thinking my defence team hadn't done enough to put witnesses on the spot.

When it was Beerey's turn to give evidence, he confirmed he'd agreed to collect Vic for me and had jumped on the 1 p.m. hovercraft from Ryde. He was still wearing his work clothes – boots, khaki shorts and a polo shirt with RGM Scaffolding emblazoned across the front, along with the company's phone number. *Hardly the sort of incognito clobber you'd expect a drugs baron to be wearing.*

Beerey then told the court he'd landed at Southsea early so stood outside until a car suddenly pulled up with – to his surprise – three men inside. One of them got out, went up to him and said: 'Are you Jamie Green?' Beerey shook his head and explained I was stuck on the tide, and that he'd come over to pick up the new crew member.

The men, however, wanted to know more about the job, so they all headed for a nearby café, Mozzarella Joe's, where Beerey phoned me on the *Galwad*. That's when he told me three men had turned up, not one, and they wanted to know what the pay would be and how long the job would last.

I'd answered their questions but the men still wanted to come over to the island and meet me when I returned. Beerey then told the court he brought them over on the hovercraft, intending to give them a lift into the main town, Newport, where they could kill some time.

There was a problem with that plan, however. Beerey only had his works van parked at the hover port and that wasn't big enough to squeeze in four adults. So, he phoned his wife, Sue, and asked her to bring over their family car. He then dropped the three men – Vic, Daniel Dugic (Dexsa) and Ed Austin – in Newport, while he went to the bank and sorted out wages for his staff. Around 5 p.m., he picked them up again and headed off to the Sportsman's to meet me.

Beerey's defence counsel rammed home the obvious points to the court. Why would he have used his works van if he'd been expecting three adults to turn up? Why was he wearing a T-shirt that was making him highly identifiable – and what on earth was there to show he'd ever been in contact with any of them before? 'There's only Jamie Green saying: "Can you do us a favour?"'

Vic's evidence filled in more of the gaps, although he needed a translator so everything he said inevitably sounded second hand and not straight from the heart.

He admitted he'd come over on a false passport after working previously throughout Europe, either as an unskilled labourer in Germany – mixing glue, cutting tiles – or selling Vatican souvenirs in Rome and Christmas decorations in Vienna.

He'd heard through a pal that a man called Dexsa could find him work in the UK, so he'd shelled out €1,000 for the fake passport and headed for London. He'd deliberately not brought labouring clothes with him to avoid any suspicions at UK border control. He'd got €3,000 with him, paid for three nights' bed and breakfast accommodation on the island, and had bought some clothes when Beerey dropped them off in Newport.

'I planned to stay seven or eight months in the UK,' he told the court. He hoped to earn around €2,000 a month and intended to send money over to his wife and three children in Montenegro.

While they were in Newport, Vic admitted he'd asked Dexsa to buy him a pay-as-you-go mobile phone 'so I could call home'. Dexsa bought two, including one for himself, using false names to register them. As Vic explained this, a picture instantly flashed through my mind – him clutching the mobile, which hadn't got a cat in hell's chance of working out in the Channel, then begging me to use my satellite as he rushed out to throw up again. I swear I can still smell the puke whenever I think about those moments.

Indeed, Vic confirmed he'd been violently ill on the trip, which he described as fifteen hours of misery – especially when he could smell the fish we'd hauled on deck.

'I wasn't able to stand or sit,' he told the court – through his translator – and explained he'd spent most of the journey ferociously gripping the edge of a table. 'The heavy seas and the stench of the fish made me worse,' he said. 'I felt terrible whether I was standing or sitting.

'It felt like I was virtually dying.'

Woolls immediately grilled him over the mobiles and made it sound as though all pay-as-you-go phones were dodgy by definition. They were 'dirty phones'. I remember thinking, *Hang on, if you wander into any High Street phone shop there's great big signs plastered all over the place urging you to take their pay-as-you-go deals. O2 and Vodafone don't say 'buy our dirty phones for only £9.99', do they?*

The more I thought about those phones, the more innocuous they became. They wouldn't work in the Channel – so there was no way they could have ever been used to keep a syndicate of drug smugglers in contact with one another. Yet this was exactly what Woolls was implying. In fact, the police seized Vic's pay-as-you-go when he was arrested but never produced any evidence from it to show he'd texted, or phoned, anyone remotely suspicious.

The only reason he genuinely could have wanted a mobile was to do what he told the court – to phone his family back home. After all, he was planning to stay in the UK for eight months. OK, maybe it wasn't great that Dexsa used false names to register the phones. But what else could someone working here illegally do?

Woolls wasn't having any of it, looked Vic squarely in the face and declared, 'You were there to oversee the safe collection of the cocaine.'

'No, it's not true,' he managed to reply in his own faltering English. I remember thinking: *You've just heard that – he can barely speak a word of our language. How on earth could he tell us what to do then?*

When Dan's turn came, he confirmed we'd gone mackereling at Freshwater. He remembered seeing rubbish bags crammed with empty milk and pot noodle cartons, bottles, paper towels and fish and galley waste. 'I definitely chucked some bin bags on top of the boat,' he said. 'I assume they went over at some point as they were not there … when we got home.'

Scott confirmed he'd chucked the rubbish overboard. He then said something that just stuck in my mind for obvious reasons. After we'd all got back to Yarmouth, he said, he went off with Dan and smoked a cannabis cigarette. He told the court, 'Jamie would have never joined us. He would never allow stuff like that on his boat.' *You're god-damned right, Scotty*.

Scott then confirmed he got a call soon after, asking him to select some lobsters for the restaurant. He also told the court how, after I'd been arrested, he tried to keep our business going by taking the *Galwad* out with an old crew member. Yes, he'd kept quiet about being on the boat that night – but he'd never once thought about fleeing the island, either. 'I didn't disappear because I knew everyone was innocent,' he said.

Scott was the last of us to give evidence and, of course, Woolls piled in, demanding to know why he'd kept the lie going about not being on the *Galwad*.

'Why did you lie at the beginning? We can't believe anything you say,' she rapped. His reply left her — and the court — speechless. 'It ain't just me who lied. The police lie as well, you know.'

I wanted to punch the air in joy. *Good on you, Scotty.* It had taken a teenager to finally say what none of our bigwigs had the balls to utter. Looking back, I really wish we'd all been more like that, but we were under orders not to upset anyone. I don't give a shit about etiquette any more.

I remember phoning Julian Hardy at the end of that day and saying to him, 'This is a fuckin' lottery, this is all a charade. We might as well toss a coin in the air and have done with it.'

He didn't like that.

I had to smirk, though, when Woolls began her summing up. Yes, mistakes had been made, she generously conceded, management records and observation logs had not been completed properly and Jeans' and Dunne's testimonies had been far from ideal. She made it sound like it was all so innocent and not much to be worried about at all. *That's OK, then, thanks for explaining — hey, these things happen, Tanya.*

I could feel the word 'but' building and building as she made light of radios breaking down, statements being altered and logs being 'spoilt'. Yes, that had all happened …

But — I'd lied about Scott not being on the boat.

But — I'd lied about when I first met Vic. I was a liar and couldn't be believed.

But — it had cost Vic hundreds of pounds to get to the island and yet he barely had any clothes with him.

But — the *Galwad* was a perfect boat for this kind of operation.

But — we'd slowed down for two minutes and thirty seconds to scoop up the bags.

But — dirty phones had been bought using false names.

But – seven calls had been made from the *Galwad* inside forty-two minutes – all consistent with reporting back at key stages of the operation. 'All these calls were about receiving instructions for jettisoning the holdalls into the water,' she declared.

But – I'd personally called Dexsa at 0038 hrs. That was to tell him we'd got the bags.

But – Beerey had been the go-between, pulling it all together, introducing me to the 'Balkan Gang'. 'Jon Beere is there so he can introduce the skipper, Jamie Green, to Austin and Dugic,' she proclaimed.

But – the bags at Freshwater had been tied together by someone used to tying lobster pots.

But – we had planned to pick them up under the cover of darkness later that night.

But – I'd called Beerey soon after we'd dumped the bags at Freshwater, telling him they were in the water. 'The *Galwad* had never been to that spot in the Channel before and it had never been to Freshwater before to go mackereling,' she concluded.

She was rat-a-tat-tatting again and all we could do was sit still and listen to it. I glanced towards the jurors: they looked like they were lapping up every word as wave upon wave rolled over them. I then turned towards Christopher, who was sat, passive, with no hint of a reaction. I kept expecting him to shake his head from side to side or throw his arms theatrically into the air – something, anything, to show utter contempt for what Woolls was saying. There was nothing. He didn't even turn and, as I stared at his back, I thought, 'Our freedom rests on that man's shoulders.'

Chapter 24

WHO'S THAT MAN?

There was one unexpected moment in court that still haunts me, right to this day. On the surface it's actually funny – in a sort of gallows humour kind of way. For me, it embodied everything we were up against.

We needed Julian Christopher to come out fighting, especially after Woolls had given all she could in her summing up. To be fair, he saved his best for last and gave us hope. He spoke passionately – like he truly believed we were innocent and wasn't just going through the motions. I even felt our trial had forced him to question some of his own deeply held beliefs about the justice system. Maybe the police weren't as honourable as he'd always assumed. That was a tough place for someone like Christopher to go but he definitely bombarded the jury with facts and arguments that, all piled together, sounded pretty persuasive.

We've got a chance here.

However. I couldn't get out of my mind an unexpected moment when one of the jurors wanted to ask a question. Sat on the back row of the jury box, in the left-hand side top corner, was an elderly woman, possibly in her early 70s. She had short, curly, grey hair and she wore glasses with a fancy, no-doubt-expensive, black frame – the sort that arched upwards towards her temples. The sort that can make someone look a bit snooty, a bit above themselves.

She was concerned about something and wanted to ask a question so she very obviously scribbled something down on a piece of paper, folded it in half and her note was handed to the court usher and finally the judge.

'This'll be interesting,' I thought to myself. 'This'll give us a clue which way the jury's thinking.'

I was expecting something technical she'd maybe not understood – perhaps to do with the Olex machine and mapping, or the way I'd tried to keep the *Galwad* under control in the heavy seas. Possibly something about the way I tied the strings and how I chose where to leave pots.

My mind was racing through all the possibilities: the depth of the water at Freshwater, maybe, or whether I'd ever steered the *Galwad* into 2.2m before. Perhaps the phone calls were confusing her – which ones had connected, which ones hadn't. That sort of stuff.

I could barely believe what I was listening to, however, as the question was read out.

'Did I not have any concerns about the environmental impact of throwing bags full of rubbish into the sea?'

What the fuck?

I sat open jawed, turned to Scott and shook my head in total disbelief from side to side. Was this what we were going to be judged on? Was this what it had all boiled down to?

There'd also been another strange incident involving a juror. Throughout the trial, a man had been sat on his own every day in the public gallery. Nobody knew who he was, why he was there – and none of us thought to ask him outright.

Towards the end of the trial, we all went off one afternoon for a debrief at a riverside pub – I think it was The Ram in Kingston – and sat outside by the towpath. We were chatting away about the case when I looked up and, to my amazement, saw the same mystery man walking past us – hand in hand with one of the female jurors.

'My God, look – that's the bloke from the public gallery, isn't it? He's holding hands with one of the jurors. What's all that about, then?'

Our alarm bells were ringing. As with all court cases, there were moments when the jury had been asked to step outside so legal arguments could be heard in front of the judge that the jurors were not entitled to hear. Had this man heard these discussions while he sat in the public gallery and possibly passed them on to the juror he'd been holding hands with? What was their relationship and why was he there all the time?

My old man and Nicky had also recognised them so, the following morning, they told one of the court officials what we'd seen. The man was quizzed but insisted he had no involvement whatsoever with any member of the jury. His word was accepted and that was the end of the matter.

We weren't happy and tried to get hold of CCTV footage from along the towpath. Unfortunately, it had already been erased; there was nothing more we could do.

Nevertheless, it preyed on my mind. *Was it all part of a great, big, conspiracy to nail us?* Thankfully, Christopher helped me forget such thoughts. His summing up concentrated on the sheer absurdity of the allegations and the impossibility of what the prosecution claimed we'd pulled off in such atrocious conditions. I thought he summed it up quite neatly when he faced the jury and said, 'A lobster fisherman has turned into a multi-million pound drugs smuggler overnight.'

His underlying theme was that none of the allegations made any kind of logical sense.

Why had we somehow plucked the drugs out of a Force Eight sea – only to chuck them back into the water again at Freshwater? Why risk them getting water damaged or floating off with the tide?

Why, at the very least, hadn't we submerged the bags at Freshwater, so nobody could spot them? If anyone knew how to properly weigh them down, it was me.

Why would I leave them there in any case? I couldn't possibly get the *Galwad* close enough to the shore and they'd be better off hidden inside lobster pots.

Why was a floaty rope used for the back line to hold the rucksacks together? I never used that type of rope and there were no leftover bits found on the *Galwad*.

Why were the lengths of the eleven legs – each one attached to a holdall – all uneven? No lobster fisherman would do that. It was the work of an amateur.

Why were the legs 16m apart from one another? If I'd used a winch to offload the holdalls – as Jeans and Dunne had claimed – the legs would need to be the same length as the *Galwad* itself or they'd get tangled up. My boat is 12m long, not 16m. This is bread and butter to me.

Why were the knots attaching the holdalls to the legs not the same as the ones attaching the legs to the back line? 'Mr Green would never do that,' Christopher told the court. 'He would have tied the knots in the same way he's always tied them for years and years. The knots on the rucksacks are not how he ties knots on a back line.'

Why was the weight used to hold the bags in position at Freshwater nothing like the ones I used? I had loads of weights and none of them looked anything like the ones discovered – a pair of old railway track couplings.

Christopher was on a roll by now: 'If Mr Green was in charge of this step of the operation, he would have relied on all his knowledge of the sea and everything he knew about tying lines and strings.

'This was the most expensive cargo he'd ever handled in his entire fishing career and yet – inexplicably – he's used none of the tried-and-tested techniques he's relied on for his own livelihood.'

Good point, Julian.

Christopher continued piling on questions that cut to the core of the allegations.

Why was no radar evidence provided to confirm exactly where the *Oriane* actually went?

Why hadn't I switched off my Olex completely so there'd be nothing to prove where the *Galwad* went that night?

Why was I being accused of 'erratic movements' when everything I did was completely consistent with mapping. My previous trips proved that I frequently went into the shipping lanes, sensible or not. There'd be fewer rival crews there – meaning more crab and lobster for me. Trip 23 was slap, bang in the middle of the shipping lanes, so was 24, 25 and 26.

Christopher underlined this point, saying, 'The *Galwad* was frequently going to places it had never been before and the charts prove it. Fishermen are constantly on the lookout for new locations and that's not suspicious in the slightest.' He wasn't finished.

Why would we bother shooting a line of pots at 10.30 p.m. – just as the weather was giving us real problems – when we had such a huge, dangerous and pressurised job to carry out just ninety minutes later? Why would I have risked missing the *Oriane* steaming past because I was too absorbed with lobster pots?

Why, after I'd allegedly scooped up the drugs, did I bother struggling with another line four hours later – one that gave me a real headache? Even the *Vigilant* and the surveillance plane confirmed they saw us pulling up pots at that moment. In fact, that's all they ever saw us do all night.

Why did we never get back on board the *Galwad* once we'd docked at Yarmouth? Woolls said we were planning to return to Freshwater so we could pick up the drugs under the cover of darkness – and yet CCTV of the quay proved none of us stepped on board the boat. Instead, Scott got lobsters out of the pen and walked off to Salty's, just as the police jumped on me, Dan and Vic.

Christopher wanted to emphasis this point and said to the jurors, 'Do not fill in the gaps with guesswork or speculation.'

Then he carried on, 'Why do we even believe there were any drugs on the *Oriane*? How do we know the cocaine came from Brazil? Why not Colombia? There's absolutely no evidence.'

Why did the *Vigilant*, whose only job that night was to watch the *Oriane*, not see the *Galwad* go anywhere near it? How can we know the bags were ever thrown overboard when nobody saw them – even though they were specifically watching for exactly that to happen?

Why was no evidence ever found on the *Oriane* when it was inspected on 4 June?

'The *Oriane*'s involvement is just a theory,' proclaimed Christopher.

'It is undisputed the bags could not have been thrown off the *Oriane* on a line because the line would have torn apart. Undisputed.

'Yet if the holdalls were in small bundles, it would have taken four minutes just to get one of them on board the *Galwad*. Even the Crown admits they couldn't have pulled in eleven bags individually in that time.'

There was more.

Why wasn't the faintest hint of drugs ever found on the *Galwad*? The bags weren't entirely watertight and some of the cocaine was found to be damp. If we'd picked them up, as alleged, then they would have been on the *Galwad* for seventeen hours before being dumped at Freshwater. So how come absolutely nothing leaked out when they were being rearranged, put on a string and thrown out at Freshwater. Not so much as a micro dot. The police tore through the *Galwad* forensically – and frantically – trying to find the tiniest trace. Nothing was discovered.

'It's all conjecture, working backwards, ignoring previous trips and depth data,' said Christopher, before continuing.

Why didn't Jeans and Dunne report seeing ten to twelve holdalls, tied together on a line with a red buoy at the end, straight away? There wasn't much else going on, after all. If that's what they saw, it's inconceivable they didn't think it was significant given they were there specifically to look for that sort of activity. Why did they just stroll off a few minutes later, leaving the packages unattended overnight?

Why had Jeans and Dunne never described seeing holdalls on board the *Galwad* when they allegedly had a perfect bird's-eye view of the deck? Also, they insisted they saw the bags coming off a line on the *Galwad*'s port side – and yet our winching gear was at the other end of the boat on the starboard side. Not even close.

Why did Breen call them at 10 a.m. the following morning? He knew the drugs had been found by then – but he only had their report saying 'six to seven' items. They should have been at the debrief, that was the right procedure – and he knew it.

Why did he carry on with the alleged debrief, without them, then take the surveillance management record and meet them in an East Cowes side street – in the back of his car?

Why did Breen ask Jeans and Dunne to sign the record but not check to see if they signed it in the right place? Instead, they incorrectly signed it alongside everyone else who'd attended the debrief – giving the entirely false impression they'd all been there together.

Christopher paused for a few moments to let the jurors think about what he'd just said, then added, 'Breen needed a link between the *Galwad* and the drugs. There was no debrief. This chat broke all the relevant guidelines.'

Christopher had already made a stink about this earlier in court, demanding to see the rules and regulations officers have to follow when they fill in logs and attends debriefs – something the prosecution didn't want to hand over. Something so secretive, it was even encrypted. The judge ruled in our favour, though, and Christopher was able to show how all the guidelines about the correct ways to fill in logs had been totally ignored.

Pages with empty spaces on them hadn't been filled with Z-lines – so extra material could easily be slipped in; everything was meant to have been dated and timed at exactly the moment entries were made. None of this had happened.

Christopher had come good. *We're going to win this.* Even the security guards sitting next to us were whispering 'is this for real?'

I went back to the flat that night feeling upbeat. I remember saying to my sister Nicky, 'You know what, Christopher's done all right, I think. It didn't go bad.' If I'd have had a tick board with all the allegations listed on it, I genuinely felt he'd answered most of them, covering this, ruling out that, dealing with such and such.

The more I thought about that tick-board, the more positive I felt so I phoned the missus, wanting to give her some good news for a change. 'Christopher's done well,' I told her, before going through everything he'd said.

The more we spoke, the more I realised how much I missed her. Just hearing her calm voice had that impact on me – even though she had far worse problems to contend with than I had. She even had some good news of her own to share: 'I reckon I'll be able to get to Kingston in time for the verdict,' she said. 'The chemo sessions end soon and the dates should work out.'

I put the phone down and thought about Nikki sitting in the courtroom as the jurors came back in. Everything would rest on what they thought, of course, but all they'd really heard was Tanya Woolls and Paul Davidson saying 'we believe' and 'it's a possibility'.

Surely they couldn't convict us just on that?

My defence team weren't quite as optimistic, though. While they were saying 'yeah, yeah' to everything I thought Christopher had covered well, they never said, 'Jamie, we're smashing this, this is going our way.'

'It's OK' is probably the best I got. They were positive but they weren't saying this is a home run or anything. They were way more guarded, like they were hedging their bets.

The judge's summing up, though, even brought a smile to their faces. As he went through the critical allegations one by one and what each of the witnesses had said, he turned to Jeans and Dunne.

'Members of the jury,' he said, looking directly at them. 'One might think if you were an officer on a cliff seeing ten to twelve packages being deposited in that way, you would tell someone about it. But … nothing, it seems, excited interest.

'If these officers, knowing that they are involved in an operation to detect drug smugglers, see what they have seen and are prepared to still leave the island – it does seem extraordinary, does it not?'

Bloody hell. That's got to be good, hasn't it? He said 'extraordinary'. Surely the jury has picked up on that.

Chapter 25

THE VERDICT

It was the mother of all storms.

My hands were clamped ferociously to the railings in front of me; my bulging knuckles looked like giant glaciers about to puncture through my straining skin. No Force Eight had ever been so vicious. All I could do was hang on.

I hadn't felt seasick for years but this time my senses were reeling. I'd no balance, I couldn't focus, everything was spinning and tilting, nothing was on an even keel. I wanted to puke but my mouth remained dry. My heart was pounding against my chest and a cold sweat of fear and panic spread rapidly across my forehead, sending icy shivers down my spine.

I knew my crew were nearby, somewhere. I heard sounds – a paralysing mix of anguished cries, screams and groans, their hysterical pitch echoing the turbulence that was engulfing me.

For the first time in my career, I felt crushed. My twenty years as a working fisherman were lost, drowned, plunged into the dark fathoms below. Sunk without trace.

And still my knuckles strained and still my hands ferociously gripped the rail in front of me. I started shaking my head from side to side – fuck, fuck, fuck – until, slowly, the first glimpses of my reality started to dawn.

The railing wasn't the *Galwad*'s. I was definitely drowning but I wasn't at sea. I needed to yell, 'What is this? A nightmare? Am I hallucinating? Am I pissed?'

I needed to scream, 'I'm just a fisherman.' I needed to beg: 'Please, everyone, just wake up. Wake me up. What's wrong here? What's happening? Come on. Stop this.'

Instead, I remained mute, incapable of sound or movement because the storm had won and frozen me to the core. Suddenly, one of the anguished cries made sense to me. I recognised Maisy's voice. I knew she was close yet I couldn't see her, or reach out to her. I couldn't reassure her. *Dad's OK, Maisy. This'll get sorted, I promise.*

Suddenly my stupor was broken. Hands locked tightly around my arms and yanked me down into a subterranean room where the rest of my crew were all waiting, all silent, all stunned. Below deck, so to speak, underneath the court where our destinies had just been decided. Then a door slammed shut. It's not stopped slamming shut ever since.

Guilty.

Jamie Green. Mr James Green.

On all counts. We find Mr Green …

Guilty.

Guilty, guilty, guilty. Such a small word crashing around my head like colossal waves battering the *Galwad*.

Guilty of trying to smuggle £53 million worth of cocaine into the UK. *You what?*

Mr Green. *Guilty* of not being a fisherman after all but guilty of being an international drugs smuggler.

Guilty of owning a fishing boat called the *Galwad Y Mor*.

Guilty of heading out into the Channel on 29 May 2010, with a crew of three – one of them a 17-year-old child – with no intention of fishing at all.

Guilty of waiting for a Panamanian cargo ship to cross the *Galwad*'s path. *Guilty* of waiting for someone on that gigantic boat to chuck overboard eleven holdalls stashed with cocaine. *Guilty* of somehow scooping those bags out of the boiling sea, frothing and exploding under the intensity of a Force Eight gale.

Guilty of miraculously finding a way of doing all this inside three minutes as the *Galwad* rolled and swayed and tossed and turned over the riotous waves.

Guilty, seventeen hours later, of inexplicably chucking the bags off the *Galwad* like flotsam so they'd float into shore and be discovered by a local fisherman the next day.

Guilty, therefore, of literally chucking overboard £53 million of cocaine and letting a total stranger find it.

Guilty of being utterly bemused when the police pounced. *Guilty* of telling them to fuck off and of laughing at the absurdity of it all, of the accusations and the claims and the serious faces. *Guilty* of saying, 'What on earth are you talking about?'

Guilty of thinking someone would stop this charade. *Guilty* of thinking lawyers would make every one wake up and see sense.

Guilty of believing no jury in their right minds could possibly believe any of this actually happened.

Guilty.

They never saw a fisherman, a family man, a businessman, an employer or a skipper. They couldn't see the boy who fell in love with fishing when he was 8 years old and turned it into his livelihood.

They only saw a criminal, a drugs smuggler. They were comfortable with that. When they looked at me and decided

I was guilty, the jurors were effectively saying: 'We don't believe Mr Green is actually a fisherman. None of the things he was doing were designed to catch lobsters or crab. We think he was a drug mule out to bag cocaine.'

There were basic fundamentals about my way of life, my habits, my beliefs, the way I did stuff and operated, that the jury never grasped, or were willing to accept. We were chalk and cheese, those jurors and I; we came from wildly differing backgrounds, so maybe it was no surprise. They didn't know enough about me.

Nobody, for example, ever asked me in court what I thought about drug dealers. Or whether I'd ever used drugs and how I'd feel if I ever discovered one of my own kids was either using or selling them. The mess I'd make of any dealer who ever went near Maisy, Poppy or Jesse. I overheard someone in Salty's bar one evening trying to offer pissed-up punters packets of weed. Let's just say he never came back after I'd grabbed him round the neck, dragged him out and persuaded him to stay away.

The jury never got to hear about the death of one of my closest pals, whose heart gave in after he'd taken drugs at one of the island's raves.

Yet all this struck to the core of who I am. If I ever heard one of my kids had meddled with drugs, it'd be the last time they'd ever touch them again. They all know I'd be both furious and disappointed with them. Disappointed mainly.

My closest pals know I've never done drugs; drink, yes, but not drugs. I remain way too traumatised by my pal's tragic death to risk going near them.

I'd grown up with him, we'd played football together, he supported Man United like me. During our teens, I'd got heavily into boxing and even reached amateur championship standard. Boxing taught me to look after my body; I could put up with a drink and a hangover but to be wrapped up in drugs would have totally screwed me as a fighter. My pal, however, was drawn into the many raves that took place on the island during the 1980s and '90s and at one of those the silly sod took Ecstasy or something similar. No doubt some scumbag had mixed it with some cheap-yet-poisonous powder because my pal, who was the same age as me, suffered a fatal heart attack. He was airlifted to Southampton General but there was nothing they could do – the drugs had practically torn his arteries wide open.

So no, I've never done drugs but the jury never knew that. Would it have mattered? Is it relevant? Would they have seen me in a different light had they known? Does it prove I couldn't possibly have smuggled in so much cocaine?

Maybe not but it tells me the jurors never thought, not for a second, that I might have some values. That I might have felt physically sick if I thought for one second my own kids were buying drugs off some sleazebag dealer. How would I have felt if my own kids had ended up buying the same drugs I'd smuggled in? Would I be ashamed or furious? Or not bothered? The jury clearly thought I wouldn't be bothered.

The jurors never saw me for what I was – OK, a drinker and a rebel who hated being told what to do, but predominantly a dad, a husband and, most definitely, a full-time, committed, professional fisherman. They seemed to think everything I did out at sea was strange, abnormal. In fact, it was the behaviour of someone who wasn't a fisherman at all.

If they had truly understood what the *Galwad* meant to me, and how it was opening up areas of the Channel I'd never reached before, surely they would have seen a fisherman – and not a drug smuggler – staring back across the court room at them.

I'm absolutely certain they never understood the significance of the Olex machine I installed on the *Galwad*, either,
and how I set about mapping the seabed for new areas to
plunder. I guess it was a bit like someone trying to make me
understand how stocks and shares work in the city.

The jurors couldn't or wouldn't or plain didn't want to
understand or believe why I would deliberately steam up and
down for hours on end just to map out a seabed. They preferred
to believe I was simply up to no good. That was easier for them
to digest than unravelling the logic of the Olex machine.

Guilty.

It was like we'd been broadsided by a freak wave I hadn't
seen coming. We were out there, working away, when –
unexpectedly – a surge of water had slammed down on the
side of the *Galwad*, turned the boat and tipped the gunwale
over – leaving us all desperately hanging on. Wham, bam, crash
– everything upended, everything buffeted by shockwaves. It
was just like that.

There'd been no hint of it, either. Well, nothing concrete.
The jury had come back in at some point and said they were
struggling to reach a decision. So we'd tried to analyse that. *If
they're struggling, that works in our favour doesn't it?*

Days ticked by and turned into nights and my head would
be going mental trying to imagine what the jurors were
saying. We talked among ourselves endlessly in the court caf-
eteria as we waited, or back in the flat with our friends and
family. Every conversation was the same. *The longer this goes
on, the better it is, Jamie. Yeah, yeah, it's definitely a good sign if it
takes long.*

Back the next day. Surely they'd be thinking about Jeans
and Dunne changing their statements and the *Vigilant* never
seeing us go anywhere near the *Oriane* and the fact their

log was spoilt and the police radio breaking down for no reason and the plane – I'm telling you it definitely flew over Tennyson at 7 p.m. – and what about the fact we had no proper phones on board, surely they'd see how we'd never do that if we were really smuggling drugs? In any case, none of it's even possible inside three minutes. I think Christopher got that point over well in the end, don't you?

Grab a paper, go outside, have a fag, read about the football, then talk about the trial again.

Guilty.

Except, I knew I wasn't. Nor were my crew. We were all entirely innocent.

It was a storm, all right. A perfect storm because it claimed my life, my family's life. All our lives.

All I am is a fisherman.

That's all I'm guilty of, Your Honour.

Chapter 26

5 MEN, 104 YEARS

Hang on. There wasn't even a trophy picture. I mean the police always pose for a triumphant photograph alongside whatever they've seized, don't they? How do we even know they really did find all those drugs? That was a colossal haul, so why wasn't there a picture showing a pile of cocaine and a couple of senior officers standing solemnly next to it, as if to say: 'Gotcha'?

No. All we ever saw was one holdall – not eleven – split open with some packets inside. There was no sign of all that powder. This was meant to be real high-quality stuff, as well, 90 per cent pure cocaine. They'd even mentioned that in the trial. 'The fact it is so pure indicates it's come from the country of origin,' was a sentence that stuck in my mind. So where was the bloody photograph?

I got thinking about the bags as we sat in the cells underneath Court 10, the word *guilty* hanging over us like a heavy, black storm cloud. Even the moment they were found at Tennyson should have raised alarm bells with the jury: it had taken the police a full hour to haul all eleven holdalls on board their RIB. That was on a bright, sunny morning in perfect conditions on placid water – and yet we were meant to have done it inside three minutes in a Force Eight storm in the dead of night.

Guilty.

The bags were just another blatant reason why we had to be innocent. They were in pristine condition with barely a mark on them and utterly unaffected by the fact they'd been hurled off a giant cargo ship into a boiling sea. The lowest open deck on the *Oriane* was, apparently, 13.5m above us – the equivalent of three double-decker buses stacked.

Even if they'd been thrown from there, how could they have possibly emerged thirty-three hours and fifteen minutes later utterly unscathed. Not even misshapen or distorted in any way. They'd allegedly been dropped overboard around 12.30 a.m.; after that, they'd spent eighteen hours on the *Galwad* before we dumped them at Tennyson, where they remained in the water for another fifteen hours overnight.

Guilty? Are you sure?

My memory of what happened immediately after we'd heard the verdicts remains hazy. All I know is that Julian Christopher got up, it was early – around 11.30 a.m. – and persuaded the judge to sentence us before we were taken away from court.

Suddenly, we were surrounded by big, burly security guards and not the much older and frailer attendants who'd sat with us before. I didn't even see them come in to our glass room, I just remember them escorting us downstairs as we waited for the judge to make his mind up.

We spoke between ourselves, desperately trying to fathom out what had gone wrong, why we hadn't been believed, what had convinced the jury. Our legal team came down and as much as we wanted to be furious with them, we also wanted to hear what they were thinking and what would happen next.

There was a lot of bewildered faces and shaking of heads and, 'We don't understand this, either.'

'The jurors obviously chose to believe the policemen over you.'

'What sort of sentences are we facing?' and someone said 'maximum eighteen years' and we all fell silent to let that sink in.

H.H.J. Dodgson insisted on taking a lunch break until we were eventually hauled back into the courtroom. Before revealing the sentences, though, the judge explained what he believed our individual roles had been – and therefore what punishments we were to be given.

The original court papers seemed to suggest I was the ring-leader. The indictment stated 'Green and others'. However, H.H.J. Dodgson turned that round. He bought into what Tanya Woolls had suggested. As far as he was concerned, Beerey was the mastermind, the man connected to the 'Balkan Gang'. He had introduced me to them and persuaded me to go out and do their dirty work in the *Galwad*. Dan and Scott were the foot soldiers.

Paul, how could that be? I mean, there wasn't one single phone call, letter, email, text – nothing to show Beerey had been in touch with a bunch of overseas drugs smugglers beforehand. In any case, if he was the mastermind, why wasn't he out on the cliff tops checking we weren't being watched? Why wasn't he at Yarmouth when we came in and docked? Why didn't he rush down and pick up the bloody drugs himself at Tennyson if that's where we'd dumped them?

In fact, why wasn't he out with us on the *Galwad* to oversee the entire operation? Surely that would have been his job, if he was the ringleader? Christ, he didn't even flee the country when we all got arrested. You'd have thought he might have done that. Worse, you'd have thought some pretty nasty people would have come looking for him if they thought he'd just screwed up a £53 million drugs operation.

I couldn't get my head around what H.H.J. Dodgson was saying. Beerey was – is – one of my best mates. How come I didn't phone him, then, at 12.40 a.m. to tell him the good news? *We've got the drugs, Beerey, well done, you've really pulled it off.*

Then I thought about Vic. *Hang on, judge.* If you're right, and Beerey was the boss, why the hell was Vic even there? What was the point? He couldn't speak English, he wasn't in charge – according to you, that was Beerey – so what function did he serve?

My mind was spinning with all of this when I became aware that, somewhere in the distance, my name was being called. I instinctively rose, the first of us to stand, my thoughts literally out to sea.

'Twenty four years.'

I can still hear the silence.

What? What was that? Excuse me?

Two years and four months … twenty-four months?

I looked towards Beerey and the lads. They were frozen, heads down.

Did you just say twenty-four fuckin' years?

I didn't move, I couldn't move, I just stood there staring out of the glass panel, looking at nothing really. I couldn't take anything in. Then I heard Beerey's name being called and he rose.

'Twenty four years'. Next it was Vic, 'twenty-four years'; then Dan, 'eighteen'; and finally Scott, who got fourteen. It all happened so quickly and then hands were grabbing our arms and we were being shovelled back downstairs again.

Our legal team was waiting and this time we weren't so patient. 'What the fuckin' hell's just happened? You said eighteen – max.'

'Yeah those sentences are unusually harsh.'

'Harsh. How the hell have we lost this? What went wrong?' They offered no answers, though; we didn't even get a debrief. I think I yelled, 'We want this appealed' but there was no response. Nothing. Was it my imagination, or were they already clearing their papers and getting prepared for their next case and their next pay day?

There were a few others waiting in the cells below the court and they were quick to give us their opinions as we waited to be shipped out. I remember one of them, younger than us and a bit of a motor-mouth, saying, 'You've got royally stitched up there. My mate only got sixteen.'

Then came the prison talk. 'Oh, you'd better hope you get such and such a prison. You don't want Whitemoor, that's for sure.' I couldn't compute any of it. I was too numb to think.

We were eventually led, handcuffed, into the back of a van. I can still hear the silence: we never spoke a word for the entire length of the following twenty-minute journey. Maybe we would have, maybe we'd have crammed in as many words as possible, had we known we'd never talk to one another again.

Some instinct within me made me study their faces, though. It wasn't difficult to spot the common denominator. Burning deep within their eyes, and stamped brazenly across their foreheads like the seared marks cattle farmers brand on their animals, were the words 'we've been shafted'. They would have seen them on mine, too.

Dan, the fitness fanatic who felt, like me, the same thrill and sheer joy of living outdoors, was sat slumped against the side of the van, his spirit broken, his mind lost in a maze of thoughts that were as black as his closely cropped hair.

Then Beerey. The alleged mastermind who'd persuaded me inside twenty minutes to attempt one of the crimes of the century. He adored Formula 1 racing but right then he looked more like a man who'd just crawled out of a high-speed car crash and was hanging on for life.

I turned away from Beerey to study the real baby in the pack, Scott – my son Jesse's best pal. His face, usually mischievous and cheeky, was just blank, sucked of life and sparkle and the sheer optimism of youth. I wanted to give him a fatherly hug and assure him it'd all be OK and he could still have a life ahead of him. Meet a girl, have a family, help me build an empire around the *Galwad*. I didn't.

Finally, I looked at Vic, who, like all of us, was motionless and utterly mute. Who was this man? Was he to blame for everything or, like the rest of us, was he simply in the wrong place, at the wrong time? If our hands weren't cuffed tightly together, would we be beating the shit out of him for leading us into this mess with his fake passport and dodgy mates? Or was the utterly bemused, confused expression on his face closer to the truth? In that moment he looked like a man stranded a million miles from home, with no hope of going back to his wife and kids. He didn't look like a drugs baron.

I was jolted back into life as the van bounced over a lump in the road and started to slow down. Within minutes the rear doors were opened and we were led from a courtyard surrounded by towering, ugly grey walls into the labyrinth of our new-yet-temporary home: Wandsworth prison. Straight away we were separated, led down different corridors, taken into different rooms where we were stripped, inspected by a doctor and put into an induction unit, never to see each other again.

Somebody ran through the basic dos and don'ts but I was in no mood to listen. I was led into a cell, where I immediately clambered on to the top bunk. I half noticed someone on the bottom but we didn't speak.

I started closing my eyes but then a screw walked in to tell me I could make one phone call but no more unless I'd got a PIN, and that'd take a few days to sort out. I knew that already, same as Winchester. But his interruption made me think of Nikki and, of course, I got up to phone her.

It was in that moment, as I stood by the wall where the phone was hanging, that the sentence really hit me. I'd been given twenty-four years; between us we'd been jailed for 104 years, and yet they were just distant numbers with no shape or meaning. I hadn't yet put a value or scale on them. What does twenty-four years feel like? How do I measure it? In days? It's 8,760. In hours? It's 210,240. In income? Is there a financial worth on it? Before the arrest I was turning over £180,000 a year so it's nearly £4.5 million and that's not allowing for expansion and new ways to increase revenue.

As soon as I saw the phone I realised it was none of that. As soon as I mechanically punched in my home number and held the receiver to my ear, I instantly knew how to measure twenty-four years. As soon as a voice answered and said 'hello', I knew. As soon as the tears invaded my eyes.

'Hello, Nikki, it's me … you alright?'

I was 43 years old, I'd be 67 by the time I got out – maybe less with parole. The only certainty within that period would be the death of my wife. I wouldn't be by her side, cramming her with crazy vitamin pills until she rattled each time she stood up; I wouldn't be there to make cups of tea, to carry the shopping, to ease the burden of ordinary life, to hold her hand when the pain was too much, to lie by her side when tears and loneliness crept in during the middle of the night. I couldn't even give her hope.

Now I understood just how devastating my sentence was. I gripped the receiver in my hands and squeezed it ferociously, unable to find any words. Was my Nikki going to die while I was in prison? Would she lose the battle against this bastard disease with nobody by her side?

I tried to say something, anything, 'Nikki, I ... I ... '. She interrupted, I think she knew and even though her voice sounded so far away – like we were already in two parallel worlds that could never connect again – the strength in her voice pushed me back from my indulgent, selfish despair. She wasn't crying. There was no faltering as she spoke. Instead, she said, 'You've got to hold it together, Jamie, for all our sakes. I can cope with you being in prison. I can't cope with you cracking up.

'We will get this sorted, we will get the appeals in and we will fight it.'

Then she found the words I will never forget.

'And don't start worrying about me, either.

'I will see you out again before this gets anywhere near me. I will not let this beat me until you are out.

'This is not the end.'

I lay in my bunk that night and thought long and hard about those words. I missed my wife like never before in that moment.

Chapter 27

RIGGED

First they sentenced me – and then, the next day, they did the same to the *Galwad*. Only that smacked of conspiracy. That smacked of deliberately withholding information that could have significantly influenced the jurors.

On the very day I was locked up – 2 June 2011 – the Maritime and Coastguard Agency (MCA) sent a letter announcing the *Galwad* wasn't seaworthy and that its licence was being revoked.

It was the timing that stank. The MCA is a government agency that often works hand in hand with the police. In fact, it's the very same agency their marine expert, Paul Davidson, had worked for as an enforcement officer. Every boat has to be issued with a licence by them in much the same way cars must have an MOT.

Although they'd granted the *Galwad* a licence six months before we were arrested, that was now being overturned because – in their expert opinion – there was insufficient visibility from the wheelhouse. We couldn't see where we were going because our view was obstructed by the high sides attached to the boat.

To be fair, they were probably right. Whenever I looked out of the front of the wheelhouse, I could only ever see over a low gunnel on the starboard side where the pots would go over. That strip was probably no more than 15ft long: the rest of the boat was all high sided to help protect the lads from crashing waves and severe weather.

The more I've thought about this, the more sinister it's become. Why on earth did the MCA wait until we were sentenced to reveal their decision? They must have sat on that letter for almost a year. Nobody from any of the maritime authorities went anywhere near the *Galwad* once it was stripped and searched by the police and then sent to the Portsmouth naval docks. The boat was returned to Yarmouth, around June 2010, and it was never inspected from then on.

What if the jury had been told that the governing body for safety standards at sea had declared the *Galwad* unfit because the visibility was severely hampered? Would the jurors have thought: well, if the skipper can't see out of his window, and the sides of the boat are so high that nobody can lean over to grab anything, how on earth could they have scooped up eleven holdalls in a Force Eight?

It certainly wouldn't have helped the prosecution's case.

It would have been tantamount to the MCA saying, 'You know what? We've checked this boat over and, quite frankly, what you're saying is impossible. It can't be done. There's not enough visibility. In fact we've had to get it out of the water because it's not safe. They can't see anything from that wheelhouse.'

'Did you say, "Someone chucked eleven holdalls overboard in the middle of a Force Eight storm and this lot scooped them up. Off the sides of the *Galwad*?"

'Nah, sorry.

'You know what?

'You must have got the wrong boat.'

Chapter 28

TERRORISTS

It's the most-dangerous and terrifying prison in the UK, dubbed a breeding ground for the Taliban and an 'al-Qaeda recruitment centre'. It has housed – and still does – Britain's most violent and evil killers, executioners who live shoulder to shoulder with notorious extremists and terrorists. Criminals handed life sentences for brutal murders or plotting to blow up tube stations and passenger planes.

Whitemoor prison is where terror fanatics and murderers serve life sentences; it's where prison staff have been viciously attacked and beaten with pool cues until their bones have been broken – and it's where inmates have killed other prisoners by slashing their throats with razor blades. It's also where many inmates have been cruelly held in solitary confinement for periods that have exceeded United Nations guidelines.

There are no limits to the insanity and the evil inside Whitemoor.

It's where they put me for a crime I didn't commit.

I saw with my own eyes how terrorist prisoners enjoyed cult-like status and the adulation of fellow inmates; I felt the intimidating knife-edge atmosphere every day. I stared into the faces of the insane and the fanatical and saw how they all shared the same look: each of them ready to snap at the faintest provocation. They were like human pressure cookers; you could feel their temperatures rising and rising through the course of a day, simmering and bubbling and reaching dangerously high levels, usually over something as petty as a misinterpreted glance or a badly chosen word.

One of the most notorious was on the wing opposite me. He wasn't powerfully built but he had a cold, unwavering stare that could stop you in your tracks, even across a prison concourse. He'd belonged to a terrorist sleeper cell that had plotted to bomb a London tube tunnel using a limousine packed with explosives. I watched inmates salute as they walked past him; he was revered by his devoted followers. Terrorists had kudos in Whitemoor and those with the longest sentences commanded the biggest respect.

Another revered ringleader was older and had been jailed for forty five years after planting a bomb in his pregnant fiancée's hand luggage on a flight from Heathrow to Tel Aviv. Then there was a prisoner who'd plotted to kill a British soldier in the same way tragic Lee Rigby was executed.

Then there was me.

Not everyone in Whitemoor was an Islamic extremist. The notorious killer/kidnapper Michael Sams was in Whitemoor and Soham murderer Ian Huntley had been imprisoned there as well. But there was definitely a dominant Muslim population – I'd say at least 50 per cent of the inmates. Like all of us, they had their own kitchenettes and would order in their own food. In fact, one of the biggest and most common flashpoints would be if a non-Muslim prisoner was cooking pork.

I saw hot oil chucked over inmates who were cooking bacon and while I never witnessed someone being stabbed in a kitchen dispute, I was told it had happened many times before I arrived. I'm sure it had. In fact, a year earlier there'd been sixty-one assaults inside the prison. These had included stabbings, slashed throats, beatings with dumb-bells – even guards threatened with beheading. In January 2020, five members of staff were brutally attacked by two inmates wearing fake suicide vests. None of this surprised me, there was something in the air inside Whitemoor that instantly told you this was a dangerous and terrifying place to be.

I often saw new inmates being targeted by jihadists eager to find new recruits. One, a 20-year-old kid, arrived at Whitemoor looking nervous and afraid, with a long sentence stretching out in front of him. He was immediately surrounded by new pals happy to share their food and let him into their gang. Six months later, he was saluting just like the rest.

I didn't really speak to them but I saw what was going on all the time. All that bothered me was why on earth was I there – and how could I get out as quickly as possible?

I'd spent six weeks in Wandsworth after we'd left court and then, out-of-the-blue, I was told to pack my stuff and get down to reception. 'You're going on the bus.'

'Where to?'

'Can't tell you too much, just get ready.'

Strictly speaking, I was a Category B prisoner. That meant I wasn't a high-security risk and theoretically could go back to Parkhurst on the Isle of Wight, which was what I was praying would happen.

Instead, after sentencing I was shunted off to Swaleside on the Isle of Sheppey, which is also Category B. 'Why can't you just send me to Parkhurst, then I can see my family and see my missus?' I asked.

'No, you ain't going there. They don't want you back there.'

'Why the hell not? I have problems at home, Nikki's ill. I have good reason. What happens if I refuse to go to Swaleside?'

'Well if you refuse, we'll put you in the Block.' That meant the isolation unit and I didn't want that.

So off I went to Swaleside. I was there for ten days when, again unexpectedly, there was a bang on the door as I sat in my cell watching telly. 'Pack yer bags, you're going tomorrow. Get yourself down to reception in the morning.'

I'd begun to realise this was how the prison system worked. They liked to ambush you as late as possible so you'd have no time to work anything out or make any dramas out of it. As ordered, I turned up at reception and asked, 'Where am I going, then?'

'Belmarsh.'

'But that's London. What am I going there for?'

'It's just for one night. Then you're going to Whitemoor.'

'Where the hell's that?'

That's when they started laughing.

'What's so funny?'

'You'll find out when you get there.'

Then the penny dropped. I'd heard that name before – at Kingston when we came down after sentencing. When the other defendants had said, 'You don't want Whitemoor, that's for sure.'

As I waited for the van to appear, I started chatting to some of the other inmates and asked if they knew anything about it. Their reactions made me fear the worst.

'What you done wrong then, mate?' and they started chuckling. 'You're going to the Big House.'

'What do you mean, the Big House?'

'That's where all the terrorists and the bombers go, all the lunatics and nutters, the lifers looking at thirty to forty years minimum. It's where the real bad Cat As go.'

You what?

I first spent a night in Belmarsh, then headed for Whitemoor the next day in a normal prison van, or sweat box as they're called. It's basically a transit, only inside there's a cubicle with fibreglass seats that are bone hard on your arse. I was in one of those.

I remember looking out of the window as we pulled up and noticing the heavyweight security all around the perimeters. More guards, more fencing, more spotlights. The buildings themselves looked much more modern and lower than I'd expected. Not at all like Winchester or Wandsworth. We were really in the middle of nowhere as well – deep in the Cambridgeshire fens.

Once again I went through the usual registration and induction. 'Right, pick yer stuff up and an officer will take you through to the wing.'

That's when I got my first proper look at my new surroundings. Everything seemed to be encased. There was no sense of an outside world. All the corridors were internal: it felt like I was in an extremely secure box with the roof and walls screwed tightly together to keep out any unwelcome intruders – including fresh air. It was what I imagined one of those Supermax prisons in the United States would be like.

All the while I was thinking: *This is a Category A prison but I'm Category B. So what the hell am I doing here? Has there been some kind of mistake?*

I got on the phone to Julian Hardy as soon as I could. 'Why on earth have I been put here? It's full of nutters and terrorists. How is Nikki ever going to visit me in this place? She can't get out here, it's too far away. Why can't I go to Parkhurst? You've got to get me transferred.'

Hardy eventually came back with some answers. As far as SOCA was concerned, I was a serious escape risk. They hadn't discovered any drug money in my bank accounts but that was clearly because I'd managed to hide it from them. With God knows how much stashed away in a place they couldn't find, I'd definitely be able to finance a James Bond-style prison breakout, no doubt with helicopters and small armies to back it up.

You couldn't make it up. That was why I was now locked up alongside the worst criminals in the country.

They also tried to play clever dicks with us by claiming Whitemoor was technically classed as a dispersal prison, which meant it could legitimately house category A and B prisoners. *Bollocks.*

I was put on B wing. Each wing had three spurs – green, red and blue – all separated from one another with heavy iron bars and mesh netting, presumably to stop inmates being hurled over balconies on to the concrete floor below. Everywhere looked cordoned off and enclosed and menacing.

I was on the top, third floor on green spur with a cell to myself. It was probably 12ft by 6ft but there was one small perk. In the middle of the far wall was a window that you could push open. OK, it had a barred cage immediately outside but at least there was enough room to keep a carton of milk cool outside.

I sensed an atmosphere of fear and looking-over-your-shoulder straight away. Whitemoor was a 24/7 tense place to be. The only way to survive was to keep your head down, trust very few people, talk to even fewer – and go to the gym as much as possible. That was the only area where you might earn some respect.

If you did a bit of training and kept at it, then some of the suspicious glances and hardened stares would soften. You didn't have to lift mega weights – although plenty did – you just had to keep at it.

My entire focus was spent on trying to get a move. Whitemoor was 200 miles from Freshwater and the journey

– including the ferry crossing – was at least five hours long. I went to the chaplain, told him about Nikki, and pleaded with my personal officer, who was a decent bloke. They just didn't have the sway. I kept pressing Hardy, who was sending letters and explaining I was a Cat-B prisoner stuck in the wrong sort of prison.

There were times, especially during the first few weeks, when I definitely felt myself sliding into despair. *Who could blame me?* There I was, wrongly convicted, rubbing shoulders with murderers and terrorists, my business and livelihood in tatters, hundreds of miles from my family, unable to even see and help my kids take their first nervous steps towards adulthood. Besides, what kind of a father figure was I any more?

If that wasn't bad enough, my wife was back home, battling terminal cancer on her own, and unable to visit me because Whitemoor was too far away given her condition. Every part of my body ached to help her, to look after her and yet I was utterly incapable and powerless.

At night, as darkness filled my cell, I could feel my mind succumbing to even blacker thoughts: what use was I? I'd nothing left to offer, I was no longer a breadwinner, a provider, I couldn't be strong, I couldn't rule the roost, I couldn't run my business, think about the orders, purchase bait and new pots, map the seabed, shoot strings. I couldn't even reach out and touch Nikki's hand or put my arms around my kids' shoulders. Everything I had ever been, and worked for, had vanished; I'd been stripped of my dignity, my power, even my desire to stick two fingers up to the world.

Nobody could see me and nobody could hear me from inside Whitemoor.

I'd gone from someone who'd provided to someone who was nothing. I was reduced to shouting down the phone at

Julian Hardy and then counting down the days until I got a visit from my sister or parents, bless them. They did absolutely everything they could to inspire me and motivate me and keep me on track. They still do. But at night time, especially in Whitemoor, all I had was my cell, my bed and my darkest thoughts.

Even though I didn't see Nikki again for at least another year – when she was finally strong enough to tackle the journey – it was her words that kept pulling me back from the darkness. Each time I felt the despair sweeping in, I'd remember what she'd said over the phone when I'd called from Wandsworth and the promise she made to stay alive long enough to see me released. *I will see you out again before this gets anywhere near me.* I can't begin to express what those words meant to me. How ironic – there was me, desperate to help her battle a terminal illness, when she was the one keeping me alive.

No matter how harsh the injustices, I knew that if I wallowed in them, I wouldn't last ten minutes. I'd burn my head out. I'd be a jibbering wreck.

That's why so many inmates hit the gym. They want to burn themselves out so when they get back in their cells they're out like a light as soon as their head hits the pillow. That's the way they handle it and I don't blame them. Lads will spend hours lifting massive, horrendous weights – I've seen some bench-press 200 kilos plus. It's the only way they can deal with tomorrow and the day after that.

Of course, you worry. You worry all the time. I've seen nippers cut themselves in prison, probably because they didn't have close friends and family who could connect them, in some small way, to the tiniest possibility that there might be something better in the outside world. They had no hope.

If you haven't got any sounding boards like that, then prison will crush you. That's what could easily have happened to me in Whitemoor. It's why it's such a good recruiting ground for extremists. Who else do you listen to if nobody is visiting? I was lucky, though: I had strong people surrounding me from day one and, as the Greens do, we goaded each other into fighting the system all over again. Fighting for a transfer, fighting for an appeal, fighting for justice. That's what kept us all sane.

Like all the inmates, I was expected to get a job at Whitemoor, where the daily routine was rigidly structured. In fact, it was probably the most organised prison I'd been to.

You had to work at set times and every time you left the wing, you'd go through airport-style security – holding out your arms while a screw waved one of those metal detector wands at you. Then it'd be repeated wherever you were going – and then again on your way back to your cell. We'd start around 8.30 a.m. and either go to a class or workshop. I attended some maths and geography lessons at first and then did a cleaning course because I knew it was the means to getting a paid job. I had to learn how to wash floors correctly and use an electric buffer, and I even got a certificate to prove I'd reached the required standard!

There were times when someone would be telling me how to put the right amount of water in a bloody bucket and it'd feel completely demeaning and humiliating. *Is this all that's left of my life? Is this all I can do?* So I'd imagine being back in my wheelhouse, king of the seas again, shouting orders at Dan and Scott and lining up to shoot a new string. It was the only way I could claw back my dignity.

Lunch would be at 11.30 a.m., then we'd all be locked in our cells again by midday and stay there until 1.15 p.m. while the screws ate. After that, we'd go back to work or classes at 1.30 p.m.

I ended up with a cleaning job on the wing in the mornings that suited me fine – emptying rubbish bags into wheely bins.

That gave me some time to myself just before midday, which I spent phoning people. There were only two or three phones on the wing for sixty inmates so that was one of the quieter periods to use them.

I was always on the lookout for a job that came with some privileges. Cleaning the gym was a good one because it meant I could go there whenever I wanted and use the equipment. There was also a CD shop at Whitemoor, where all the CDs that hadn't sold on the High Street were sent to be broken and recycled. We'd take them out of their brand new, unopened packaging, scratch up the discs and then smash them to pieces. That was one of the better-paid jobs: I earned around £30 a week doing that, which is good money in the prison system.

I spent a large chunk of it, around £20 a week, on phone credits, which were incredibly expensive. Then I'd buy stuff such as toiletries and, most importantly, food. Lifers could never survive in Whitemoor if all they ate was the prison food. You'd get a menu sheet at the start of the week with three or four options and fill that in. Lunch might be soup one day or a tiny cob roll with a packet of crisps. In the evenings, we'd get a main meal with an unrecognisable slice of meat plus chips and veg, then a little carton of milk with some tea bags and sugar.

It was all very basic, usually tasted shit and was never filling. So inmates buddied up into groups of two or three, bought food and cooked it together. That way you could tuck into whole chickens and joints of meat instead of the scrag ends you were normally served. It also helped pass the time.

You weren't exactly dining with saints inside Whitemoor, either. One of my unlikeliest buddies was the hitman Paul Cryne, given a life sentence for the infamous Sharon Birchwood murder. He'd allegedly been paid to kill Birchwood by her former husband and was found guilty at the Old Bailey after being extradited from Thailand, where he'd been living.

Cryne wasn't a well man when I met him and was living off pills following a heart-bypass operation. Strangely, it was the sea that connected us. He was a former bodybuilder – you could still see hints of that in his stocky frame – and he'd once set a world scuba-diving record. He was fascinated with boats so I gave him some old photographs of the *Galwad*. To my amazement, I got a letter from him long after I'd moved to another prison. Inside was a painting he'd done of the *Galwad*, which I still have to this day. He died in January 2019 from sepsis.

In some ways, I was lucky. I got out after three years, despite the system's best efforts to keep me there. Everything was a firewall; if I wanted a transfer, then I'd have to go through such and such a person, only he'd just been seconded to another prison and wouldn't be back for three months and then he'd be on holidays. That sort of stuff. Every tiny request had to be needlessly written down in meticulous detail; everything was a process and it was all geared to slow me down because, hey, nobody gets out of Whitemoor in a hurry.

Then suddenly – as is always the way – I was told to pack up and get ready to be moved. Only there was a catch. I'd begged and begged to be sent to Parkhurst, but the system wasn't going to let me dictate the terms. Instead, I was sent to Lowdham Grange in Nottinghamshire, a Category B prison just like Parkhurst. Except it's nowhere near the Isle of Wight.

I will always believe I was sent there out of spite, simply because I'd never stopped arguing about being in Whitemoor. What on earth was their logic for transferring me even further away from my family? They'd already kept us five hours apart by dragging me off to Cambridgeshire – now they were adding another thirty minutes to the journey.

How could Nikki possibly cope with that? Where was their compassion? Their humanity?

Chapter 29

INNOCENT FROM EVERY ANGLE

It sounds a bit crazy but I guess it's what happens to you when you're banged up for a crime you never committed. After you've spent years going over and over every tiny detail and exhausted every conceivable reason why it simply couldn't have happened, you start to look at it from a different angle.

I actually got to wondering: *How would I have carried out this crime if I really was involved?* If I gave this serious thought; maybe it would cast some further light on my innocence.

I've had plenty of time to think it over after all – ten years.

Ten years staring at prison walls and prison doors. Ten years doing mind-numbing prison jobs and lifting weights to earn some respect from feral inmates. Ten years drinking prison tea and eating prison slop. Ten years of only being able to see my kids during visiting hours. Ten years lying in my bunk night after night, staring through prison bars and trying to remember what the fresh sea air felt like in my lungs.

Well, it sets my mind thinking.

One thing I know with absolute certainty: I would never, ever have done it the way the prosecution said it was done. Their way was impossible.

For starters, I wouldn't have used the *Galwad*. It's probably the worst type of vessel I could imagine for such a task. Too big, too slow, too cumbersome. It's also high sided, to protect us from weather, but that makes leaning over to scoop up bags practically impossible. It also makes it inconceivable that I could have spotted, from my wheelhouse, tiny bags being hurled around on crashing waves. *Doesn't it prove my innocence straight away?*

The Olex machine would also be a bit of a giveaway, given it keeps a constant record of our movements. It'd be like having a running commentary of everything we were doing and then storing it for the police to find.

I'd have wanted a fast boat out there, something I could manoeuvre, something way more agile and nimble, probably a RIB. These are rigid-hulled inflatable boats, nice and light-weight but with a collar designed to maintain buoyancy, even in bad seas. The military use them, lifeboat crews use them – even patrol boats looking for drugs operations like this. They ain't half sturdy and they ain't half nippy.

The prosecution claimed the bags would have been thrown off the back of the *Oriane* because all the side doors were alarmed and none of them went off.

If that's true, there's no way those bags would have mer-rily bobbed along in a nice tidy line waiting for us to calmly pick them up. If the bags landed in the prop wash, which – combined with the weather – would have been heaving that night, they would have instantly dispersed. Within seconds, they'd have spread way beyond the width of the boat, which is 40m wide; the turmoil of the *Oriane*'s wake would have hurled and chucked them – without any logic or pattern – left, right and centre.

Once that happened, it'd be impossible for me to retrieve one of them, never mind all eleven, inside three minutes. Especially on the *Galwad*. It can take two or three attempts just to pull a buoy up on the end of a string of pots – and that's a fixed object in the water. The *Galwad* would be like a dinosaur in that situation: a monstrous hindrance, painfully slow, when I'd need something instantly responsive, fast, lightweight – something I could turn on a sixpence in the blink of an eye.

Even if we saw one of the bags, I'd somehow have to get close enough so one of us could lean out with a grapple or hook or something. How do you do that off the sides of the *Galwad* in that weather? God help the poor bastard who tried. It'd be a miracle if he didn't go overboard. In the time it would have taken, the other bags would have been long gone. At least in a RIB I could go haring after them.

Maybe the bags were thrown over in one great, big, mesh cargo bag? Maybe they were – but it's definitely not what I would have accepted. Even if we were in a RIB, or the *Galwad*, how on earth would we be able to drag such a monumental weight on board?

Pushing such a lump off the *Oriane* in the first place would be hard enough, but once it hit the water it'd just carry on plummeting, getting heavier and heavier as it soaked up more and more water in the depths below. It certainly wouldn't merrily bob along on top of the surface. It'd just sink like a great big anchor.

Even if it did eventually bob up – and we'd be waiting a long time for that to happen – we'd somehow have to separate all the bags and that would take forever, especially in the weather. We'd also have to remain totally stationary – impossible in those waves, whatever boat we were in.

No, I wouldn't have wanted the bags chucked off the back because of the *Oriane*'s prop wash and the chaos that leaves in the water. I wouldn't have wanted them tied together in one large lump, either.

Instead, I'd have demanded the bags came off the side of the *Oriane*. If they couldn't be, because of the alarms, then find another cargo boat – or another mug instead of me.

It would be the only way to swerve the prop-wash mayhem. Once the bags were chucked off the side, and therefore heading towards the back of the boat, they'd get pushed away from it. The RIB would let me get up tight against the side of the *Oriane*, and then I could try to weave in and out to pick up the bags. It's not perfect and it's not foolproof and the weather would still cause havoc. But if I was really trying to make this work, it's what I'd do.

I would also have insisted that location devices were attached to the holdalls – or, at the very least, lights. Without either, I'd be looking for needles in a haystack.

My next priority – actually my number one – would be communications. I wouldn't have gone out that night relying on mobiles that I knew damned well couldn't possibly work in the Channel – or a clapped-out satellite phone that was ten years old and forever losing its signal.

I would have demanded a continuous and uninterrupted link to whoever was on the *Oriane* so when the pivotal moments came for the drop-off and pick up, we were both 100 per cent co-ordinated and certain what each of us was doing – and, critically, where we were both positioned. In those conditions, my senses and my experience would have been stretched to their limits: I'd have to make quick, instantaneous decisions every time a random wave crashed into us and potentially threw us off balance. I'd need to be 100 per cent sure the bloke dumping the bags could see me and hear me and wait for my instructions. Timing and accuracy would be everything.

I'd also need to be 100 per cent certain he was genuinely in on the operation and not just some random voice on the end of a line. We'd need to have an ID set up in advance, perhaps a code word that only we would know about – something to prove our identities to one another. Our lives, our freedom would be dependent on each other, after all.

Everybody knows an operation like this comes with the total certainty of a crippling prison sentence if you get caught. At the very least, I would have demanded encrypted phones, the sort used by the military, and I would have wanted to test them out first to make sure they worked – and they were untraceable. You've got to be some sort of imbecile not to realise the police could easily trace mobile and satellite records through the service providers.

I also wouldn't have let Vic on my boat. He was the alleged overseer but he could barely speak a word of English; he didn't even have a phrasebook with him. What possible use was he? If I needed to confirm the job had been completed then I would have made that call myself on my encrypted phone. I didn't need Vic for any part of the exercise whatso-ever. He brought nothing to the table. I would have insisted on being the only person in direct contact with the man on the Oriane and we wouldn't have put our phones down on one another until the operation was over.

I've tried laughing at the absurdity of Vic being the over-seer, with his £9.99 mobile bought at the last minute in Newport. The laugh keeps getting stuck somewhere between my stomach and mouth. The guffaws simply don't come out. I just feel tears welling in my eyes.

I'm assuming, I think fairly, that there would have been plenty of funding for an operation this big. I can't believe someone tries to deliver £53 million worth of cocaine on the cheap. This can't be some dozy little backstreet amateur thing.

There were millions of pounds at stake and I suspect some pretty unpleasant characters at the end of the line. One fuck-up and somebody dies. Those sort of people. Would they really leave it to a bunch of lobster fishermen they've never met – and a bloke with no English armed with a mobile that doesn't work? Would I have gone along with such a suicidal shambles?

I've spoken to plenty of drug dealers since I've been in prison. Getting the right phones is elementary to them – it's almost like an investment in their line of business. They don't buy pay-as-you-go shit from Carphone Warehouse and they don't rely on clapped out ten-year-old satellite phones.

Assuming I managed to pick up the bags successfully, I'd then be faced with what to do next. I certainly wouldn't have been dropping them off at Freshwater in broad daylight, only to pick them up again a few hours later, that's for sure. If I was stupid enough to do that, I would have strategically placed some pals on Tennyson cliffs purely to look out for anyone watching us. That's just basic.

I wouldn't have steamed out to where the pick-up allegedly happened, either. I would have sat my RIB on the other side of the Channel and waited for the *Oriane* to come on through. That way, I could have lined it up, passed it side-on – where the bags would be thrown – and then continued on to England, instead of turning around in atrocious seas. Everything would have been in one straight, uncomplicated line. Then I would have raced straight into any one of the little creeks scattered along the south coast and delivered my cargo – completely eliminating the need to dump them first on the Isle of Wight and then worry about how they get transported from there.

Yep, that's how I would have done it. The secret is in the details. It would take an immense amount of thought and planning and it definitely wouldn't be hatched inside twenty minutes around a table in a pub garden. *Cheers mate, see ya tomorrow, what can possibly go wrong?*

The prosecution and the jury weren't interested in those details, though. By eliminating them, it became easier for them to find us guilty. We were out on the sea that night, so was the *Oriane*. Therefore: Guilty.

Yet the details are what prove our innocence because they're so fundamental to what we did every day of our working lives. The way I tied knots, the ropes and the anchors I used, the mapping, the destinations and tracks, the bait, the lines and the pots, the way I steered the *Galwad* in bad weather, my knowledge and understanding of the sea. It's all embedded and ingrained in my hands, my brain, my body, my soul. It's ingrained in all of us. I wouldn't know how to change this bread and butter stuff, even if I tried. I'd only know how to carry on living like that, like I know how to breathe oxygen.

Yet, inexplicably, I abandoned all this knowledge and did all sorts of crazy, nonsensical stuff I'd never done before.

If you're going to find me guilty, at least find me guilty of the way I would have done it – and not the way you think it was done.

Your way is impossible.

Chapter 30

THE MISSING LOG

Right now, the truth is lying under impenetrable blocks of black ink that conceal its secrets like gigantic slabs of granite covering a churchyard grave. If we could peek underneath, we would prove our innocence.

The truth is this: A top-level police report exists that details every single minute-by-minute moment of Operation Disorient. I call it the Bonfield log, after its overseer, because that's what it is: an ultimate official diary of what everyone did, when they did it and what was happening over that entire weekend.

The truth is this: We barely knew the log existed and its contents were never explicitly revealed during our trial.

The truth is this: When we did actually see it, key information was redacted. Great blocks of black ink obliterated entries so nobody could read what was written underneath.

Incredibly, the Bonfield log wasn't the only revelation we discovered after our trial. My sister, Nicky, threw herself at our case, demanding paperwork that none of us had ever seen. A great chaotic mound of it – largely from Christopher's office – ended up on her lounge floor, none of it filed or sorted, much of it on handwritten scraps of paper that made little, if any, sense or barely seemed to be connected to anything.

Nicky spent hours and days and weeks and months and – ultimately – years ploughing through it all, painstakingly piecing together sections and bits that had been separated but, when put together, made some sort of logic. It was like a gigantic jigsaw puzzle made up of documents and emails and notes and single pieces of paper and tattered bits of note-books. Slowly she put the pieces together, itemising and then grouping them, transferring what she could to her computer and even managing to construct a timeline of the entire case. What she did was phenomenal and I'll never find a way of paying her back.

Once sections were sorted, she passed them over to me in Whitemoor and I'd pore over them, hunting for anything that might make a difference. Between us we slowly uncovered one bombshell after another. Sometimes we'd spot neatly typed passages in crucial documents we never knew existed; some-times we'd spot a scruffily written side note, hastily scrawled in almost-illegible handwriting by the margin of a page.

The log's overseer was Miles Bonfield, Operation Disorient's land-based silver commander, pretty much the man in charge. Everything that breathed and moved that night was reported back to him straight away and every single detail of it was writ-ten down in his log. *His radio link never mysteriously broke down.*

His entries prove conclusively that the *Vigilant* was watch-ing the *Oriane*, waiting for a boat like ours to suddenly appear and get too close. Around the same time the prosecution claimed we were picking up the drugs, the Bonfield log clearly states: 'UKBA cutter has visual on the MSC *Oriane*.'

Significantly, Bonfield makes no mention of the *Galwad*, and there's absolutely no mention of us scooping up bags.

That entry was made at 0141 British Summer Time (BST). Confusingly, Bonfield was using BST because that was the time on land. At sea, where Greenwich Mean Time (GMT) is used, it would have been logged as 0041. Both times are the same.

We didn't have this information during our trial. Then there's the stuff that *wasn't* in the Bonfield log that really should have been – if they'd actually happened. There's no record of us throwing anything overboard at Tennyson. At no time were any of Jeans' and Dunne's observations noted down. *Strange.*

There was another Bonfield shock to come as well.

Christopher knew of its existence but never really explained it to me. I was vaguely aware there was a document some-where in the background but I'd no idea how important it was. In fact, I do remember seeing something on his desk one day and asking, 'What's that?'

'Don't worry,' he replied. 'It's nothing of any concern.' *Was it the Bonfield log, Julian?*

He obviously had it, because it was buried within all the paperwork Nicky retrieved from his office after our trial. He knew its secrets but never revealed them in court. I suspect he had no option: he'd probably been allowed to know what had been written so long as he never referred to it, or used it as part of our defence. It was all part of the great carving up pro-cess behind the scenes: we'll tell you this, but you can't use it.

The legal system's very own black arts.

That pissed me off more than anything else. Why wasn't my defence allowed to refer extensively to the Bonfield log in court? Why couldn't we see what had been written down? If it helped prove our innocence, why couldn't we have access to its contents?

That was the stitch-up. How could something so funda-mental to a case – an official police log of what happened – be protected and kept secret when men's livelihoods and freedom were at stake? *How was that justice?*

My defence should have had the right to stop the trial at so many stages. When we learned about the spoilt log, the broken radio and the fact Jeans and Dunne had altered their statements. When the existence and contents of the Bonfield log became known to Christopher. At any of these stages, he should have been legally allowed to say, 'Hold on. We've got this information, it's come to us far too late, we can't work with it, my client's not even seen it, we haven't got time to go through it and build a proper defence. In the interests of justice, the trial needs to be stopped so we can have time to respond.'

There was none of that. If anything, my defence team carried on being obsessed with not upsetting the judge or anyone else for that matter.

The Bonfield cover-up still haunts me today. Without realising it, I was fighting with one arm tied behind my back. I still am. Even today, we've never seen what lies underneath the blacked out redacted passages. Why not? What are they hiding? The fact entries are blacked out is suspicious enough. Would I be wrong to think those slabs of black ink are hiding evidence that would destroy the police's own case? What other explanation could there be?

If I'm wrong, then prove it. Show us the Bonfield log without the redactions. It's my belief the log simply proves we were never there – and therefore totally destroys the case against us. It's indisputable that the *Vigilant* never saw us scooping up bags. If it had, it would have recorded that fact immediately in its own log, and not simply inserted the word 'spoilt'.

Next, it would have launched its RIB, zoomed in and boarded us before we'd had time to turn and head off. The UKBA regularly posts videos on YouTube of the very same cutter, *Vigilant*, doing exactly that. Racing up to boats in its RIB and boarding them so they can catch crews red-handed with whatever cargo they might have on board.

Why didn't that happen to us? It's so obvious it would have happened – had we done it. Being caught in the act pretty much makes their case watertight.

OK, let's pretend the *Vigilant*'s crew – that's all twelve of them including senior SOCO officers – were having a cup of tea at the time and simply weren't watching the *Oriane* when we unexpectedly pootled up. Let's pretend they incompetently failed to keep a constant eye on the only ship they were watching that night and simply didn't see us. Let's pretend that happened.

Let's forget the crew would have been in all sorts of shit for that alone. Instead, let's fast forward to the moment they do eventually spot us – lobster fishing – some four hours later. From then on, they are ordered to carry on watching us until we get back to Yarmouth. Which is what they did.

So, given these senior personnel on board the *Vigilant* have already screwed up the biggest single moment of the night, how come they make exactly the same mistake again fifteen hours later? How come, when we are allegedly throwing bags overboard at Tennyson, they don't zoom straight in and grab those bags out of the water? Even though it's a beautiful evening with crystal-clear visibility, how come that's not in their log – or Bonfield's – either?

Or were they all having another cup of tea?

Nicky was in no mood to surrender, though, and lodged an appeal with the Independent Police Complaints Commission (IPCC), this time focusing on the evidence given by Breen, Jeans and Dunne. She urged the commission to demand phone records and to visit the island, specifically Tennyson Downs.

She asked them to investigate the flightpath and take-off time of the surveillance plane.

At first, the IPCC seemed to be responsive and used some of its investigative powers to dig out more information. They actually got hold of DI Storey's phone billing records, which clearly showed Dunne *had* phoned two or three times around 7 p.m. – just after allegedly seeing us dumping bags at Tennyson. This had been denied in court. Dunne even phoned again later on in the evening, after we'd been arrested.

However, when the IPCC asked to see Dunne's records, they hit a brick wall. The data had inexplicably been stripped out. Yes, *stripped out.* Not deleted or expired. Someone had actually contacted the service provider and got the records removed.

The IPCC also managed to track down ten officers, all part of Operation Disorient, who hadn't given evidence in court. They confirmed they'd heard Dunne over the radio telling the loggist that 'six or seven bags' had been thrown off the *Galwad* at Tennyson.

It all sounded promising – until the whitewash. The IPCC released an intensely confusing sixty-page document that barely made a word of sense – other than there was no case to answer. The officers had, apparently, been working under difficult circumstances and yes, there may have been some management issues – but nothing a training course wouldn't resolve. OK, there'd been some 'inconsistencies' in what Jeans and Dunne had said but that didn't prove they'd made it all up.

Just as I'd feared, the IPCC were no different from the Court of Appeal – they never had any intention of rocking the boat, or upsetting their chums. They were simply firewalls designed to protect the system: the police, SOCA, the CPS, the prosecution, the judge, the jury … the verdict.

We remained guilty.

It felt like a stitch-up, although I'd seen it coming. I knew everyone back home would be devastated but, unlike them, I'd been surrounded by prisoners who'd been through similar appeals and seen them all brushed away. They'd warned me this would happen, so when it did it didn't hit me as hard as it did my family.

As much as I knew they'd shafted us, I resolved not to surrender. If I did, it'd eat me apart. I'd become resentful and angry overnight. If I allowed that to happen then being in prison would send me crazy.

I needed help though. Me, Nicky, my family – we were all trying our best but we were mugs waiting to be mugged by a system determined not to admit any mistakes. We didn't know how to play the game, we didn't know what legal rights we had or whether we could have access to any funding.

We were also about to discover more revelations that had been hidden away from us …

Chapter 31

FIGHTING BACK

The *Oriane* was a *third of a mile* away from us. It never got close enough for us to scoop up any bags.

We never crossed paths because the cargo boat had changed its course. It wasn't steaming through in a straight line at all; it wasn't manoeuvring in the way the jury had been told.

Unlike the *Vigilant*, the *Oriane* had seen our bright lights blazing away in the black night, it had noticed our blip on its radar screen and it had started turning away to make sure it kept a safe distance from us.

There was more.

Somebody had tampered with my Olex machine. Vital data that should have been embedded deep within its memory banks had simply vanished. Digital evidence that would have proved where we were – and where the *Oriane* had gone – was inexplicably missing.

I will never forget the moment Nicky told me all this. She'd walked into the visitors' room at Whitemoor, we'd hugged, like we always did, said a few 'how are yous' – and then sat opposite one another across a nasty melamine table.

We were clutching plastic cups of sweet tea, which Nicky had bought from the kitchen serving hatch, along with a polystyrene tray full of pasty-looking chips cooked by some of the inmates.

For a few moments I thought *Christ, she looks knackered*; her hair and coat were weather beaten, like they'd just come through a Force Eight of their own, and I thought about the five-hour slog she'd just endured to come to see me. Was I worth the effort? 'I'm sick of that A47,' she groaned. 'Bloody roadworks everywhere and, besides, it's pelting down outside.'

I stared into her eyes and I swear I suddenly saw the big sister I'd grown up with. There was mischief there and the ever-so-slight signs of a sparkle. I could tell Nicky had news – but what?

'What you up to then?' I asked. 'You got something you want to tell me?'

Suddenly there was no more small talk. She jumped straight in. 'The *Oriane* moved to the south at least ten minutes before it got anywhere near you,' she said, excitedly. She no longer looked quite so tired.

I let what she'd just said slowly sink in and, as I absorbed the news, I could feel my heart starting to pound heavily against my ribcage, like it wanted to explode from my body and ask a few questions of its own.

In court, the prosecution had never produced any physical data to prove where the *Oriane* was. All we had was Davidson insisting it had travelled in a straight line and then we'd crossed paths. There was no actual evidence, however, to show he was right.

'Bloody hell,' I mumbled. 'That makes total sense. That explains why I never saw it anywhere near me.

'It's the most basic, fundamental rule of the sea – all over the world. The *Oriane* was the overtaking vessel, so it *had* to give way to us. It's like following the Highway Code, any skipper would do it automatically. It moved to the south to get away from us.'

We fell silent for a few moments while I carried on thinking about what she'd just said. Even the suffocating tension inside Whitemoor suddenly didn't feel quite so oppressive.

Davidson had convinced the jurors that the *Oriane*'s course never wavered: it had moved across the Channel in pretty much one straight line. By edging over to the south, however, the *Oriane* was breaking that line and making the one and only manoeuvre guaranteed to keep us well apart.

There was a cluster of big ships in the Channel that night and the *Oriane* was one of the fastest, travelling at roughly a mile every three minutes. I'd already studied their tracks and, at times, they were slaloming with one another – overtaking just like cars on a motorway. You could never be sure which boat would be where at any one time; sometimes the gap separating them was so small, it'd be suicidal to nip in between them.

If I'd genuinely wanted to scoop up drugs, I'd have ideally wanted the *Oriane* to inch out to the north, away from the shipping lane and therefore away from any other boats. According to Nicky, the *Oriane* was doing the polar opposite.

Then I calmed down and my heart stopped beating so fast. 'Hang on, Nicky, how come you know all this? How on earth are we going to prove any of it?'

Her reply took my breath away. 'I found it while I was ploughing through all that paperwork,' she replied. 'I found some emails.'

Nicky then explained what she'd uncovered. Almost immediately after we'd been arrested, SOCA officers had contacted the company Davidson worked for, the international marine giants Brookes Bell. 'They wanted their advice,' she explained. 'They wanted to know what data they needed to take off the *Galwad* and the *Oriane* to prove your positions.'

Brookes Bell had replied, Nicky continued, and one of their experts, Mark Keenor, had told SOCA to get hold of data from the Electronic Chart Display and Information System (ECDIS).

I knew what that was: a hi-tech computerised chart – instead of a paper one – which shows a boat's position, speed and heading. It stores information mainly from radar and satellite readings, like GPS, and is basically an incredibly accurate electronic record. It's so powerful it can pick up and store the movements of just about everything for miles around – on the sea, or even in the air. The police were able to get most of that information from my Olex machine. However, they never presented in court the same data from the *Oriane*. *Why not?*

In fact, Davidson never once referred to ECDIS in court – even though Keenor had alerted him to its existence. In fact, Davidson's assistant, William Smith, had even downloaded the ECDIS data from the police spy boat, *Vigilant*. Nicky discovered a handwritten note Smith had scribbled down the side of a page that proved he'd used the *Vigilant*'s data to study where I'd steered the *Galwad*.

So how come the same data wasn't used to prove unequivocally where the *Oriane* went? It was a huge – and deeply suspicious – omission in the prosecution's case.

Nicky must have been reading my thoughts as I inhaled heavily, leaned back and stretched my arms out wide. 'There's only one thing for it, Jamie. We'll have to get the *Oriane*'s data ourselves,' she said. Which is exactly what she did. With funding from the *Mail on Sunday*, she paid the same Dutch marine company used by Davidson, QPS, to hand over their

GPS maritime records. That's when she discovered the *Oriane* had altered its course after seeing us that night.

It felt like we were unravelling material that could and should make a real difference but we still knew, deep down, we needed legal and professional help. Had we got something here that could give us grounds to appeal? Could we get the paths of the boats reanalysed by someone who had the credentials to be taken seriously? Could we find a way of challenging everything Davidson had stated as a matter of fact in court?

Again, Nicky came to the rescue. The *Mail on Sunday* had devoted a huge double-page spread to our story and the reporter who'd written it, David Rose, recommended we got in touch with a legal charity, Appeal.

That's when Nicky met the campaigning lawyer Emily Bolton, who specialised in miscarriages of justice and human rights cases. She listened to what my sister said, visited me in prison – and eventually all the lads individually – and agreed to represent us. It was a gigantic step forward.

Emily was softly spoken but I could see the fire in her eyes: this was a woman on a mission, someone intensely driven and determined to expose cases just like ours – where the non-disclosure of key evidence had led to a wrongful conviction.

She threw herself straight into the case, demanding material we never knew we were entitled to see, and in 2014 lodged an application to appeal with the CCRC, knowing it would take at least fourteen months simply to get a case officer allocated. That gave us time to carry on unearthing new evidence, especially stuff that would challenge what Davidson had said.

Nicky and Emily were sure the Olex machine was critical to a potential appeal but, understandably, they struggled to understand all the complex data that it contained and what it actually meant. My sister had even started randomly Googling Olex dealerships every time she had a question, then ringing them in the hope whoever answered might be able to help.

I remember her visiting me one day in Whitemoor and saying, 'Jamie, I've had a right result.'

'Oh, yeah, what's that then?'

'I phoned one of the Olex dealerships and they gave me the number of someone called Mal, who'd just retired and was an expert in this sort of stuff.'

'Go on … I'm listening …'

'So I called and the bloke who answered thought I was someone from his old office who was also called Nicky Green, so he heard me out!'

By the end of that conversation, Nicky had found our marine expert – someone who absolutely understood the innards of an Olex and all the technical complexities of GPS, ECDIS, satellite data, radar readings, charts, courses, tracks, bearings. Someone who knew the sea. Someone who had all the professional qualifications not to be brushed aside or ignored.

Emily phoned Mal shortly afterwards and he committed to helping us. His first priority was to focus on where the *Oriane* had really gone. We now knew it had started turning to the south whereas Davidson had kept it on the same, straight course. Our man looked at what the *Oriane* did once it started to turn, where it moved to and how far it kept away from us.

By doing that, he was able to present a completely different track to the one Davidson had given. The *Galwad* and the *Oriane* weren't close together at all – in fact, metal to metal, we were between 400 and 550m apart. That's at least a third of a mile.

Our tracks, he said, also proved this. The *Oriane* was first on the scene, and even though it had long gone by the time I steamed up, its track remained in the water. Our expert was now saying the track from the *Oriane* and the track from the *Galwad* were at least 180m apart.

Mal also uncovered something else – something more sinister. He wanted to examine the *Galwad*'s Olex machine but all the police returned was a cloned copy of the hard drive and, straight away, he could see something was wrong. Telltale signs only an expert could detect indicated stuff was missing; the police's cloned version didn't contain all the information that should have been there.

Data that would have also confirmed the *Oriane*'s exact position was mysteriously missing.

We knew the police had brought electronics experts on board the *Galwad* as soon as we were arrested and we knew they'd examined the Olex. We didn't know who they were or what they'd taken, though. *Had one of them tampered with the Olex?*

All Mal's new marine evidence and findings were added to our appeal but we realised it would trigger all sorts of questions. Would some smart-arse say, 'Even if your expert is correct, those bags would still have drifted straight towards the *Galwad*, wouldn't they?'

That was something we needed to tackle, so Emily contacted the Plymouth Marine Laboratory, which had a computer model capable of analysing such a scenario. By inputting the position and direction of both the *Oriane* and the *Galwad*, and by adding data about the weather, wind and tidal conditions – even the dates – they were able to recreate the scene and work out where the bags would have gone once they hit the water.

The laboratory concluded the bags would definitely not have merrily bobbed along in a nice neat line straight into our hands. In fact, they would have immediately drifted away from us in an east–north–east direction. Their report was added to our appeal – along with something else …

Chapter 32

NAMED AND SHAMED

It felt like two *fuck-you moments*. Two key pieces of additional information that would surely swing the CCRC appeal in our favour.

The first concerned two of the main police witnesses against us. They weren't squeaky clean – far from it. They'd been named and shamed by an appeal judge in another, unrelated trial. He'd ruled that one of them had persuaded local officers to make up evidence, while the other had misheard what she'd been told over the radio. Sound familiar?

The judge was so appalled by their behaviour, he even mentioned my name and said it was possible the pair had done the same in our case.

The other *fuck-you moment* concerned the *Oriane*. Not only could we prove it wasn't where police marine expert Davidson had said, we could also prove it wasn't in the Brazilian port where the cocaine had allegedly been loaded.

You've got to hang on, Nikki.

I was truly gobsmacked when my sister told me about Chief Observation Officer Gary Breen and the Police Loggist

Louise Parry. *Remember them?* Breen was the one who'd asked Jeans and Dunne to meet him in his car after the debrief. That's when they altered their statements. That's when they said they hadn't seen us throwing six or seven dark bags overboard, they'd actually seen ten to twelve holdalls attached to a rope and a bright red buoy.

Breen then got them to sign the debrief record and didn't spot that they'd signed it on the wrong page, therefore giving the entirely false impression they'd attended.

Parry was the one who said she'd misheard what they'd said and written it down incorrectly. She was the one who told the court, 'Seven and ten can sound the same on a fuzzy radio.'

I'd always suspected the jurors found us guilty because they fundamentally believed the police would never lie but we probably would. However, would they have felt the same about Breen and Parry had they known about their track record and how their behaviour mirrored exactly what happened in my case?

Again, it was a drugs trial. Alexander McGuffie was one of five convicted of importing cocaine from the Caribbean. Surveillance officers at Gatwick Airport claimed they saw a woman, allegedly carrying the drugs, make eye contact with McGuffie as she walked through the arrivals hall and pump her fist, as if to say, 'I've got them.'

Breen was the bronze commanding officer on that case and Parry the loggist, while two local coppers were the surveillance officers – just like Jeans and Dunne had been.

McGuffie was found guilty but appealed. My sister Nicky sent a load of our paperwork to his legal team to show the obvious similarities. Once again, Parry admitted she may have made a mistake when recording what the two local officers reported seeing.

Also, when Breen was asked whether he was under investigation in any other cases (i.e. mine), strangely he said 'no'. He never mentioned us, even though he was very much at the heart of our IPCC complaint, along with the whole fiasco of the altered statements.

McGuffie won his appeal and, significantly, the judgment stated that a jury could conclude both Breen and Parry 'were prepared to break the rules as regards compiling observation logs'.

Then came the killer bit. Referring specifically to our case, the judgment continued:

> There is a sustainable basis for a court to conclude that DC Breen had taken steps to persuade two local officers to give false observation evidence that linked the fishing boat with the holdalls that were later discovered.

That really did feel like a *fuck-you moment*; I wanted to punch the air as my sister Nicky told me the details. 'Are you telling me the judge actually said that in his summing up?' I asked, barely able to believe that could be the case.

'Yes,' she replied. 'That's pretty much what he said and we can include it in our CCRC application.'

There was more we could add to our CCRC case, as well. One question had always plagued me, Christopher had mentioned it in his summing up and there'd never been a convincing answer. How do we know there was ever any cocaine on board the *Oriane*? After all, it couldn't possibly be the mother ship unless there were drugs on board. Take away the drugs and the case collapses. Even if there were, who put them there – and who threw them off?

The prosecution had somehow managed to sweep aside the fact there were no phone calls, or emails or texts or anything at all that linked Beerey to the unidentified masterminds of this operation. They simply announced he was the Isle of Wight supremo and to hell with the fact there was nothing to show he'd made any contact with a mystery international drugs cartel beforehand.

The prosecution couldn't be quite so cavalier, however, when it came to the *Oriane*. They couldn't simply say, 'This is the boat that carried the drugs' without making some attempt to explain why they were so sure.

So, midway through the trial and without any prior warning, they suddenly had a stab at doing just that. 'We've some important new evidence that shows a link to Brazil,' they triumphantly announced. *What the fuck?*

We'd no idea this was coming and had been given no advance warning. Christopher immediately leapt up to protest. The judge asked the jurors to leave the courtroom so he could rule on whether the prosecution's new information would be admissible.

They'd got hold of statements from the Brazilian police that suggested a Serbian, Damar Simic, was one of the possible drug suppliers. He'd been in two ports where the *Oriane* had docked – Navegantes and Santos – and he'd apparently met an unidentified member of the ship's crew in one of them, Navegantes, on 12 May.

A statement from officer Renato Prado claimed Simic had been under surveillance and had used a RIB to transfer drugs to a cargo ship in Santos. The Brazilian statements hinted at a large police operation and even mentioned thousands of phone taps.

Christopher argued that we'd had no opportunity to check any of this out and the judge, to his credit, agreed. The jury would not be allowed to hear any of the details.

However, the mystery man in the public gallery, the former police community support officer we saw hand-in-hand with one of the jurors, would have heard every single word of what the judge had just been told. I've often wondered: *Did he pass it all on to the jurors while they were having a cosy coffee together?*

Nicky and I were discussing all this during one of her visits. 'Surely there must be records that show where the *Oriane*'s been, which ports it docked in – and when,' she said. 'How do we even know it was definitely in Brazil?' A few weeks later she came back with the answers – and it blew the prosecution's picture to smithereens.

The *Oriane* was never where they said it was on the dates they said it was.

On the day it was meant to be in Navegantes it was around 600 miles away at a completely different port. In fact, it *never went* to Navegantes. Furthermore, it was meant to have arrived in Santos on 13 May – but didn't actually get there until four days later.

The Brazilian police statements and the 'thousands of phone taps' never once mentioned the *Galwad* – and never once indicated the drugs were being sent to the UK. As for the cargo ship in Santos that Simic had allegedly transferred drugs on to, it turned out to be the … MSC *Nuria*.

Apparently it's the largest container ship to have ever been built in Romania. It was under Brazilian police observation – but the *Oriane never was*.

All this was added to our CCRC case. Some part of me actually thought we'd produced something pretty convincing. Maybe Nikki would actually get to see us walk free.

Then, suddenly, none of it seemed to matter any more…

Chapter 33

HANDCUFFED IN THE PULPIT

They sent armed police to my wife's funeral. Just in case I tried to make a run for it.

Hundreds and hundreds of mourners turned up to say goodbye to my Nikki. They squeezed into the chapel until there wasn't any more room and the doors had to be kept open so people outside could still follow the service. Then there was the police.

They sat in vans, clutching guns, just in case.

Even when I clambered up to the pulpit to say a few words, they kept me handcuffed. I stood in front of a packed congregation chained to a prison guard, who was squatting behind me, desperately trying to duck out of view. Everybody could see he was there.

They honestly thought I was going to do a runner at my wife's funeral.

Nikki would have gone ballistic. She'd have told them all to 'eff off' and she'd have said it straight to their faces, too. 'You've no place here, this is my bloody funeral, sod off the lot of you.' That's what she would have said.

It was just the same when they begrudgingly let me see her as she lay dying in a hospice on the island. I tried to stroke her face but that's difficult when you're handcuffed to a prison guard. They thought I might do a runner then, as well.

Prison did its best to separate us from the moment I was sentenced. I didn't see Nikki for at least eighteen months once I'd been needlessly transferred to Whitemoor. Her chemo was intense during that period and there was no way she could have endured the five-hour journey. So every day we talked on the phone instead, clinging to our memories, talking about the kids, our parents, the case. We rarely talked about her bastard disease.

I knew what she was doing. I knew her tactics. She was picking up the phone and thinking, *If he thinks I'm all right, then he's going to be all right.* She had too much grace to tell me about her own pain. So she made sure we talked about the case and not the cancer.

Nikki believed in my innocence 100 per cent. I know that with complete, overwhelming certainty. She believed in all of us. She never hesitated or wavered once. She never even asked me, it was simply understood. It didn't need questioning, it didn't need saying. She'd seen it in my face, in my eyes, in my body language, in everything I'd said and done after our arrests.

I'm also certain of this: she'd have known if I had done it. She'd have been able to tell with just one glance; any one instinct would have found me out. I couldn't have pulled off a lie as big as that in front of Nikki. She knew me too well: she knew my mannerisms, my telltale signs. She knew what my guilt would look like, smell like, sound like.

I couldn't have faced her, day in and day out, and kept the pretence going or the lie alive. She wouldn't have forgiven me, either. She wouldn't have said, 'Never mind, Jamie, it was worth trying.'

She would have unleashed all shades of hell instead. She would have been so furious with me for tossing away our lives on something so stupid, so insane, so ill-prepared, so badly organised and so illegal. 'What about Maisy and Poppy and Jesse? What about me?' she would have screamed.

Instead, she stood solidly by my side throughout and the only agony was the distance the system kept between us. There was no way she could have handled the arduous journey to Whitemoor and I fully understood that.

So I kept protesting and arguing and pleading to be transferred somewhere closer to the Isle of Wight. The system wasn't having it, though, no matter how cruel the decision. However, it did eventually show one tiny chink of humanity by letting me accumulate visits so I could sometimes be temporarily transferred to a jail closer to the island – usually Winchester. As much as I hated that dump, it was worth it.

I'll never forget the first time I saw Nikki again. I hadn't seen my wife for almost eighteen months, I hadn't seen what cancer and chemotherapy and steroids had done to her. I hadn't even guessed it because every time we spoke on the phone she made damned sure I didn't start worrying about her. Then she walked into Whitemoor. The main doors into the visitors' room opened and the usual rush of families and friends poured in. I couldn't see Nikki anywhere at first until suddenly a painfully thin woman started slowly walking towards me through the chaos of bodies and tables and chairs. She was trying to smile, trying to lighten up my life.

She must have seen the shock in my face. I still hate myself for that. The next day I rang her first thing. 'Nikki, you must come again, I'm sorry that was such a bad visit, I have to keep seeing you.' She did, of course, in between more relentless bouts of chemo.

The more she visited, the more accustomed I became to seeing how the ceaseless treatment would play havoc with her body. Sometimes I'd see her and she'd be painfully thin, other times she'd balloon under the weight of steroids. It was like seeing a different person every time.

Even then, we fell into a trap of not finishing sentences when we talked. If Nikki was trying to say something that I instinctively thought would be too painful to hear, I'd interrupt and finish it for her with something like, 'Don't worry, I know what you mean, there's no need to say it.'

Nikki understood what was going on far better than me. In 2015, she started making plans; at first, I didn't realise what she was up to. In September she suddenly went away on a family holiday abroad with her mum and dad, the kids and her sister. She'd never been one for foreign holidays before.

Then, as autumn approached, she managed to clamber back on one of her beloved horses. They'd meant so much to her throughout her life. Looking back, I now realise the holiday, and riding that horse, they weren't simply sudden impulses. Nikki was shrewd, she was having a last hurrah. Me? I was in denial, not wanting it to happen and not facing up to it.

The last time I saw Nikki face to face was in Winchester, before I was transferred to Erlestoke, near Devizes. It's Category C and much closer to the Isle of Wight than Whitemoor and Lowdham Grange. It's less hostile, too – except the door still slams shut every night.

Nikki and I had kept talking on the phone but I'd begun to realise the medication wasn't working like it had before and the chemo wasn't having the same effect. It wasn't until I saw her on that visit, though, that I saw how devastating her weight loss had become. She hadn't been able to eat properly, she couldn't hold food down.

'Look, I've been to see Dr Marshall, I've had some scans and …'

'Don't Nikki, I know what you're telling me. You don't have to say any more. I understand.'

I realised the CCRC appeal had become a target for her; she was clinging to the hope that she'd see me released before the cancer got her. The last thing I wanted was to take that hope away.

'Is there any news, Jamie? Only …'

I rushed to finish that sentence for her as well. 'I know what you're trying to say, Nikki. I'm pushing as much as I can, believe me. The lawyers are all over it.'

Nikki and I never *talked* about dying. That visit was the closest we got. When we finished each other's sentences, there'd usually be a silence between us – as though we were saying the missing words over in our minds but not speaking them out loud. That's when we'd *think* about dying.

Nikki was taken into a hospice on the Isle of Wight in November 2015. A week or so later, a member of staff called Erlestoke and said, 'You'd better let Jamie come over.'

I was allowed to see her the following Friday, escorted by two prison officers. I stayed handcuffed to one of them as we walked into Nikki's room. She was half propped up against a pillow and I just about managed to lean over and give her a cuddle before I could feel the chain tugging against me.

Every movement I tried to make from then on was governed by that chain: if I stood up, the guard stood up with me, if I walked round Nikki's bed, the guard had to do the same. It felt like the Grim bloody Reaper was in there, casting his black shadow over us. When there was no conversation, and the room fell quiet, it was his breathing that filled the silence. If he moved, or fidgeted, I'd suddenly feel my body getting yanked back towards him.

I remained cuffed even when I used the toilet – we some-how managed to get the chain to stretch under the loo door. I mean, really? Where was I going to go from a toilet with no windows?

I'm sure he was uncomfortable with the situation, too, but there was no escaping the fact he was in the room, watching my wife's final, precious moments, seeing her at her most vul-nerable, witnessing something intensely private. Something no stranger should have been there to observe.

Nikki was just like me: she automatically kept her feelings and emotions to herself, even in such extreme circumstances. She wouldn't have wanted to share weakness and pain with anyone – least of all a prison guard. She wouldn't have wanted him to hear, or see or get to know the personal stuff. So the words Nikki and I should have exchanged that afternoon were never said; our space had been invaded and it was too suffocating for both of us. The shadow in that room was too big, too overwhelming.

I'm not blaming the guard. He had a job to do and orders to follow. He tried to look away, he tried to pretend he wasn't listening, but it was all a charade and we all knew it. There would never be a moment when it would just be me and Nikki saying goodbye to one another. In fact, we never said 'goodbye' to one another. We craved that solitude and that space but it never came.

We would have talked about our kids, we would have reminisced, we would have laughed about our first dates and all the happiest memories. We would have reminded each other why we fell in love and why we'd never lost that devotion. We'd have remembered life when we were always together, and we would have told each other we wouldn't have swapped those days for the world.

I was allowed to stay for two or three hours. Nikki was tiring by then and it felt the right time to go. I leaned towards her and – as the chain pulled the guard closer to her bed, so close I could sense his body leaning over behind mine and his stale-coffee breath exhaling against my neck – I whispered: 'I love you, Nikki.'

When I returned to Erlestoke, the duty governor on the wing came to see me and said, 'I'll arrange for you to go back again on Sunday.' It was a rare moment of sensitivity and I immediately phoned my sister and said, 'I can come back on Sunday, make sure Nikki knows will you?'

One of the screws knocked on my cell door the night before and said, 'I'll see you tomorrow, Greeny, I'm coming down with you in the morning.'

'I'll be ready, don't you worry about that.'

I got up nice and early on the Sunday, but nobody came to get me. Surprised, I went down to the screws' room and asked, 'What's happening? We're supposed to be leaving for the hospice. Where is everyone?' They didn't know what I was talking about; I started getting agitated, so they called the duty governor, who turned up thirty minutes later. She marched in, took one look at me and said, 'You can't go.'

'What do you mean, I can't go?'

'We haven't got the staff to take you.' It sounded like an unconvincing lie; she looked nervous and uncomfortable.

'But the bloody guard told me himself last night that he was taking me. What's happened since then?'

It didn't take me long to work it out. To this day, I remain convinced the police, SOCA, the system – whoever it was – stuck the boot in. *Jamie Green was a security risk. He's got millions stashed away somewhere. The only reason he wants to see his wife again is because he's planning to do a runner.*

I'm convinced that's what happened and everything that was to follow only underlined my suspicion. Nikki died on 30 November, three weeks after I'd been allowed to see her.

She was 50. The chaplain came and banged on my cell door
about nine in the morning and, as soon as I saw his face, I knew.
I'd always called her Stormin' Norman, she was bulletproof
to me and in many ways she proved that. First they gave her
six months, then eighteen months – but she'd hung on for almost
six years, enduring chemo and treatment all the way through.
I don't know how she found the strength or the courage.

The system did everything it could, however, to turn
her funeral into a nightmare. I didn't know whether I'd be
allowed to attend until the morning itself. I was going crazy;
once again, I was sure someone in HQ was saying, 'He's plotting to escape.'

The fact I'd behaved myself every single day in the prison
system, the fact I'd gradually gone from a Category B prisoner
to Category C, made no difference whatsoever. They genuinely thought I had the money and the callousness to do a
runner at my own wife's funeral.

First I was grilled by the main security governor, who read
me the riot act, spelling out what I could and could not do.
Then he added, 'Don't think for one second you can have a
drink, either.'

'You what?'

'You heard me, don't start playing silly buggers with us.'

'You honestly think I'm going to my wife's funeral so I can
go on the piss? Is that what you're saying?'

'Just forget any thoughts about going to the wake. Don't
get your family and friends to start pressurising my officers
into letting you go. That's what I am saying.'

'For Christ's sake …'

'You'll have four prison officers with you all the time.'

'Four? I'm a Cat-C prisoner, why the hell do I need
four officers with me?'

'Because that's how I say it is. If you keep on like this, you won't be going.'

Those were his final words on the matter and those were the words still bouncing inside my brain when I woke on the morning of the service: 15 December 2015. I'd genuinely no idea if they'd let me go, or whether they'd try to fob me off like they had with the hospice.

That's one of the hardest realties of prison life. You're stripped of everything. You've no rights, no say, no influence. You're totally at the mercy of the regime. Even when I realised they were going to let me go, I was given another lecture: 'You're not going to do anything stupid today are you, Jamie?'

'Like what? It's my wife's funeral, for fuck's sake.'

'You're not going to take anything, or try to bring anything back with you?'

There we had it. Not only were they paranoid I'd try to escape, they were also worried I'd either try to gulp gallons of alcohol, take drugs, or, worse, try to bring some back with me. That was all I was in their eyes. They didn't see a man who was grieving for the only woman he'd ever loved.

I wasn't entitled to be human in prison.

The next shock was the amount of security they put in place. I left Erlestoke with four officers but I'd no idea there were loads more on the ferry as we crossed over to the island.

Even they never anticipated what lay ahead. As we turned off the main road to enter the crematorium, there were cars wedged tightly together along the road edges and long lines of mourners walking slowly towards the chapel. The four officers sat with me couldn't believe what they were seeing. 'Christ, how come there's so many people here? What's all this about then?'

It was the only time I laughed. 'They're here for my Nikki. This is what she meant to them.' I could see the guards were beginning to look nervous, especially when people started looking up and recognising me through the van windows. 'Jamie. Look, there's Jamie. We're here for you, mate.'

We were in a little, dark-blue people carrier that parked up behind the chapel. One of the guards jumped out to assess the situation and came running back within seconds. 'Bloody hell, there's hundreds of them out there.'

And there was. We sat in the van waiting while the mourners filed into the chapel. I asked whether I could be allowed to carry Nikki's coffin as it went in but that was refused. However, one of the screws did have the decency to say, 'Do you want to get out and see some of the people?'

I was grateful for that so I stood by the chapel doors. One after the other came up and asked me how I was, or told me how sorry they were. Some even tried to give me a cuddle, despite the fact I was chained to a guard. A lot of them were from Nikki's side of the family. 'It's good to see you, Jamie. We can't believe this has happened.'

Then there were mates of mine, who I'd known from schooldays and, of course, my own family.

That stopped when the tide of people walking up the road started to part and a horse and cart began to appear, getting ever closer. That was a big moment. That brought it home. I walked over and stood on a grass verge with the screw, alongside the flower beds. Once it had halted outside the chapel doors, I saw Jesse, my old man, Nikki's dad and her brother-in-law, Steve, go to the back and slowly lift her coffin on to their shoulders. At that point, a bugle sounded, just like it would have done at one of the many hunts she'd always loved to attend.

I just stood there, cuffed and chained, too conscious of the shackles to raise my arm and wipe away the tears filling my eyes. For a second, I wanted to believe it was just a terrible scene in a terrible dream. It was like watching my life coming to an end. Who was I without Nikki? How could I carry on without her? *Come back, Nikki.*

Once the coffin was inside the chapel, I walked in. Row after row was packed, there was nowhere left to stand and it was clear many more mourners were left outside, trying to hear the service through open doors. There must have been at least 500 of us in total. I walked down to the front where I was allowed to sit, still cuffed and chained to a guard, with the families.

The service began, there were readings and music – including one of Nikki's favourite songs, Ronan Keating's 'Life is a Rollercoaster'. Then I got up to speak. That's when I climbed up to the pulpit, still cuffed, still chained to my guard. He was trying desperately to crouch and stoop and keep out of sight. He did his best but I doubt there was a single person, including the lot outside, who didn't see him there.

I was incredibly aware of the cuffs and the chain, and their degrading grip. I desperately wanted to stand there, in front of Nikki's family and friends and all the people we loved and cared for and not let them see what the prison system and justice had reduced me to at my own wife's funeral.

It was humiliating. Those hideous restraints felt like intruders, they had no right to be present. I looked towards the mourners, then turned to see Nikki's coffin. I wanted her to see me as she had when we were together, free, happy, in love. Not shackled, not shorn of everything I'd ever been to her.

It was like a final, demeaning, public sentencing. *Jamie Green, you are sentenced to twenty-four years and to stand at your wife's funeral wearing handcuffs, chained to a prison guard.*

I did all I could to keep the cuffs and chain as low as possible behind the pulpit and talked about how Nikki and I had met, how we'd started a life together, how happy and comfortable we were in each other's company, how we saw the world. I talked about the pride and joy we felt for our kids and how we'd always told one another that our life was a bit of a rollercoaster – just like Ronan Keating's song: 'We found love, so don't fight it, life is a rollercoaster, just gotta ride it.'

In my own quirky, embarrassed, probably clumsy way I finished by saying how much I already missed her. 'You'd better have a spare ticket ready for the next ride on the rollercoaster, Nikki, because I want to be sat right next to you.' It was hard to say.

I didn't know about the armed guards until we were leaving. As the mourners left all the access points on the roundabout close to the crematorium, there were police vans at each of the main turnings. Inside, for all to see, were police and guns.

Even the guards with me could see how wrong that was. How out of place and unnecessary. We weren't 500 terrorists leaving a convention. People were leaving Nikki's service in tears; armed police were the last thing they needed to see as they headed off to the wake. One of the guards turned to me and said, apologetically, 'That shouldn't have happened.'

I shrugged. Nothing surprised me any more. A system that told me I could visit my dying wife for a second time in the hospice and then changed its mind on the morning I was about to leave; a system that wouldn't even let me know until the last minute whether I could attend my wife's funeral; a system that kept me in handcuffs and chains as I spoke from the pulpit in a crematorium. That same system wouldn't be bothered about sticking a few armed guards bang in front of mourners as they left a chapel in tears.

'I haven't been judged on how I've behaved and acted within the prison system,' I said. 'I've been given no bloody credit for the person I am and how I've handled being locked away all this time.'

Chapter 34

VICTIMS

Nikki never got to hear the CCRC's verdict. The bastards took four torturous years to announce their decision. My wife had been dead for nearly three of them.

That four-year wait was soul destroying. As much as everyone told me to get on with life, and not think about it, that was pretty much impossible. There's nothing inspirational about being in prison; when visitors come you can't tell them about all the fantastic things you've been doing inside. Prison makes you a Not Very Interesting Person.

I got sick of asking, 'What's going on?', knowing deep down that there was no news but clinging to the tiniest hope I could be wrong. I hated myself for urging Nikki to hang on, that we were pushing hard, it wouldn't be long now.

It still sickens me that the appeals system was that slow; it felt like some sort of cruel, perverted punishment with so much at stake. Was someone, somewhere, laughing at me, daring me to dream about going home, holding Nikki, seeing the kids, repairing the *Galwad* and going back out to sea? How could

I erase those thoughts of freedom when that's exactly what the appeal was ultimately all about?

I'd never realised the system could be that inhumane. For God's sake, four years. It was like another sentence on top of the one I'd already got.

Sometimes inmates would stop me in a corridor, or in the gym, and say, 'What's happening with the case then, Jamie?' I might as well have carried a little tape recorder with me and pressed 'play' each time they asked. 'Well, we're waiting for this, we're waiting for that.' One look at their faces told me what they were thinking: *You must think we're fuckin' stupid. You told us that six months ago and nothing's happened.*

My sister, my mum and my old man, my kids – they all kept coming to see me but I'm sure I wasn't much company. I hadn't got anything meaningful left to say.

It felt like my life – all our lives – were on hold. There was never any feedback, no sudden questions because maybe someone wanted something clarifying. That would have been OK, a sign, at least, that our application was being debated. All we got – every three months – was a snivelling letter saying, 'You won't hear from us for another three months, unless we've reached a decision'.

Then, after all that time in limbo, a provisional state-ment of reasons suddenly appeared out of the blue and, in a split second, we realised four years had just been flushed right down the pan. The appeal was rejected but, worse, was the manner in which they did it.

Their reasoning made little sense. In fact, it was like they'd barely read or understood the points we'd made and totally misinterpreted the entire application.

The McGuffie case, and the fact Breen and Parry had both been damned, was written off as irrelevant. Even though the bloody judge had singled me out and said Breen and Parry could have been up to the same antics in our case. *Sorry judge, we're the CCRC and we don't care.*

Then, they totally dismissed the evidence that proved the *Oriane* had never been in the Brazilian ports named by the prosecution. Instead, the CCRC said that was also irrelevant because the drugs could have been transferred to the *Oriane* anywhere between South America and the UK. It didn't much matter where. *You what?*

It absolutely did fuckin' matter where. The prosecution had identified Santos and Navegantes and intended to tell the jury the *Oriane* was in both ports on specific dates. If the judge hadn't stopped them, that's what they'd have presented in court as fact. That's how they were connecting the *Oriane* to the drugs.

We'd unearthed new evidence that proved that version of events was fundamentally wrong. The CCRC, however, simply glossed over this by coming up with their own alternative explanation. 'Oh well, maybe the drugs went on board somewhere else.'

Yeah, and maybe the drugs were never on board the *Oriane* at all, which means it was never the mother ship, which means the entire case against us was false. *Are we making this up as we go along? Is that how this appeals lark works?*

If the very basis of the prosecution's case was fundamentally flawed – and the cargo ship they said was carrying the drugs was never in the ports they named – doesn't that mean they've got the wrong boat all together, or there were never, ever, any drugs on it? *Isn't that what you bastards should have been worrying about?*

How could it be an appeal body's job to come up with an imaginary explanation to help shore up a massive hole in the prosecution's case? The CCRC isn't there to help the prosecution's case by filling in missing gaps and correcting their basic errors. *Is it?* The CCRC is meant to be an impartial safety net to make sure fundamental principles of the British judicial system are rigidly followed. *Isn't it?*

Not long after, using the Freedom of Information Act, we discovered the CCRC had even held private little chats with the SOCA officers we'd accused of stitching us up. The CCRC never had any chats with me, though.

They just brushed it all under the carpet. The system had done what it always did: protected itself from people like us.

In 2018, the CCRC Commissioner, David James Smith, was interviewed about our appeal on Victoria Derbyshire's BBC morning chat show. I can't recall his exact words but it was effectively: 'The only way I would have sent this case on to the Court of Appeal would have been if the *Galwad* had never left the harbour.'

There have been many times when I've wondered whether the system is deliberately winding down the clock and the CCRC was simply the start of that process. They didn't need four bloody years, they could have made their minds up inside six months, easily. They just strung us out.

Scott and Dan are now both out on parole so that's two of the lads sorted. I've done ten years so far, same as Beerey and Vic. Parole is on the horizon for all three of us, so is the system just letting us burn up time?

Is it simply planning to humour us by pretending to consider our appeals so, once the months have turned into years, it can generously say, 'Good news, lads, you're up for parole. Keep your heads down, be good and you'll be going home soon. No need to fight for justice any more.'

Is that the game? Are we just scraps of rubbish in a great big recycling bin that will eventually churn us out in little bits?

The system is designed to sweep up people like us. It needs convictions, or else questions will be asked. Once we're safely locked away, it's then designed to keep us there – guilty or not. Who cares?

The last thing the system wants is to admit mistakes so it makes sure all these appeal bodies are manned by the right sort of people – former policemen ideally, ex-magistrates perhaps, men and women who've served on committees, pillars of the establishment. Anyone who doesn't need reminding, when they see a quiet nod or a gentle wink of the eye, where their loyalties must lie.

These people don't know, or can't see, when the police have done something wrong because it's the same way they were taught as well, so it must be correct. They're not looking to embarrass their mates down the road or turn upside down all the values to which they've spent their lives adhering. They are backing their own. If a defendant says, 'This never happened,' then he's automatically lying. If it's one of their own who's screwed up, then it's, 'Oh he must have made a mistake, maybe he was tired.'

Why are there no ex-convicts, or inmates who've had their convictions quashed, ever on these panels? After all, they've got real insight into what goes on. They've been on the receiving end of it, just like us.

That's how it goes round. What a shower of shit. Organisations like SOCA eventually get a bad reputation because so many cases keep going to appeal, so what do they do? Change their bloody name, or rebrand as they like to say. Now they're calling themselves NCA (National Crime Agency) but it's the same group of people. And each time they rebrand, they can bury a load of shit. Each time someone else who's been wrongfully convicted asks for disclosure of evidence never made available, they can say, 'Sorry. That's not available any more, that was the other lot, SOCA. We're the NCA.' Just watch, they'll be called something else in a few years' time. That's how they insulate themselves.

I'm sorry, Nikki. We were shafted. The CCRC was a sham and we were the victims. Casualties of the fuckin' system, that's what we all are.

Chapter 35

PROVING OUR INNOCENCE

We submitted a new appeal in 2019. I've told Nikki all about it; I've told her this one's got a real chance. It'll be going in front of an appeal judge and not the bastards from the CCRC. I speak to Nikki every day, of course I do. I couldn't survive without knowing she's still there.

This is what I've told her:

* We can now *prove* a surveillance plane *did* fly over Tennyson at 7 p.m.
* We can also *prove* a rigid-hulled inflatable boat (RIB) zoomed straight to the same spot at the same time – just minutes after Jeans and Dunne allegedly saw us chucking bags overboard. Nobody ever told us about this.

This brand-new marine evidence is the crux of our latest appeal, which was submitted in April. It only came to light after Emily fought for the right to see it, even though it should have always been made available to us. Immediately after our arrests, William Smith (Davidson's colleague) downloaded the ECDIS data from the spy boat, *Vigilant*. He saved the files on floppy discs but they were never heard of again – until Emily came along.

That this happened makes me sick to the core: it's non-disclosure in its vilest form. It's a clear example of evidence never surfacing that could have kept innocent men out of prison. How much lower can the system sink?

It's not the only example of non-disclosure that we've had to stomach, either. There were also the more subtle forms, like deliberately not interviewing key witnesses and experts, or choosing not to demand records and statements – such as the flightpath of the ghost plane. *We're victims of it all, Nikki.*

The ECDIS data is the standout most crucial, however. It not only shows every move the *Vigilant* made that night, it also reveals exactly where the *Oriane* went – and conclusively proves it didn't do what Davidson had said in court. The cargo boat never carried on in a straight line that dissected our track. Instead, it took evasive action and altered its course to keep a good distance between us. Just like the QPS data had revealed. Just like Mal had said. Only this time the information was coming directly from the police's own spy boat.

According to the *Vigilant*'s data, the track for the *Oriane* was nowhere near Davidson's line. By manoeuvring to the south in the way it did, the *Oriane* created a gap of at least 500m – which means I could have never been close enough to pick up any bags.

It's indisputable, Nikki.

Unlike us, Davidson knew this information was available. He could have used it if he'd wanted. His own assistant had downloaded it, and yet he never once referred to it in court. *How come?*

Why didn't he use it to prove where the *Oriane* went? Why didn't he use the same, definitive source when it mattered the most?

There's another mystery concerning Davidson's court evidence, as well. It's disappeared. Emily applied to see all the transcripts of every witness. They were all made available, except for one. The one whose evidence probably got us convicted. Davidson's evidence has simply vanished, apparently because the company that transcribed his testimony went bust and his records were never returned.

Emily asked whether anyone else had ever applied to see his transcripts. To this day, she's never had a reply to that question.

The ECDIS data also answers – once and for all – the mystery of the ghost plane. The one I saw with my own eyes yet the police insisted was never there. It was. The radar on their own spy boat Vigilant logged both its time and path as it flew over.

The same data also revealed something else, something entirely unexpected that we never had a hint of. About 50 minutes after we had gone mackereling off Tennyson, a RIB – or something else small and nippy – raced straight to the same location. It even looked like this mystery craft had been launched straight off the *Vigilant* itself.

If that wasn't the case, it must have been witnessed by everyone on the spy boat because it was so close. And yet there are no police records of this anywhere. Logically, it was the real culprits racing over to dump the drugs – or it was a surveillance boat checking out the bags Jeans and Dunne said they'd seen us throwing overboard.

Remember, all of this information was digitally stored by the police spy boat's own high-tech radar. It's beyond dispute and yet we were never told it even existed.

The ECDIS data fills in all the missing gaps, Nikki. It establishes once and for all that the police swarmed all over Tennyson by plane – and probably boat as well – and clearly found nothing. If they'd spotted bags of drugs, then they'd have photographed them from the plane flying incredibly low overhead – or they would have known about the RIB they never told anyone about.

Like me, Nikki always believed it was blindingly obvious the police would have done all this. Their entire operation was based around a belief cocaine was being smuggled into the UK. Why would they not have fallen over themselves to check out bags that could well have been the very drugs they were hoping to seize?

The trouble was, when they discovered there was nothing there, they had a huge problem. They had no way of linking the drugs that were found at Tennyson the next day to the *Galwad*.

By hiding the fact a plane and a RIB had checked out the area, the police could keep alive the fantasy that we'd thrown eleven holdalls overboard attached to a rope and buoy. By claiming they never went to Tennyson, they wouldn't have to admit there was nothing there.

The ECDIS data shows the exact time the plane flew over and the time the RIB set off. The data also shows the routes the plane and the RIB took, and where they circled.

The first 'blip' is timed at 1902 hrs and is clearly the plane flying across the water at Freshwater Bay, then following the coastline from the Freshwater inlet towards the Needles. At 1905 it circles anticlockwise and by 1907 it's over the Needles, flying along the cliffs. In court, they insisted the plane was still at Bournemouth airport at 7 p.m.

The ECDIS data then shows another radar blip appearing – the RIB. It's certainly extremely close to the Vigilant and yet there's no mention of this in the cutter's logbook.

This is the same logbook, Nikki, which had the word 'spoilt' written where entries should have been made.

There's plenty more we've found out, largely thanks to Emily and, of course, my sister, Nicky. The police have never returned the *Galwad*'s satellite phone – in fact it's mysteriously disappeared – but, nevertheless, we can now prove it wasn't even working properly that night. Tanya Woolls convinced the jury it was being used to liaise with Dexsa through all the key stages of the operation and that seven calls between 2235 and 0038 hours were made specifically to co-ordinate the final, crucial moments of the operation.

She never told the court, however, that the phone was in such a bad state it actually indicated we were on dry land in the Picardy region of mainland France at the time – and not in the middle of the Channel at all. Paris is just down the road, although I don't know how we'd have driven there in the *Galwad*.

Despite being asked over and over, the police still haven't handed the phone back. *Wonder why, Nikki?*

Then there's the call durations. The police provided a load of figures in court to show how long the calls to my satellite phone had lasted. They never explained where they got that information from, though. Surely, the service provider? After all, if I wanted an itemised mobile phone bill and I'm on the O2 network, then I'd go to O2 for that information. I wouldn't go to Vodafone.

Strangely, the Metropolitan Police didn't use the official service provider, Iridium, but instead relied on records supplied by AST Systems. *This is where it gets messy, Nikki.* Three of the calls logged by AST were significantly longer than Iridium's records showed.

Of these, the final call is perhaps the most telling. According to Woolls, this was when I phoned to confirm the operation had been a huge success, the bags had all been successfully picked up, everything was on board and we were heading home. According to AST, this call lasted thirty seconds – which given what I was allegedly saying, would probably have been about right. According to the actual service provider, however, the call only lasted ten seconds.

Calls four and five on the table overleaf also show the police source logging much longer calls than the official data supplied by Iridium. This is particularly significant because it would be fair to say these calls would have coincided with the very moments when I'm allegedly manoeuvring the *Galwad* into position for the pick-up. The fourth call (0012) is eighteen seconds longer than Iridium logged, so is the next (0018).

None of this was explained in court. Instead, the jurors were given one set of call statistics, which seemed to be indisputable and official. Nobody mentioned Iridium or AST or discrepancies over how long the calls lasted.

Emily, however, managed to unravel the truth by directly contacting Iridium in 2017. She also discovered that call durations are from the moment when a caller presses the 'connect' button – and not from the point when someone answers. They therefore include the time the call takes to physically ring and connect – which means it's highly possible they never even connected, especially the shorter ones. Especially in the conditions that night – and especially on a clapped out satellite phone that thought the *Galwad* was heading down the Champs-Élysées on its way to the Arc de Triomphe.

Call Log

	Iridium	AST	Discrepancy
2356	41 sec	No data	No data
	OUTWARD		
0003	37 sec	37 sec	0 sec
	INWARD		
0005	1 min 28 sec	1 min 28 sec	0 sec
	INWARD		
0012	1 min 1 sec	1 min 19 sec	18 sec
	OUTWARD		
0018	53 sec	1 min 11 sec	18 sec
	OUTWARD		
0029	9 sec	9 sec	0 sec
	INWARD		
0038	10 sec	30 sec	20 sec
	OUTWARD		

All the calls in to the satellite phone were from Dexsa's number but nothing clarified whether they were missed calls or call alerts to indicate missed calls.

One thing is for sure, however. Vic had been trying – and failing – to contact him. We now know this because contents from Vic's pay-as-you-go mobile – the one branded a 'dirty phone' in court – were eventually handed over. It clearly showed six text messages, sent by him to Dexsa between 2316 hrs and 0023, which simply said: 'I want to go home.' None of these were ever produced as evidence in court.

There's a couple more things I've told Nikki about as well. Jeans and Dunne weren't the only officers who signed the debrief but who were never actually there.

Andy Marwick was caught on CCTV footage at Yarmouth harbour when the debrief was allegedly taking place. With him were two other officers: Jason Fox and Paul Seeley. All three signed the official debrief record – again leaving the false impression that they'd attended.

Nikki, don't you remember? They were the three officers who ordered you not to move my lobster pots from the quay. You were effing and blindin' at them and it made me laugh.

I'm not stupid enough to think our latest appeal is a shoo-in. Do I think it has a real chance, though? Yes. The ECDIS evidence is unequivocal and the barrister who won the McGuffie appeal, Joel Bennathan QC, has agreed to represent us at the Court of Appeal, thanks, of course, to Emily. He's an appeal specialist as opposed to a trial specialist.

He will focus solely on the ECDIS data and not so much on all the police inconsistencies and errors. That means this appeal is based on indisputable, hard facts – digital, radar evidence taken from the police's own spy boat that really can't be ignored or argued with. Nobody has plotted some co-ordinates on a chart and then connected them with straight lines using a pen and ruler to announce, 'This is where the boat went.'

Chapter 36

FAILURES

After the trial, Julian Hardy told me something I'll never forget. 'I can tell you this, Jamie,' he said. 'The police never expected to win.'

'What do you mean?' I snapped. I'd barely seen anything of Hardy in court and I wasn't much in the mood for anything he had to say. 'Well, I had a visit from one of them,' he explained. Suddenly, Hardy had my attention.

'Go on then, I suppose he was bragging, was he?'

'Actually, no, far from it,' continued Hardy. 'He'd come round to return some stuff and we got talking about your case.

'He told me he'd never expected the jury's decision. In fact, before it was announced, he was actually in the middle of writing a report to his bosses to explain why he thought they'd lost the case.'

I fell silent. *Even the police thought they'd lose. That's how much confidence they had in their own case.* 'Was he gloating or something? Why did he tell you that? You sure he wasn't just being sympathetic or something?'

'No, he was chatting open and honestly. I just thought you'd like to know,' and with that Hardy picked up his papers and left. I've no reason to doubt he was telling me the truth but, hey, who cared any more about the truth?

I've no doubt we were stitched up. Our fate was sealed not so much by what was said in court, but rather all the stuff that was never mentioned or deliberately withheld – and all the questions that were never asked and all the key witnesses that were never interviewed.

It was only after our convictions, when Nicky and then Emily got involved, that critical information and evidence slowly dribbled out: stuff we never knew existed at the time. Stuff that would have made a difference; stuff that would have swayed a jury. Emily stopped us being mugged. She opened doors we never knew could be opened – or even existed – and she's done it all for free. Appeal is a charity and, unlike our defence team, she isn't guaranteed a fat pay cheque irrespective of whether we win, lose or draw.

With the benefit of hindsight and experience, I can't help being critical of our defence team. They didn't probe deeply enough, they failed to make witnesses squirm who deserved to squirm, failed to make the court see and understand the absurdity of the allegations. Failed to fight as ferociously as they should have done.

Evidence presented by the prosecution – especially Davidson's – was simply accepted on face value and never vigorously challenged or queried.

The sheer impossibility of what the prosecution was alleging wasn't stripped down to its tiniest components and then ripped to shreds. The only constant seemed to be a desire to offend nobody, to behave like gentlemen and not to cause too much of a stink. Jesus. Our lives were at stake and yet all my defence wanted to do was play by the rules.

Even police statements that were altered, and logs that were 'spoilt' and radios that were broken and a plane that was never there and a straight line a cargo ship never took – none of this was ever disemboweled in the way it deserved to be. In the way I'd expected.

Why was nothing made of the questions I was asked when I was interviewed at Fareham police station, for example? That's when I was first accused of throwing holdalls attached to a red buoy into the water at Freshwater, only to be told seconds later, by interviewer DI Richard Crouch, that I'd been observed chucking 'black items' overboard.

The words 'black items' were exactly what Jeans and Dunne had originally described seeing, until they changed their stories the following morning and insisted they'd actually witnessed eleven holdalls attached to a buoy go overboard.

Yet Crouch's question proved that Jeans and Dunne *must* have phoned in to report seeing black items. Why else would he start interrogating me about them otherwise? Where did he get the words 'black items' from, if it wasn't what Jeans and Dunne had reported? Why didn't anyone go to town over this?

It proved the police altered what they'd seen – to what they actually found.

There's more. Why weren't the *Oriane*'s digital radar readings ever produced in court? Why wasn't the pilot of the surveillance plane made to produce his flightpath? Why weren't the entire contents of the Bonfield log made available (without the blacked-out bits)? Why wasn't the trial heard at a coastal town? Why weren't the jurors taken to the island to see Tennyson for themselves?

I expected our defence to jump up and down over stuff like this. I wanted to hear them scream, 'This is disgusting. This case is a sham. These men are being framed. This evidence is false. There is no evidence. Why are there no trophy pictures? We demand to see phone records. Why have these statements changed? Who wrote the word 'spoilt'? Why did they write it? Why didn't the *Vigilant* see the *Galwad* and *Oriane* cross paths? Nobody can do all that in three minutes, it's impossible. We demand to see the *Oriane*'s digital radar readings.

'This trial must be stopped because crucial information is being withheld.'

I wanted to hear real anger and outrage but we got none of it. Just Christopher's impassioned summing up, which was great at the time but was probably too little, too late.

Then there are the jurors, who were each interviewed after Richard said they'd been fed information they shouldn't have been told. We now suspect four of them had links, of sorts, to the police. One was the wife of a retired Metropolitan Police officer, another had a close relative who worked for revenue and customs – then there were the two involved in Richard's complaint. One was a member of a social club used by SOCA officers; the other was the woman living with a former special constable.

Is all of that simply a coincidence? Am I imagining a conspiracy that isn't really there? One thing's for sure, none of them were the partners of bloody fishermen. I mean, a retired policeman's missus? Whose side is she going to be on? Christ, she even admitted during questioning that she still uses the police gym.

We didn't know the half of what was going on. Now, ten years on, we are a lot wiser. OK, more cynical, but our latest appeal feels better prepared and much more pertinent to the marine evidence than ever before.

Chapter 37

THE WHITE EMBER

I've got to go fishing again. I've got to get back on the *Galwad*. I miss the sea like I miss being free. Like I miss my wife and my family. They're all I've ever known that's ever mattered to me.

I'd go out with the same crew and, yes, I'd even include Vic, so long as he'd conquered the seasickness. The only positive that's come from our ordeal is the solidarity between us. The police tried everything to separate us, trip us up, get us to contradict one another. They worked particularly hard on Dan and Beerey, trying to squeeze out of them the tiniest detail that might have made us all look like liars.

They failed miserably. They failed because we all knew, in our own individual ways, that we were entirely innocent. Nobody could tell another version of the story because there wasn't one to tell. Nobody was willing to make stuff up; nobody was willing to do a deal by lying for the police in order to get a lighter sentence – and two fingers to everyone else.

I miss that camaraderie. I miss the one-for-all, all-for-one togetherness you get among a good fishing crew, especially when the weather's a pig and the work is tough and long and you're knackered and the bloody string's got snarled up but you have to carry on and you're icy cold and the freezing spray and waves are smacking on to your skin and stinging your eyes until every part of you is screaming to go home. It's fuckin' hard graft, believe me.

Being there, being in control, bellowing orders out to the lads, beating whatever the weather might be chucking at us, that was the challenge, that was what being alive meant. That was freedom. That was what breathing felt like.

Then there'd be the moments when we'd be heading home and I'd be happy everyone had worked their bollocks off, only this time we'd landed a decent catch and I knew everyone had earned that first pint back in the Bugle. That was a good feeling, it really was.

Nobody ever taught me, or showed me how to strive for that, or how to achieve it. It just came from somewhere deep inside, the need for that moment possessed me and drove me on so I would want to keep on repeating it, over and over.

It was something the jurors never accepted or understood; after all, they'd never seen, or experienced it. My defence counsel actually got a better glimpse of my world before the trial when I took a couple of the junior barristers out in the *Galwad*. They wanted to see what an ordinary day looked like and how it all worked. So off we went one evening, about 10 p.m.

They were lucky, the weather was OK – a bit bumpy but not wild – so I steamed out to the grounds, did a bit of mapping and tried to recover some pots that been left out at sea. It was full on: we found a string snagged on the seabed and spent five sweat-drenching hours trying to drag the pots up. Even though there were only eight, they were worth every muscle-sapping second to me – otherwise I'd have to kiss goodbye to £600 of kit. Fortunately, I had Scott with me as well.

There was a moment, though, when I looked at the two barristers, standing on deck in their Barbour anoraks. They'd had enough, poor sods, I could tell. Their designer hair was sodden with sea spray and looked like black paint dribbling down from the top of their heads; their eyes were begging me to turn around and go home but their mouths remained firmly shut because they didn't dare say what they were thinking. So I said it for them, 'You think I'm going to abandon these pots? I'm not leaving them here and I don't care how long it takes. None of us are going back 'til this is sorted.'

I worked through the night with no kip and we came back late the following afternoon, with no product on board – just the recovered pots. I let the barristers sit in the wheelhouse, where they tried to cull their shivering by clutching endless mugs of tea. They'd had enough but inside I was smiling: they'd seen a glimpse of what really goes on out at sea and they'd begun to appreciate our values and our way of life – which was totally alien to theirs. As we got off the boat in Yarmouth, one of them turned to me, shook my hand and said, 'I'd no idea. I could never have begun to comprehend what you do, and what you go through.

'How come you're not knackered?' he added.

'It's just the way I am, it's the way I manage it. I'm used to it.'

Ten years in prison have starved me of all that. Without my family, my parents, I wouldn't even have the *Galwad* any more. They've carried on paying the mortgage on the boat, bless them; it's still on the island, exposed to rain and sleet and shit. But it's still there, stubborn. Just like me, just like all us Greens.

There was a lad who I knew who came to see me in Erlestoke towards the end of 2017 with a plan. He was willing to renovate the *Galwad* and bring it back to life so long as I'd let him go out fishing in it.

I said, 'OK, we'll do a deal. If you can do it up, you can fish it. If I come out in the meantime, we'll sort it so you don't lose any money. We'll get over it one way or another but I have to end up getting the boat back. I can't let go of it.'

'Yeah, yeah – it's a deal.' The lad left, brimming with excitement. I vaguely knew him, and his father, because they'd bought one of my old boats off me way back when. He got stuck in, brought boat builders in and some of the rotten timbers were stripped out. Then fate intervened; the lad was taken seriously ill, and he's had to abandon the project completely.

That was a real shame because, like me, I could see he was captivated by the *Galwad* and his heart was in it. But I'm determined to pick up what he started; the thought of rebuilding the *Galwad* and getting back out to sea is what keeps me going.

Right now, the boat's out of the water in Cowes, after we lost an eighteen-month battle to keep it in Yarmouth. The harbour masters there took away our mooring because, they argued, nobody was using it any more. Every which way I turn, it seems the system keeps on finding a new way to screw me.

My biggest aim is to go fishing with Jesse. It's in his blood, he feels the same freedom in his lungs that I once did. The boat he's currently skippering probably turns over £1.25 million a year and is one of the top five in the UK, doing solely crabs and fishing out in the North Sea.

The *Galwad* – and me – remain the missing links. My daughter, Poppy, has taken over the crab processing side of the business (which Nikki used to run) and is really making it work; she's even converted a 20ft ship container into a little factory of sorts with sinks and fridges. Her day starts around 4 a.m., she finishes fifteen hours later and now has three other girls working with her.

As well as devoting herself tirelessly to my case, my sister somehow managed to keep Salty's up and running throughout.

Every summer it would be packed to the rafters with yachties and day trippers and locals. But it was a relentless slog, especially as she could no longer rely on the fresh fish I used to bring into the restaurant off the *Galwad*. In the summer of 2020, my family all agreed enough was enough and Salty's was sold to a couple who plan to keep the business going.

I am staggered Nicky kept it going for so long yet still found time to fight for justice and slog down motorways and A-roads to keep on visiting me. Yes, it was sad; in many ways our restaurant became another victim of our bastard sentence.

My other daughter, Maisy, has also stayed on the island with her partner Sam, and they have a 2-year-old son, Arlo. I'm so proud of them all – and, of course, of my mum and dad. They've stood by me, throughout. They've never stopped visiting. They've never stopped believing.

Prison deprived me of the chance to see my kids become adults, it deprived my family of their main breadwinner and it deprived me of precious, final moments with Nikki. The sheer injustice of it all could easily make me bitter and twisted; it's not like being inside has somehow given me a new purpose in life. How could the prison system possibly rehabilitate someone of my age and generation? It's hardly going to teach me a new, meaningful skill. Especially after it's stripped me of the one I already had.

Instead, I get up every morning determined to fight the bastards and to prove our innocence.

I'll leave you with this thought.

When a huge cargo ship, like the *Oriane*, overtakes you in the middle of the night all you really see is a great, big, hulking silhouette ploughing past. You can hear the ferocious power of its engines and you can feel the sea churning and quaking but you can only make out a ghostly outline and shape, feebly illuminated by lights at the front, middle and rear. It's quite a hypnotic sight and I've often carried on watching as the boat's slipped further and further from view. Eventually, all that's left on the horizon is a tiny white stern light stubbornly refusing to be snubbed out by the surrounding blackness.

That moment always reminds me of a little white ember when it's all that remains of a once-roaring fire. That pinprick dot is so totally out of proportion to the gigantic, heaving beast to which it's attached; it doesn't offer the faintest hint of the brutal power and majesty of what it represents. In fact, on its own, it seems the exact opposite: fragile, even serene.

When I close my eyes at night, just as I'm about to fall into sleep, that light is the last thing I see, faintly flickering away, always threatening to vanish yet somehow hanging on, never quite burning out.

Nikki, we have a chance. We really do. Get ready, girl, because when I leave that court a free man, I want you there – right by my side.

Chapter 38

NON-DISCLOSURE

The more I think about it, the *Galwad*'s just like me isn't it? It ploughed head-first into a bitch of a storm, it was stripped and smashed and beaten up and then it was locked away, broken and shattered. All that remained of its bright vivid livery, the blues and the whites I adored, were little pinpricks of colour that defiantly poked through ever-increasing layers of decaying wood and rust.

There have been many times when I've felt exactly like that – battered but just about hanging on. Only this time the tide might be turning, for me and my boat. At this moment, I'm sat in my new cell at Ford Open Prison, counting down the days as I wait for a phone call that will determine the rest of my life. If we win the appeal, I'll be out and – if I have anything to do with it – back at sea. ASAP.

The *Galwad* is also facing a new lease of life. The rotting hulk of flaking wood it rapidly became has been painstakingly restored by my kids. They stripped it bare, gutted it completely and then basically rebuilt it from scratch. It now has a smart coat of paint and to me it's coming alive all over again.

That boat means everything to me at the end of the day. It's me. It's everything I stand for and what I have done and what my life consisted of before this nightmare happened. OK, it still needs fitting out with machinery, but I reckon I could have it back in the water inside four months if I was back on board. I could sort the engine, pipework, plumbing and deal with all the bloody authorities. I haven't forgotten how.

The kids sent me photos of their work as it progressed and I've put them all into one of those ring folders so I have a permanent record. I love looking at them; it's like the colour coming back into my world after 10 years of blackness. Besides Nikki and our family, going out to sea on the *Galwad* is what I've missed most and right now I'm chanelling all my hopes and dreams on the day when I can do it again.

Maybe it's a bit sad, but I've also kept on reading the weekly fishing paper ever since I was banged up. It's been my only tangible link to the world I once inhabited and I still pour through the pages for anything and everything that reminds me of what was snatched away.

If I see an article I like the look of, then I'll tear it out and keep it. It might be something about a bit of kit that I could imagine having on the *Galwad*, or a news article about someone or some firm that I vaguely know. The fishing paper even helped me land a proper job, one I'm doing right now – making lobster pots down on the quay in Shoreham.

The sea is some way off down river but I don't need to physically see it. The smell is all I need. When the wind's in the right direction, that smell is heaven to me.

Then there's the boats, just like the *Galwad*, all brightly coloured and tied up to the quay wall with little flags fluttering away in the breeze, and the clattering and clanging of fishermen repairing engines or touching up paintwork. I was one of them once.

I get up at 4.30 a.m., leave prison at 5.15 and start work bang on 6 a.m. I'll then work through until 5 p.m., with an hour for lunch when I'm free to go wherever I want and eat whatever I fancy. The pay is minimum wage, but I'm not complaining. Except the bastard prison took 40 per cent off my first wage packet – on top of the tax! They wanted it for some fund of theirs, but I complained and told them I needed every penny to pay off my mortgage and the legal aid bill I was landed with after my first trial. They accepted my argument and I've not paid it since.

I can make four or five lobster pots in a day. It's pretty labour intensive, a lot of fiddly stuff, but it's nothing I haven't done before. The frame is usually already made so all I'm doing is wrapping the net over it and then adding some heavy-duty rope to give it protection. Next comes the entrance, with an elasticated pull which keeps the shellfish inside the trap. Then I'll add the base, which has a metal weight inside, and, finally, wrap the bottom with bits of old car tyres because they're hard-wearing against the seabed.

The company I'm working for is Monteum Ltd, which is owned by a real old seadog, Jim Partridge. I swear he loves the sea just like me and he tries to encourage nippers to learn the trade. I read about him in the fishing paper and wrote to him, asking if he'd take me on day-release work. 'Course I will,' he replied. 'Get yourself down to Ford Open and then get back in touch.'

He was true to his word, although I had to rely on the local MP, Tim Loughton, to make it happen. When I first came to Ford in September 2020, nobody was in any rush to help me get out to work. It's odd coming to a place like Ford because it really is open and you're free to walk in and out and cross the main road outside as if you were back in the real world. But, just like everyone else in the entire prison system, nobody is in a rush to help. They much prefer it if you lie in bed all day and do nothing.

Well, I wasn't having that so I wrote to the MP, told him I could work at Monteum, and he got on to the governor here. That did the trick.

Doing the pots has been a life saver, especially as I wasn't allowed to physically attend the appeal in person. That was a nightmare. I had to rely on either Emily or my sister Nicky to give me a call whenever they could to run me through what had happened each day. If I hadn't had the job, I'd have been pulling my hair out. It's amazing how you start listening to the tone of someone's voice in a situation like that, rather than what they're actually saying. Do they sound upbeat, happy, angry, despondent?

It was definitely despondent at the beginning. The appeal date was originally set for Friday, 18 September 2020, and we all thought we'd be free men by the end of the day. Home for Christmas. That's how good we all felt about the new evidence. Stupidly, I dared to dream.

That was quickly shattered, though, when the judges brought everything to a grinding halt and insisted our expert witnesses met the prosecution's experts to see if there was any common ground they could all agree on. Here we fuckin' go. Why hadn't that been sorted already?

'Everyone's now got to check their diaries, Jamie, and see if there's any dates when they are all available,' explained Nicky. 'It's going to take at least three months to sort this lot out.'

Which it did. Another Christmas, my tenth, was spent in jail and a new appeal date was eventually set for Tuesday, 23 February 2021. Surprisingly, a new appeal judge was put in charge as well – and not any old appeal judge, either. This time it was Sir Julian Flaux, who'd only just been promoted to Chancellor of the High Court – making him one of the most senior judges in the country. Bloody hell. We never saw that coming.

Second time round and the appeal started as I had imagined. Because of the Covid lockdown, the amount of people who could attend the court was severely restricted, so most of my family watched it from their homes on the Isle of Wight via a live video link. The same applied to Jon, who was allowed to watch it from his prison in Wolverhampton because the appeal was in his name. I had to rely on Emily and Nicky again.

It lasted four days in all. There were highs and lows, of course, and moments when I'd be yelling at Nicky, 'are the judges listening? Are they reacting? Are they getting the message?'

'God knows, Jamie,' she'd reply. 'It's impossible to tell what on earth they're thinking.'

I'm convinced our QC Joel Bennathan gave it his best shot. From what Nicky told me, he clearly hammered home the key point: the *Vigilant*'s ECDIS radar data was never made available at our original trial, none of us knew it even existed – except the bloody police – yet it would have proved we were never close enough to the *Oriane* for anything to have happened.

Further, it would have also revealed that a surveillance plane definitely did fly over Freshwater Bay at 7.02 p.m. – just as I'd said – and that a mystery RIB zoomed to the same area about 50 minutes after I'd allegedly dumped drugs there.

That wasn't all, either. Remember the police's marine expert, Paul Davidson? It was his evidence that screwed us most at the original trial. He insisted we definitely crossed paths with the *Oriane* and, to prove it, he produced a chart which he said showed where our tracks went. The jury trusted every word he said.

Well, Joel made sure the appeal judges heard an entirely different story. For starters, Davidson never told the jury there had been a huge 11-minute gap in the radar readings he had used, and he'd simply drawn a straight line right through it to show where the *Oriane* went. He couldn't be 100 per cent certain whether it was correct.

Davidson also never revealed that the *Vigilant* had taken its own accurate reading of the *Oriane*'s position that night – and the cargo ship was much further south than where he had said it was. He knew this – but never mentioned it.

Then Joel turned to the Bonfield Log, the ultimate record of everything that happened that night – the one that had been heavily blacked out so we couldn't see what had been written down.

According to the log, the *Vigilant* had spotted a 'daughter vessel' near to the *Oriane* – at around the same time we were in the area. The *Vigilant* hadn't spotted anything suspicious about this 'vessel', in fact they noted there was 'no activity' on the stern of the *Oriane* at the time. The experts were now agreed that this boat was almost certainly us – in other words, the *Galwad*!

As Nicky explained all this I thought to myself, *Surely no jury would have ignored all that – had they been told?* That's all these appeal judges have to decide. Would this evidence have altered the jurors' thinking?

Joel also stressed that the police knew the ECDIS data existed all along. Marine electronics engineer William Smith admitted he visited the *Vigilant* at least twice: first to save the ECDIS data on 2 June 2010, then to get a copy of it on 11 June. He also admitted that he recommended the data should be backed up in case it would be needed and he even invoiced SOCA on 10 August to claim specifically for down-loading and securing it.

'It's gone well then, Nicky,' I asked tentatively. I should have known better. Once Joel had finished, the prosecution's QC, Deanna Heer, kicked off.

'She basically insisted our experts aren't experts at all and don't have the qualifications or experience to analyse the ECDIS data correctly,' Nicky explained. 'According to their experts, the radar data from the ECDIS was fundamentally flawed and giving out a false reading.'

I didn't like the tone of my sister's voice, although we knew Heer was always going to rubbish the radar data. In fact, this had already been debated before the appeal when both sets of experts met to see if they could agree any common ground on this issue. Frustratingly, they couldn't and I was worried when Nicky added, 'One of the three judges seemed really hot on this and kept firing loads of questions.'

It was complicated stuff but in a nutshell the prosecution witnesses were adamant that the *Vigilant* radar data was astray by 0.9 of a degree.

Our experts went to great lengths to analyse and research this, and cross referenced it against all the available radar data that was available from that night – including my Olex on the *Galwad*. They couldn't find any discrepancies. The *Vigilant*'s radar was working perfectly.

Nevertheless, I went to my cell that night fearing the worst. I had my own room, inside a converted shipping container, with a bed, a TV and some cabinets, and even my own toilet and shower. None of it offered any comfort though and I was paralysed by one overwhelming fear: these bastards screwed us 10 years ago, and they've carried on doing it ever since. Why would it be any different now?

Don't tell me the radar was 0.9 of a degree out. No it bloody wasn't. If it was, then what the hell was it doing on a police surveillance boat in the middle of a massive operation? Don't tell me the crew went out knowing the fuckin radar wasn't working. And in any case, if it was broken, how come there's never been any record since of it being repaired?

We're not talking about some clapped-out Morris Minor of the radar world here. This was the bloody Rolls Royce of the seas, basically naval class. They're not putting some shit broken-down radar on there, are they?

I knew what their game was. They had to discredit the radar because that's all they could do to lessen the fact that they'd hidden the data away for 10 years.

The more I agonised, the less faith I had in the system. This 0.9 of a degree business was a big, fat red herring and the system was going to hide behind it because that's what it always did – make up some shit excuse to prevent them doing the right thing. The system would protect its own, not us. We should have won any one of our previous appeals, but the system always found a reason to keep us locked up. Why would it suddenly now admit to being fundamentally flawed?

I didn't trust the appeal process one bit. Nobody would want the justice system to come out of this smelling bad. Oh no. Then it dawned on me: we'd only get a result if it left no nasty smells in its wake. If we didn't tarnish the system, then maybe we had a chance.

I didn't sleep well that night.

I knew the hearing kicked off at 10 a.m. the next day, when the prosecution experts – including Davidson – would be giving evidence. I was desperate to find out what happened but didn't get to speak to Nicky until 2.30 p.m.

'It's gone brilliantly, Jamie,' were her first words. 'Joel has torn them apart – especially Davidson.'

I took a deep breath as her words sank in. 'What happened? Tell me everything.'

'It was electrifying,' she answered. 'Davidson admitted that he never told the court 10 years ago that he'd simply drawn a straight line to connect dots. He also admitted that he had ignored a handwritten note of the *Vigilant's* radar data because he didn't think it was "relevant".

'It got better though, Jamie,' she added. 'Joel looked him squarely in the eyes and said, "Don't you think a good expert would have mentioned such a thing to a court?"'

'Bloody hell, how did he answer?'

'I wrote down his exact words. He said, "Yes, I do." He bloody admitted he should have told the jury.'

Nicky was right. It couldn't have gone any better, but not being able to gauge the judges' reactions and not being able to see whether points were hitting home somehow made the appeal feel very distant and surreal. Were we 5-0 up, or was it only 2-2? There was no scorecard I could use to log every point, no way of monitoring the appeal so we could be sure the judges were sticking to some established set of rules.

I could only imagine how Joel was emphasising key points, and I desperately wanted to see what Heer was doing. Was she shuffling papers around manically and looking despairingly at the judges? Or was she cool, calm and collected, confident the system would protect its own?

Heer would hit back, that was her job. She'd try to dismantle and discredit all the good work Joel had done.

I was right. It was Thursday, 25 February, and an afternoon session had been set aside for Joel and Heer to deliver their closing speeches. That would leave the judges free to return the next day and maybe announce their decision. Or so I foolishly thought.

Yet again I had to wait, desperate for Nicky's update, which didn't come until around 5.15 p.m. I was expecting her to tell me it had all gone pretty well and Joel had said everything we could have hoped for.

'They put him through the ringer,' were pretty much her first words. 'The judges started firing questions the second Joel opened his mouth. He held his own to be fair but they kept on grilling him about the radar data, and whether it could be relied on. They were obsessed by this 0.9 of a degree issue and whether the radar line was all wrong. I didn't like where they seemed to be going, Jamie.

'Then Heer piled in, only she was concentrating on what you'd said in court 10 years ago. As far as she was concerned, you'd accepted Davidson's line was correct and therefore that meant you must have gone across the back of the *Oriane*.'

'But that's because I wasn't given any option,' I protested. 'I was told we couldn't dispute Davidson's line, we simply had to accept it was right even if I didn't think it was. I had no bloody way of proving he was wrong. We couldn't rely on the radar data from the ECDIS because nobody told us it existed.'

Shit. That wasn't what I'd expected Nicky to say. I fell silent. Everything would now depend on the last day, when Joel and Heer would have a final chance to clarify any issues and drive home their main arguments.

I needed Joel to be everything our barrister hadn't been 10 years ago. I needed him to microscopically challenge everything Heer said and expose the weaknesses and inaccuracies. But would he be up to it, or would I just be left with another pile of questions that were never asked – and never answered? Once again it felt like an eternity before I got through to Nicky. 'It's gone well,' she said. 'Joel told the judges there'd been a "massive failure of disclosure" and the jury would have definitely thought differently had they known what we know now.

'Better still, even Heer agreed there had been a load of "failures" – a failure to understand how important the ECDIS data was and a failure between William Smith and SOCA to do anything with it.

'She admitted it would be safest to assume it was a surveillance plane that flew over Freshwater – and that's the first time they've admitted that, Jamie – and she didn't dispute that a speed boat went into the bay after you'd left.

'The prosecution made some pretty massive concessions and I'm certain the judges were taking it all on board. In fact, one of them said it had surely been Smith's job to hand the ECDIS data over.'

I let Nicky's words sink in. If this was a truly fair hearing, then, surely, we've won?

'Joel did absolutely everything he could,' my sister added. 'There was nothing else left for him to say. All we can do now is wait and see.'

And so we waited. Another four agonising weeks. The system is never in a hurry, after all. It's happy for us to keep on burning up time so we stay in nick that bit longer. Only something felt different about this appeal. Or maybe it was the lobster pots and smelling the sea air again. Whatever the reason, it felt like I was almost home.

And then came the call.

Chapter 39

THE PROMISE

I had a dream the night before the verdict was announced. It was 2011 again and I was back in the Kingston court room at my own trial – only I was watching from a distance, like a bystander. I could see all five of us behind the glass screen. We were all leaning forwards, listening intensely.

Our barrister, Julian Christopher, was pacing in front of the jury. He seemed taller, more confident and commanding than before. The jurors were following his every move. They seemed in awe of him.

'To conclude, the ECDIS radar data taken from the police's own surveillance vessel conclusively proves the *Galwad* never went close enough to the *Oriane* to be of any concern.

'More, it proves that a surveillance plane flew over Freshwater Bay at the time my client says - and not the time the police want you to believe.

'The same irrefutable data also shows that a RIB sped into the same area some 50 minutes later – something the prosecution do not now deny. Ladies and gentlemen of the jury,

I urge you to consider these critical details when you start your deliberations.

'They are critical because they prove these charges are false and without any substance whatsoever. These details, members of the jury, leave you with no option but to acquit these men.'

Good one, Julian.

The dream didn't end there. We all watched the jury disappear and then, the following morning, return to court to hear their verdict.

I carried on watching as Judge Dodgson turned to the jury chairman and asked whether they had reached a unanimous decision. 'Yes, your honour.'

'Do you find the men guilty or not guilty of conspiracy to import £53m of cocaine?'

'Not guilty, your Honour.'

Almost 10 years later, at 9.30 a.m. on 25 March 2021, I woke up to reality. I was at the quay, making more lobster pots, trying desperately not to think about the appeal judges who were about to reveal their verdict at any moment.

Sir Julian Flaux, Chancellor of the High Court; Mr Justice Andrew Baker; Mr Justice Calver. Sat in an ivory tower somewhere, with my life in their hands.

Suddenly the phone rang. It was Nicky.

'Tell me.'

'They've rejected everything, Jamie. Every single part of the appeal has been turned down.'

It was like a kick in the gut that I never saw coming. It was like hearing that word 'guilty' pounding through my brain again from 10 years ago.

I fell silent and tried to take it all in.

'Are you taking the piss, Nicky? Is this for real? How could they possibly reject everything?'

'What makes it worse, Jamie, is that they actually admitted the evidence should have been made available 10 years ago,' she answered.

I was gobsmacked. That was the real gut wrencher. The fact they actually admitted the evidence should have been made available at our original trial. How could they say that in one breath, and then in the next say 'but it wouldn't have made any difference so it really doesn't matter'? Wow.

The police's failure to hand the ECDIS radar evidence over was why we'd won the right to an appeal in the first place. Non-disclosure was the fundamental principle at the heart of our case. So how could the judges accept that it had happened – but then completely ignore it?

Even the bloody prosecution admitted during the appeal that there had been massive failures of disclosure. All these judges had to do was decide whether it would have influenced the way a jury reached its decision – like it did in my dream. *Of course it fuckin' would.*

Instead, these three men had assumed the role of twelve jurors and decided none of the ECDIS stuff would have made a jot of difference.

'What the fuck did they say, Nicky? What reasons did they give?'

I listened in horror and disbelief as she went through their report. They totally accepted that the ECDIS data was faulty and, once you allowed for the fault, then it supported Davidson's version of events.

They also agreed that one of our expert witnesses was 'not credible'. Funny they used that expression. It was exactly the same one the system used to describe the juror who had complained about what happened at the original trial. Not credible. How do they know? Do they know more about radar equipment than a man who has devoted his life and career to that science? Are they better qualified than him?

Then, inexplicably, they accepted that the 'daughter vessel' – the one mentioned in the Bonfield Log, the one that a surveillance plane and the *Vigilant* checked out and dismissed – was almost certainly us.

But instead of that proving our innocence, they insisted that it simply proved we must have gone close enough to the *Oriane* to have been spotted in the first place. Even though the man in charge at the time, Miles Bonfield, was happy to write in his live report that we were 'not a vessel of interest'. Even though their own surveillance plane and the *Vigilant* checked us out and photographed us.

'What about the plane at Freshwater and the RIB, Nicky? What did they say about that?'

It just got worse. They couldn't deny that the ECDIS data clearly showed a low-flying plane over Freshwater at the time I'd seen it – 7.02 p.m. But the crew had written in their log that the plane only took off from Bournemouth at 7 p.m. and there was no note of it flying over the Bay, so the judges believed that instead. *The radar is the undeniable truth, not the bloody log.*

Strangely, the judges then said that even if the plane had flown over, it was hardly surprising it didn't see any drugs bobbing about in the water because it wouldn't have known to look for them. *You what?* The two coppers on the clifftop, Jeans and Dunne, had phoned in to report us throwing black bags overboard. It would have been looking for those, for starters.

I was eventually sent a copy of the judges' verdict by my daughter Maisy and went straight to this point because it felt so important. I couldn't believe it when I read: 'Even then, it's only one piece of evidence a jury would have to consider against a strong body of circumstantial evidence that it was indeed the *Galwad* which dumped the drugs.'

Circumstantial evidence. That's all they ever had on us, back then and right now, and yet that's what the judges were still clinging to. Nobody ever saw anything, nobody knows if there were ever any drugs on board the *Oriane*, nobody found a micro-dot of cocaine on the *Galwad*, none of our fingerprints were on the holdalls they found – the whole bloody lot was circumstantial.

Yet here were these all-mighty judges deciding that a jury would have been more influenced by what was being made up and alleged 10 years ago, rather than what the radar was telling us right now.

Then the judges made a big fuss about what I said in court back then –that I hadn't disputed Davidson's account of whether I had gone close to the *Oriane*. Excuse me, I wasn't given a choice. I was told I had to accept it because there was no way of proving otherwise. Look at the current Post Office IT scandal –innocent sub-postmasters pleaded guilty to something they hadn't done because the system told them they had to. I was in the same bloody boat.

Call that justice? We certainly didn't get a fair crack of the whip. The judges missed the point completely because they had to miss it completely. They did what the system expected of them.

Of course they'd bloody turned us down. Those three judges were the gatekeepers of British justice, after all. They wouldn't want to see that statue on top of the Old Bailey cracking and wobbling. They wanted to keep those scales nice and straight.

The power they were wielding was phenomenal and it was completely unchecked. They were utterly beyond reproach. I'd have rather faced a bloke with a gun or a knife in the middle of the street – at least then I could have seen what I was up against.

The British justice system is a bit like the banks – too big to fail. Can't let them collapse, got to save them, got to pump more millions in. The courts are just the same. Don't worry about a few families being destroyed, just keep those scales nicely balanced.

In fact, our families are the other victims in all this. They lost the appeal as well after daring to dream and hope and thinking that there might be a light around the corner. There must have been times when my kids have thought, 'fuckin' hell, we've lost our mother and the old man is still banged up. What the fuck?'

Jon's father died very recently and I even lost my dog, Rio, a few days ago. Something he ate had got stuck and perforated his gut, so he had to be put down. I was heartbroken when the kids rang to tell me.

Jon's dad. My Nikki. Our dog. The years we should have had together with our children. Gone. There's the human cost, there's something the appeal judges can't be arsed with either. Where's the last 10 years? There are no happy memories. I can't press rewind and replace them with something better. All I've got in my head are images of bloody prisons and being cooped up with arseholes and screws – and doors banging shut every night.

So what's next? Right now, it's all a bit too raw. But one thing's for sure - I certainly won't give up. Why should I? Because it's easier to do that, than carry on fighting? Because the system has built a wall and keeps adding more layers of bricks?

Fuck all that.

I'll be out on parole in 18 months but I don't want to be forever looking over my shoulder. I don't want them dictating what I can and cannot do for the following 12 years after that because I'm still technically guilty. I want to be back on the

Galwad, I want be out fishing – especially with Jesse. I want to rebuild my business. But they won't let me do that, even when I'm out on parole. Not as the law stands at the moment. They think I might paddle off to Brazil or somewhere.

More than anything, I want people to look me in the face and know that I am innocent, the victim of a diabolical and hideous wrongful conviction. I am living proof that there is something fundamentally wrong and corrupt within the British legal system. In a word, it's rigged. I was talking to Dan the other day – he's already out on parole – and he said, 'Jamie, it's not the same as it was. This defines us now.'

I don't want that. I want people to read this story and think: 'fuckin' hell, nobody deserves what those men went through. Something's got to change.'

Where are you, Nik? The bastards screwed us once again but, I promise, I'll never give up so long as you're by my side …

SUPPORT THE FIGHT FOR JUSTICE

If there is one thing I have learned from our ordeal, it's this: You only get proper justice if you're proper wealthy.

Mercifully, there is one woman in this country who is fighting tirelessly to change that. Emily Bolton runs the legal charity Appeal, which is dedicated to exposing and reversing wrongful convictions like ours.

Although we didn't get the result we were praying for, we only got to first base because of Emily. She battled ferociously against a system that continuously wanted to slam doors in our faces. She won us the right to be heard.

I cannot thank her enough and I urge everyone out there who is either touched by our story or concerned about the British judicial system, to support Appeal and, ideally, donate to their funds. They do everything for free and that's not how it should be.

Find out more about their work at their website: appeal.org.uk

ABOUT THE AUTHOR

Mike Dunn is the author of two books: *Grey Wolf* (SJH, 2016) and *The Belt Boy* (Austin Macauley, 2016), which was listed for two UK sports book awards and made *GQ* magazine's top-10 essential reads of 2017. He is a former Head of Sport of the *News of the World*, *The Sun*, *The Independent* and *The Standard*.

IF YOU ENJOYED THIS TITLE
FROM THE HISTORY PRESS

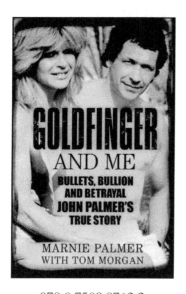

978 0 7509 8762 2

978 0 7509 9618 1